I0800142

IMAGES
of America

GROWING UP IN BALTIMORE

A PHOTOGRAPHIC HISTORY

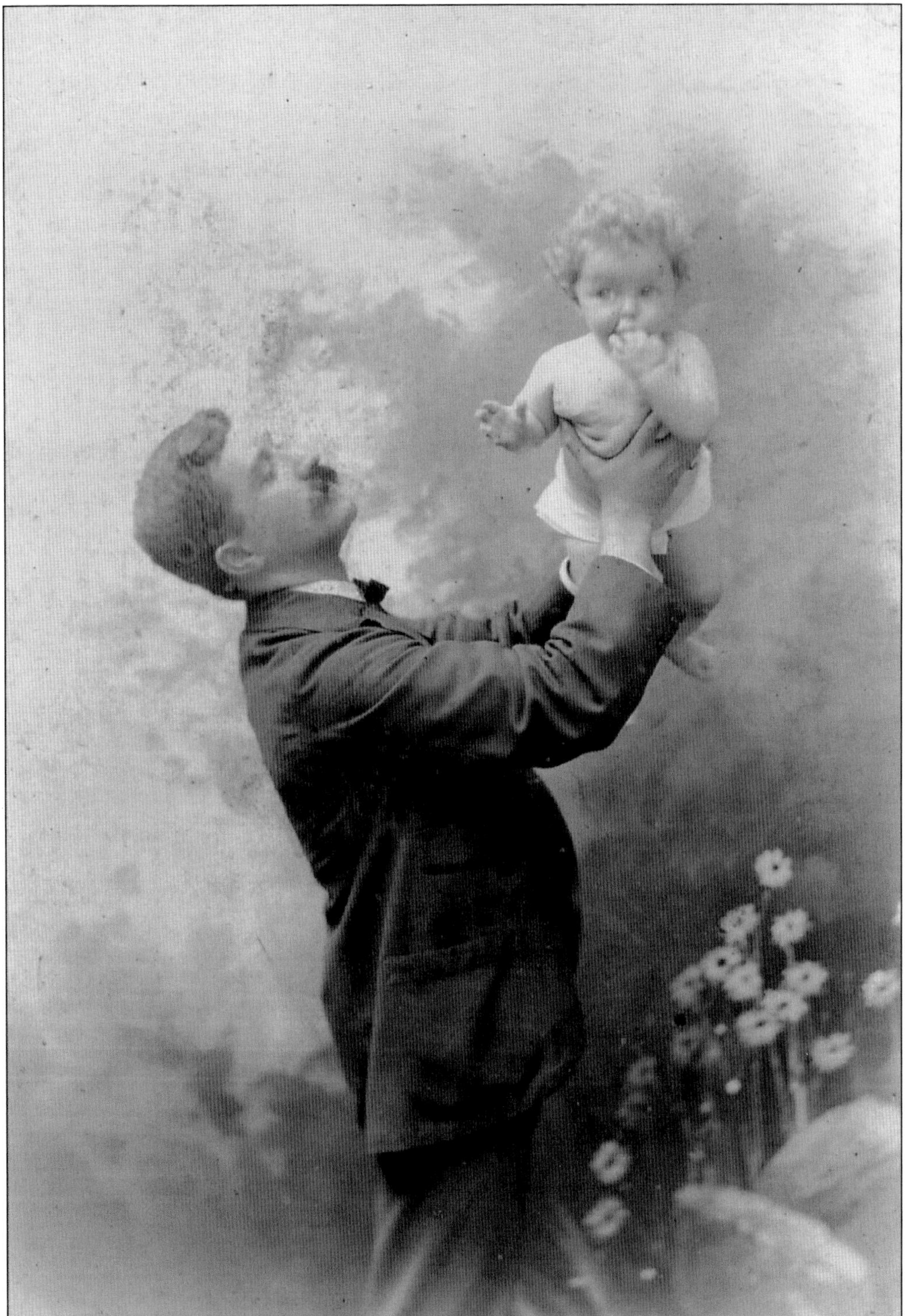

Louis Kohn is pictured with his son Walter in 1895. (Courtesy of Liz Moser.)

IMAGES
of America

GROWING UP IN BALTIMORE

A PHOTOGRAPHIC HISTORY

Eden Unger Bowditch

ARCADIA PUBLISHING

ISBN 978-0-7385-1357-7

Published by Arcadia Publishing
Charleston, South Carolina

Printed in the United States of America

Library of Congress Catalog Card Number: 2001089654

For all general information contact Arcadia Publishing at:
Telephone 843-853-2070
Fax 843-853-0044
E-mail sales@arcadiapublishing.com
For customer service and orders:
Toll-Free 1-888-313-2665

Visit us on the Internet at www.arcadiapublishing.com

For Julius, Lyric, and Cyrus, my wonderful children.

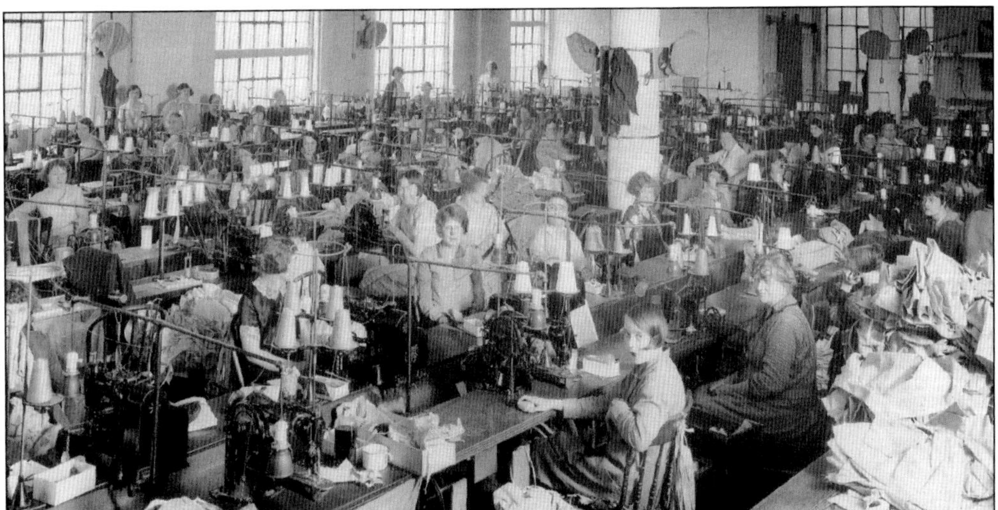

This is the sewing room of Thanhouser & Weiller Manufacturers of Boys Clothing, c. 1930. The building was located at Pratt Street and Collington Avenue. (Courtesy of the Enoch Pratt Free Library,)

Contents

Acknowledgments

This book required a great deal of research and investigation, and there are several people without whom this project would not have been possible. If any of them is not included, it is a terrible oversight and not for lack of appreciation. First, I must thank my wonderful husband, Nate, for his endless love, patience, and assistance. I must also thank my children for being my inspiration and for "helping" with the research, and my parents, brother, and sister for making my own childhood wonderful. I would like to thank Jackie O'Regan, curator of Evergreen House; Peggy Woodward, archivist of Bryn Mawr School; Liz Dausch, archivist of Gilman School; Ann Cartentuto, administrator of the Maryland School for the Blind; Mariale Hardiman, principal of Roland Park Public School; Heidi M. Blalock at Friends School of Baltimore; Barbara Krupnick, librarian at Roland Park School; Sue Welsh of Roland Park Country School; and Hillary Jacobs of the Park School of Baltimore. I must also thank Dean Krimmel; Tim Ford, Tom Beck, and John Beck (no relation) of the University of Maryland, Baltimore County; historians and authors Christopher George, Jacques Kelly, Ralph Clayton, Frank Shivers, and Philip Merrill; Uluaipou Aiono; Christian Malone; Chesapeake Systems; Karen Tamol of the Baltimore Zoo; Christine Rowett of the Maryland Science Center; and Rose Murphy. For allowing me to investigate their private collections and use some of the treasures found within, I would like to thank Liz Moser, Denny Lynch, Jack Hennessy, and Will Depfer. My appreciation extends to Elizabeth Duvall, associate editor, and Laurel Harris Durenberger, publisher, of *The Urbanite* magazine for their help and understanding. Thank you to all my friends, and their children, who have made Baltimore their home. And thanks to a great storyteller and friend, C.R. McGee.

Special Thanks

Although there were many who put their time and effort into helping me in this endeavor, Jeff Korman of the Enoch Pratt Free Library not only knew where to point me when I needed something I couldn't find, but his tireless assistance and seemingly endless knowledge of Maryland history was of the utmost necessity. The hours he spent perusing photographs and double-checking facts amongst the archival volumes that fill the shelves of Enoch Pratt's Maryland Room cannot go unmentioned. Jeff is an incredible resource and, after all the hours digging into the past together, I consider him a friend. The Enoch Pratt Free Library is lucky to have him.

INTRODUCTION

Researching this book has truly been an adventure. Baltimore is a city steeped in history. I see the city with more empathy and awe than I ever could have before undertaking this project and became totally absorbed in the task. I spent week after week poring through the 16,000 photos in the Enoch Pratt Free Library's archives and I spent afternoons with private collectors who were willing to share their photographed histories. I gained a great deal of insight into the history of the schools as I spoke with archivists and searched through old school pictures. I wiped tears from my eyes as I looked through Lewis Hine photos and found that, nearly a century later, they still evoke the reaction that was intended when Hine took them for the National Committee on Child Labor in 1909. Evergreen House generously allowed me access to their collection documenting the grandeur and privilege of the Garrett family and friends. I also found some shocking and beautiful photos at the Maryland School for the Blind.

Of course, without the great wealth of artists taking photographs in Baltimore from the mid-1800s through the 1930s, this truly would have been impossible. The Baltimore Camera Club, established in September of 1883, was one of this country's oldest camera clubs, and its members took numerous photos of parks, events, catastrophes, and post-fire Baltimore. Lewis Hine took photos of children working in the fields outside of Baltimore and families packing up to leave for the country to work at the berry farms. He took photos of children in the canneries and the mills. David Bachrach and his studio took a huge number of celebrity photos as well as shots of the parks and local families. Bachrach, who came to this country from Germany in 1848 and attended Baltimore public schools, was the photographic assistant at the Gettysburg Address and participated in the now famous photo of Lincoln, the first President to be photographed. In 1868 Bachrach opened his own studio, and Bachrach Studios photographed every President after Lincoln until the studio closed in 1974. Amiger Studios in Woodberry was located on what is now Thirty-sixth Street, then called Third Avenue, and Amiger took many of the photos from the Hampden/Woodberry area during the age of the Civil War and after. Semi-professional photographers like James Lewis created their own collections of images, many uncropped and showing behind-the-scenes views that truly capture a sense of photography *verité*. Luckily, many of these wonderful photographs have been preserved for us to enjoy.

It was my good fortune that some of these photographs had been recently collected for various centennial anniversaries and celebrations. Still, even with that luck, the hours put in to this project cannot be discounted. My husband spent many of them with me, helping with the layout and reading through everything. It was exhausting but even that was a pleasure. Perhaps the most difficult chore was choosing which photos would not be included. There were so many incredible pictures, this book could have been one of three volumes. There is something haunting about seeing the face of a child, looking so much like our own children, who has long since died of old age. Or discovering that the child in the photo that is now so familiar died shortly after having his image imprinted forever on glass. We must remember that for every child that happened to stand in front of a camera, thousands never did and are lost forever from our sight. But we are lucky that avid photographers pursued these young subjects and have left them for posterity. Seeing these children from so very long ago is really an experience not to be missed. I am so pleased to be able to share this intimate look into childhood in yesterday's Baltimore. *Growing Up in Baltimore: A Photographic History* will take you on a journey back into the lives of so many children, some we know and some we never will; all were captured for that single moment and remain there, as they were, for all time. It is quite a journey and, having taken it myself, I can say it really is an adventure.

Eden Unger Bowditch is a freelance writer and author. She currently serves on the board of directors at Cylburn Arboretum Association and formerly as editor of the *Urbanite Magazine*. Eden lives with her family in Baltimore.

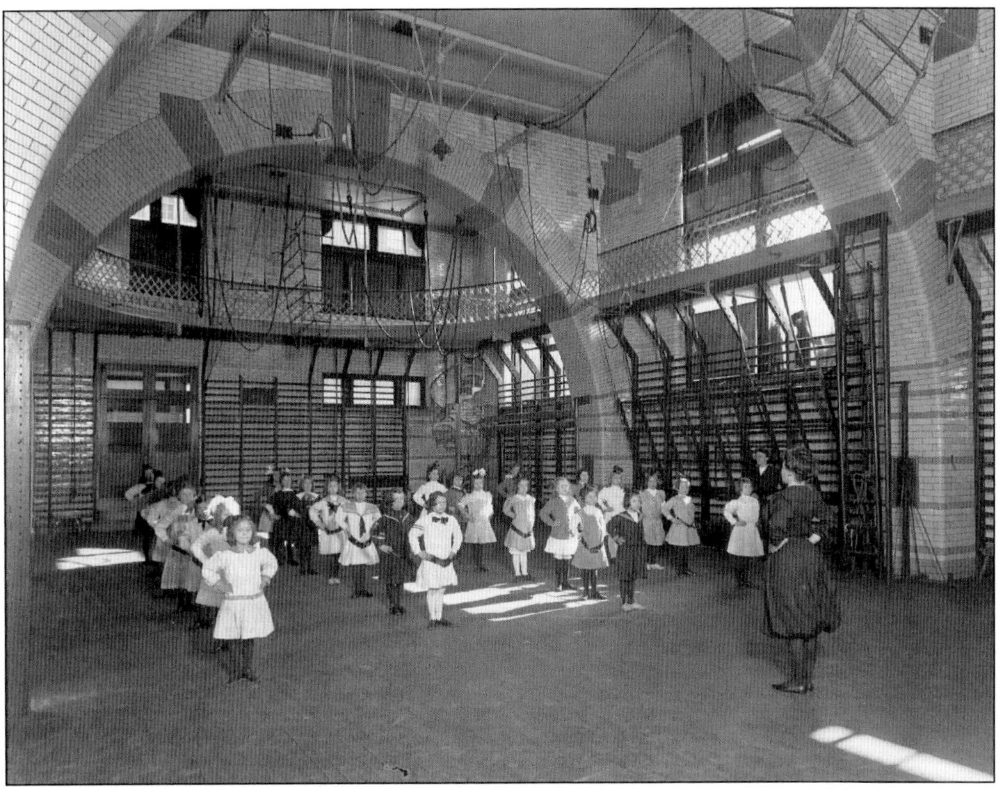

This is a lower school gym class at the Bryn Mawr School, c. 1890. (Courtesy of the Bryn Mawr School, Baltimore.)

One

Children at Home

Seeing children with their families and in their home environment gives us an intimate picture of private life during a particular time. Most often we find photos of families that had wealth since they were the ones who could afford to have photographs taken. But anonymous children were very often the chosen subjects of photographers. Many children who were captured on film by interested strangers may never have had a chance to see these images of themselves. Some of the children living in poverty may have elicited sympathy or concern from those taking the pictures. As a result, we have a chance to see both children in the most elegant, affluent stately manors and children living with their families in squalid hovels with little hope for anything better. In the times of great industrial success, there were the children of laborers who were not privy to the wealth that their parents' sweat helped to create and there were those born into families that had more than enough and would never understand want. Children born into slavery in Baltimore may have been luckier than others born on plantations in the South; yet, there was active slave trading and sometimes babies were even sold out of the arms of their mothers. There were children from families who came thousands of miles to make Baltimore their home and to give their children a better life. Those from Baltimore's aristocracy whose descendants can still be found on the registries of the city's most elite organizations. All of these children are the children of Baltimore, and they are presented here, as they once were, in the midst of daily chores or relaxing family time, at home.

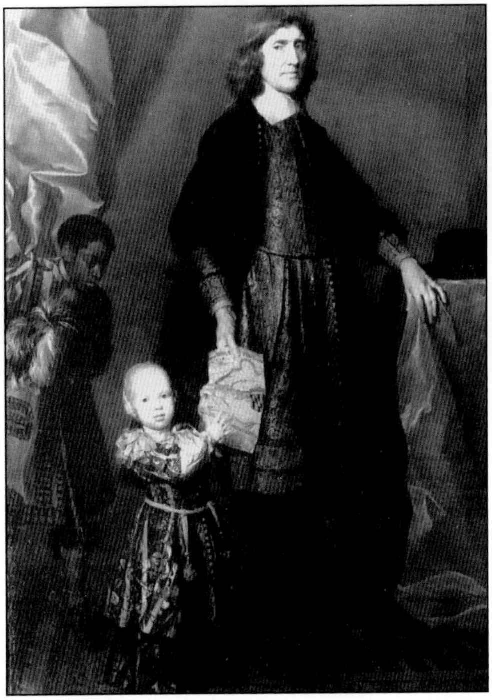

The first "Baron of Baltimore" was George Calvert, the secretary of state in the court of King James I. He was given this Irish title of nobility in 1625. Calvert had begun a settlement in Newfoundland in 1621 but, upon converting to Catholicism, lost his position. The title of Baron of Baltimore did not replace the income he lost. Preferring not to return to harsh Newfoundland, Calvert went to Virginia. He was to have been given land under a charter granted by King Charles I and he called this land *Terrae Maiae* after Charles I's wife, Queen Henrietta Maria. (We can translate the name as "Mary Land.") The charter was not fulfilled before Calvert's death so his son Cecil Calvert, the second Baron of Baltimore, was, legally, the first proprietor of land in Maryland. In this late 17th-century painting by Gerard Soest, Cecil is shown with his grandson and servant. In his hand is the charter of the Maryland colony. (Courtesy of the Enoch Pratt Free Library.)

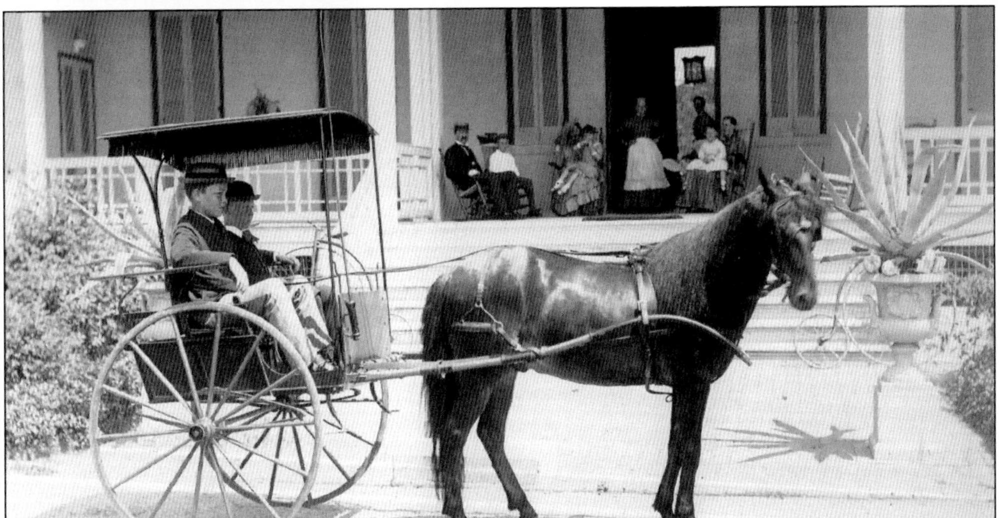

David Maulden Perine was the founder of Homeland. The 390-acre estate that he purchased in 1799, then called Job's Addition, had originally been a section of a 1,000-acre parcel patented in 1694 called Friends' Discovery. In 1840 Perine hired an architect to design a mansion in the classical revival style. It burned down one year later, and Perine had to rebuild it. This house, along with numerous farm and tenant houses, survived until 1924 when the Roland Park Company destroyed all of the existing structures in order to develop the area. Perine was a Southern sympathizer during the Civil War. It is said that he loved practical jokes. He is said to have often hidden the clothes of young village boys from Govans while they were swimming in his lake. (Courtesy of the Enoch Pratt Free Library.)

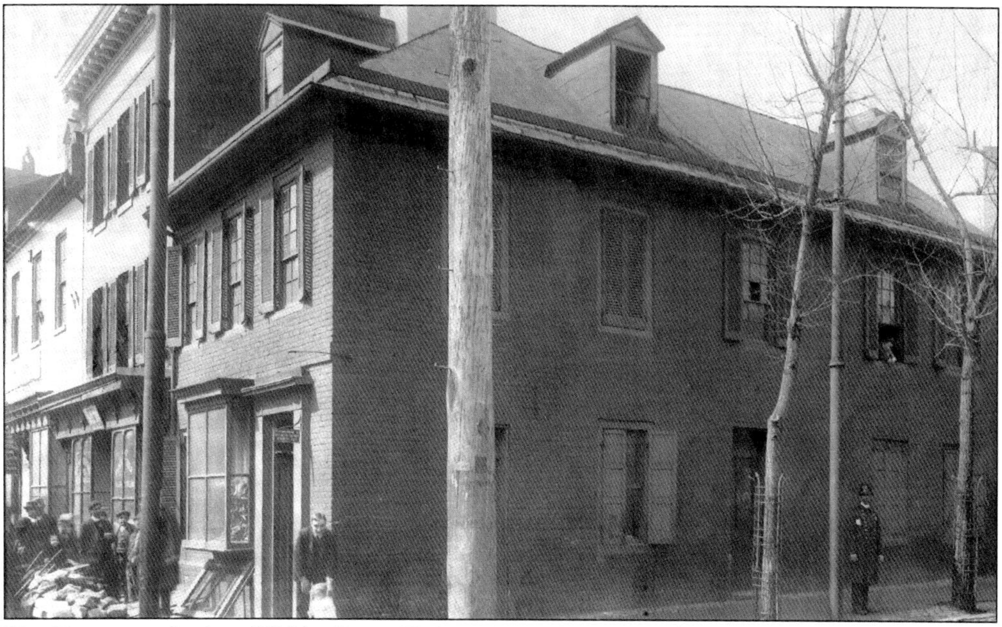

Flag House was built c. 1793 by Brian Philpot. In 1807, Mary Pickersgill moved to the area with her seven-year-old daughter and her mother, Rebecca Young. Pickersgill and her mother, both widowed, leased the corner rowhouse on Albermarle. Caroline slept in a trundle bed under her mother's bed, and it was in this room that, in 1813, Mary began work on the flag that inspired Francis Scott Key's "Star Spangled Banner." She had to use the floor of a warehouse to finish the job since there was not enough room in her quarters to complete the huge project—the flag was 42 feet long and 30 feet tall. In 1820 Mary bought the house and lived there until her death in 1857. She willed the house to her married daughter, Caroline Pickersgill Purdy. (Courtesy of the Enoch Pratt Free Library.)

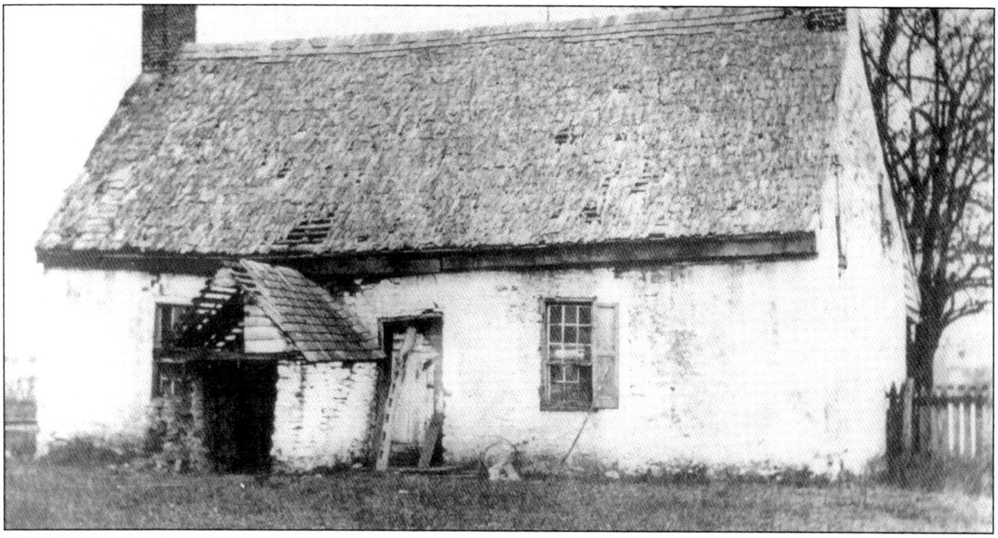

This house was built by Joshua Howard, the first Howard to come to America and the grandfather of John Eager Howard. Joshua Howard was given a grant sometime soon after 1685. Located near Pikesville, the property was originally called Howard's Inheritance and was later known as Grey Rock. The house was destroyed in the early 1900s. (Courtesy of the Enoch Pratt Free Library.)

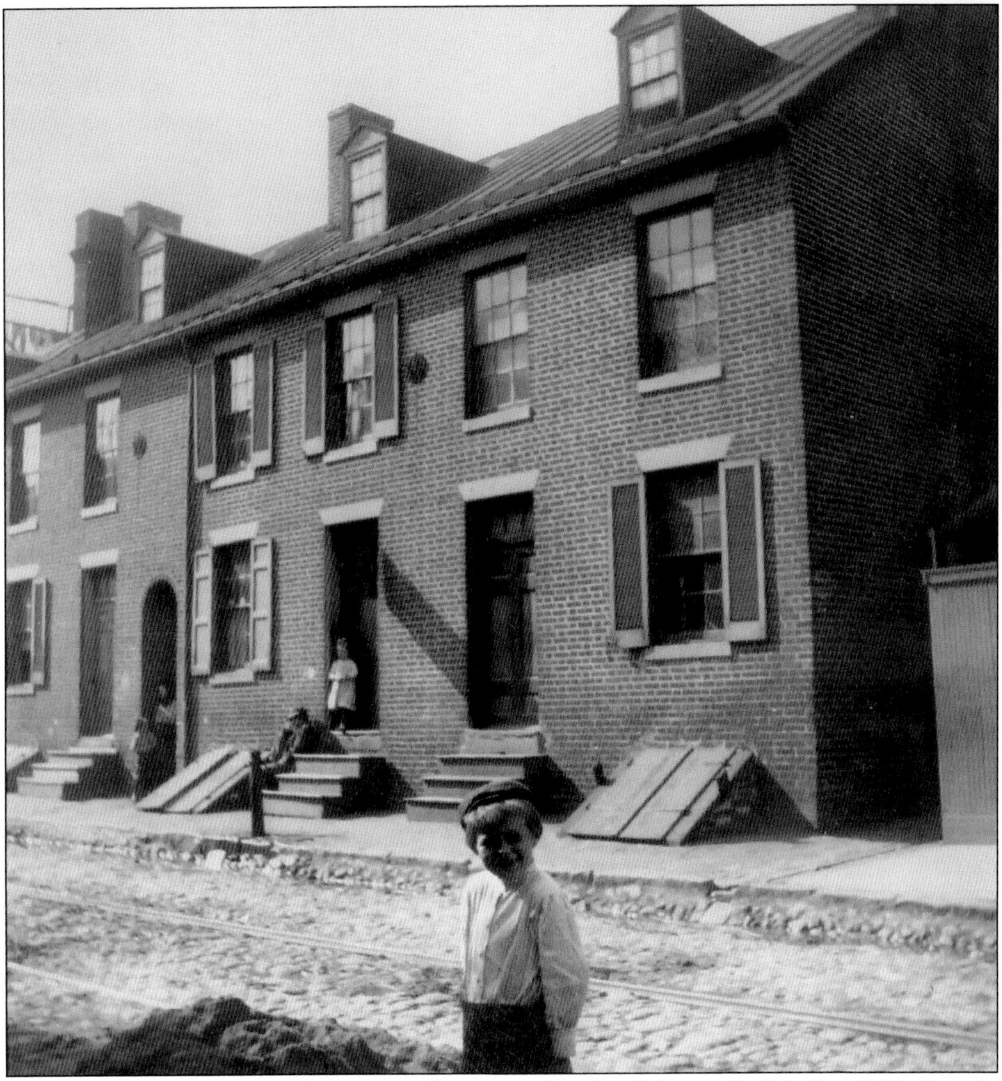

Shakespeare Street, a very old street in Fells Point, is lined with houses built before 1800. Gravely unhealthy sweatshops were also located on this street at the turn of the century. The Maryland Bureau of Industrial Statistics' findings there were condemning, and although laws were passed in the 1890s, little was done to improve the health and comfort of the workers. (Courtesy of the Enoch Pratt Free Library.)

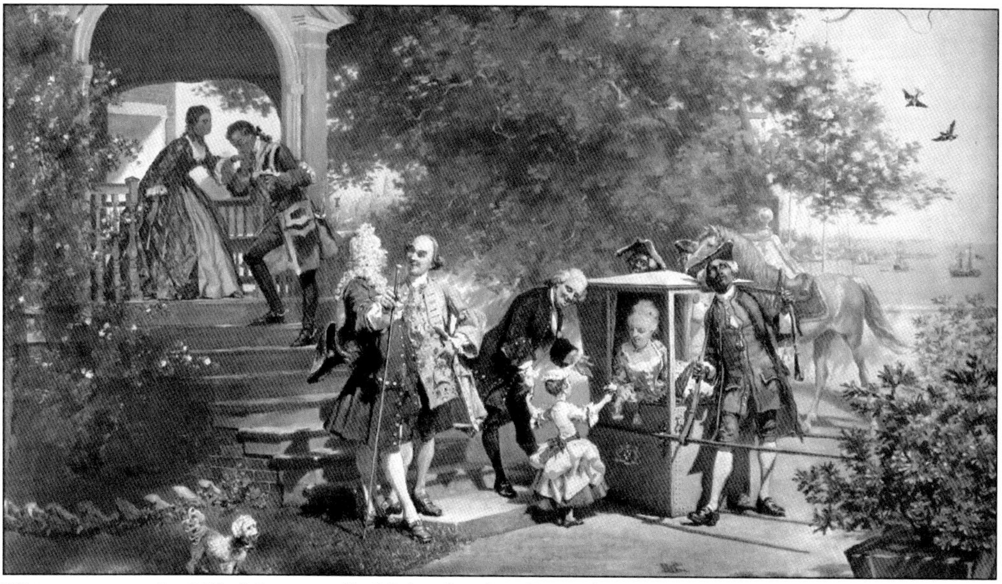

This painting by F.B. Mayer, called *Maryland A.D. 1750* or *My Lady's Visit*, depicts a typical upper-class, 18th-century Baltimore lady taking a trip to visit friends in Annapolis. The painting is in the possession of the Maryland Historical Society. (Courtesy of the Enoch Pratt Free Library.)

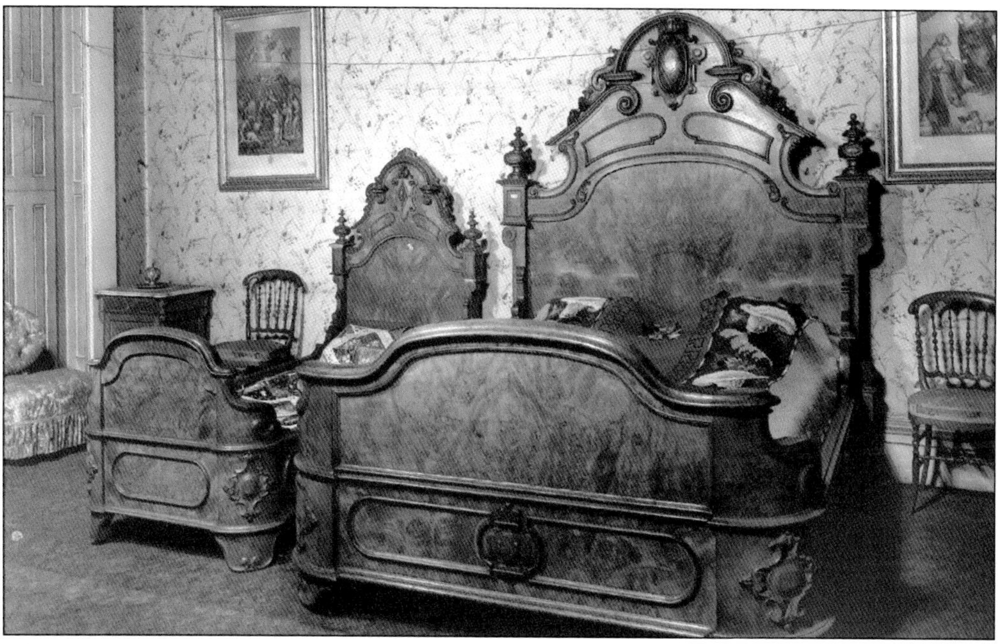

Wealthy parents often had their beds replicated in miniature for their children and placed next to their own for convenience. This elegant example is from the home of Henry Walters. The son of William T. Walters, Henry Walters was the benefactor of the Walters Art Gallery and gave money to create free public baths for the city of Baltimore, c. 1900. The senior Walters was a commission merchant and a great lover of art. His extensive collections were legendary for their content as well as their cost, and before the gallery was created, he would sometimes open his home to share his art with the public. (Courtesy of the Enoch Pratt Free Library.)

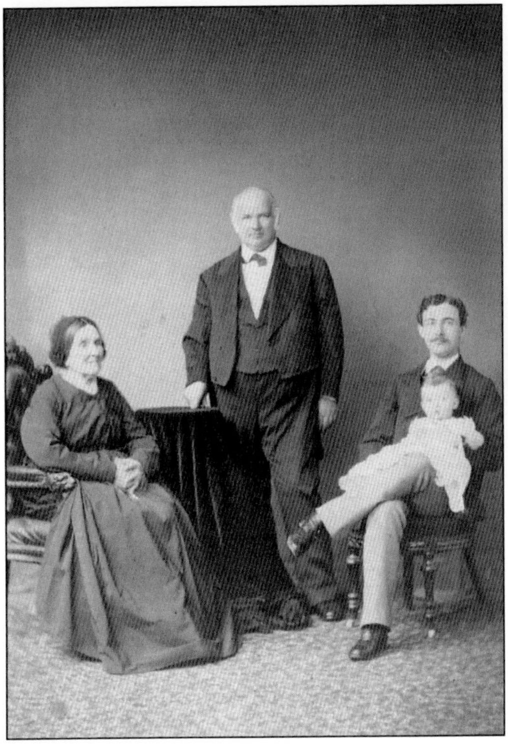

The Garrett family's business, Robert Garrett & Company, was a prosperous commission merchant house established in Baltimore by 1819. Robert Garrett (1783–1857) and sons Henry Stouffer (1816–1864) and John Work (1820–1884) made the business thrive. They played an important role in establishing the Baltimore & Ohio Railroad, and in 1859, John Work Garrett became the railroad's president. Garrett's refusal to give fair pay and rights to railroad workers caused the strike of 1877. Though unsuccessful for the workers, the strike seems to have convinced Garrett to institute B&O Employees' Relief Association in 1880. In 1884, B&O also organized the nation's first employee pension plan. In this *c.* 1873 photo are, from left to right, Elizabeth Stouffer Garrett (born 1791), John's mother; John Work Garrett; his son, T. Harrison (born 1849); and his grandson, John Work (born 1872). (Courtesy of the Evergreen House Foundation, The Johns Hopkins University.)

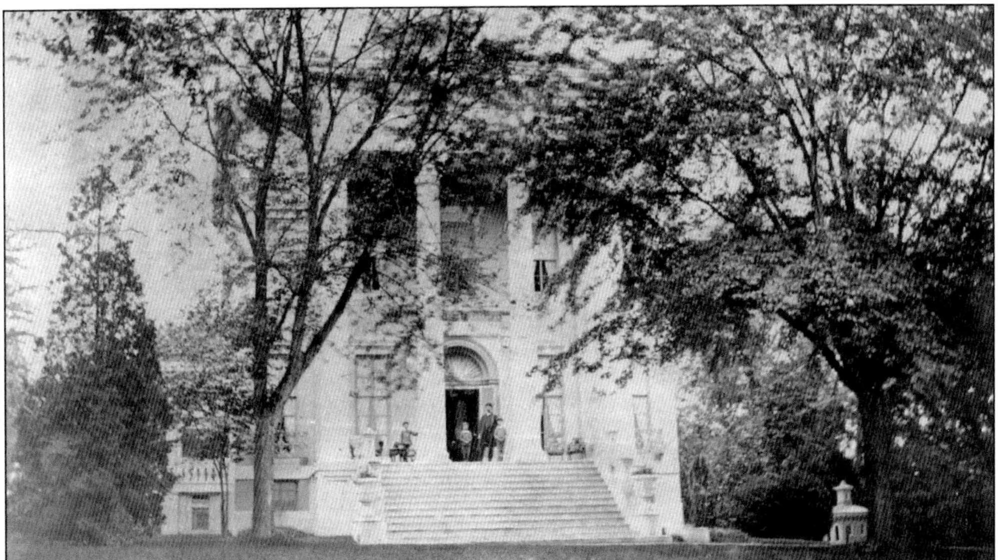

Evergreen House is seen here in its timeless splendor. At the top of the marble steps stands Robert Garrett with his sons. Two generations of Garretts lived in this house, which was purchased in 1878 by the Garrett family firm for T. Harrison Garrett, the son of John Work Garrett. Evergreen House, now a historic house museum of The Johns Hopkins University, contains over 30,000 rare books as well as other collections that include Tiffany chandeliers, Japanese lacquers, Chinese porcelains, and early 20th-century paintings. (Courtesy of the Evergreen House Foundation, The Johns Hopkins University.)

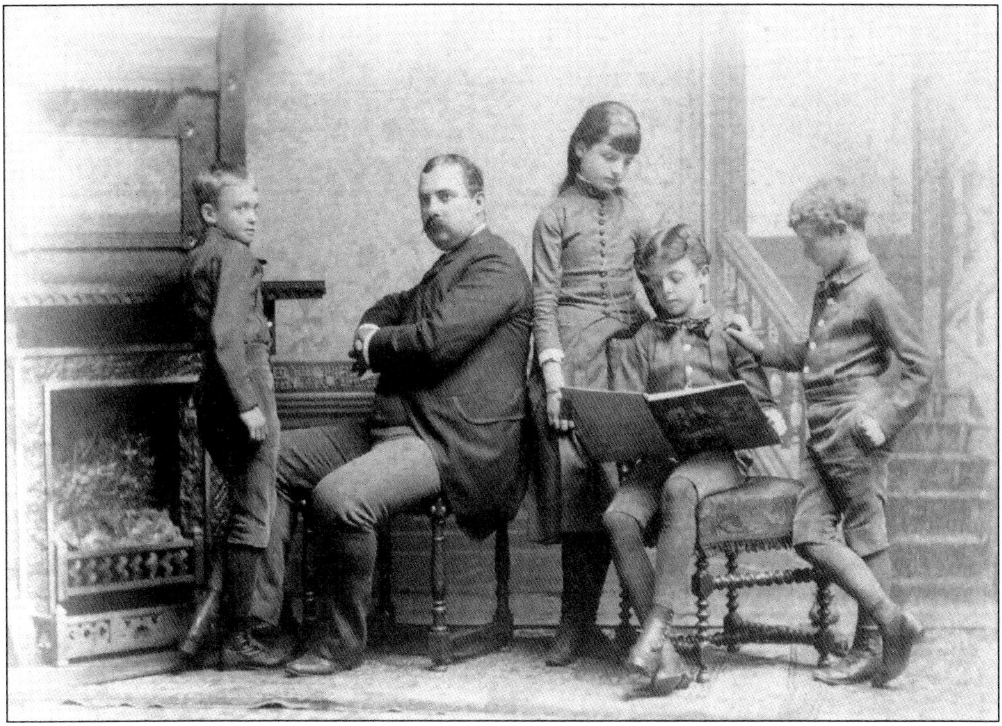

The photo above, taken in the early 1880s, features T. Harrison Garrett, the son of John Work Garrett, and his three boys, from left to right, John, Horatio, and Robert. The girl in the photo is family friend Lisa Turnbull. (Courtesy of the Evergreen House Foundation, The Johns Hopkins University.)

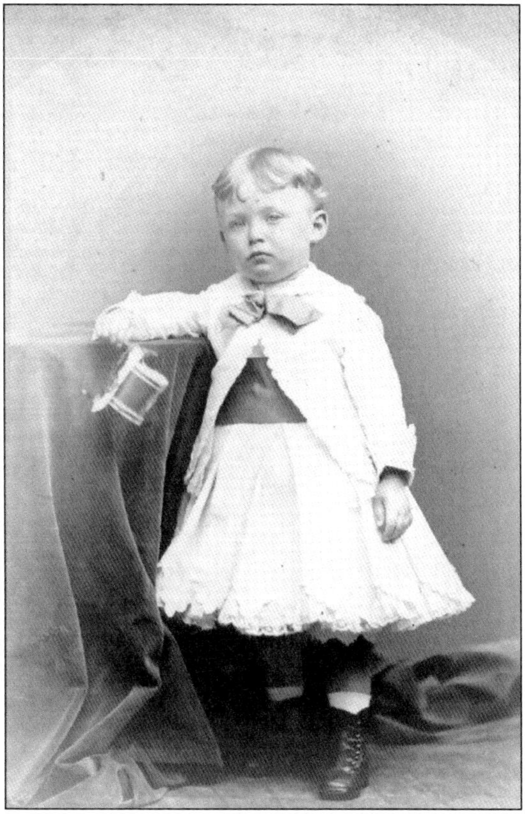

Shown at right is J.W. Garrett, the eldest son of T. Harrison and Alice Whitridge Garrett. Born in 1872, he was approximately three years old at the time of this photograph. (Courtesy of the Evergreen House Foundation, The Johns Hopkins University.)

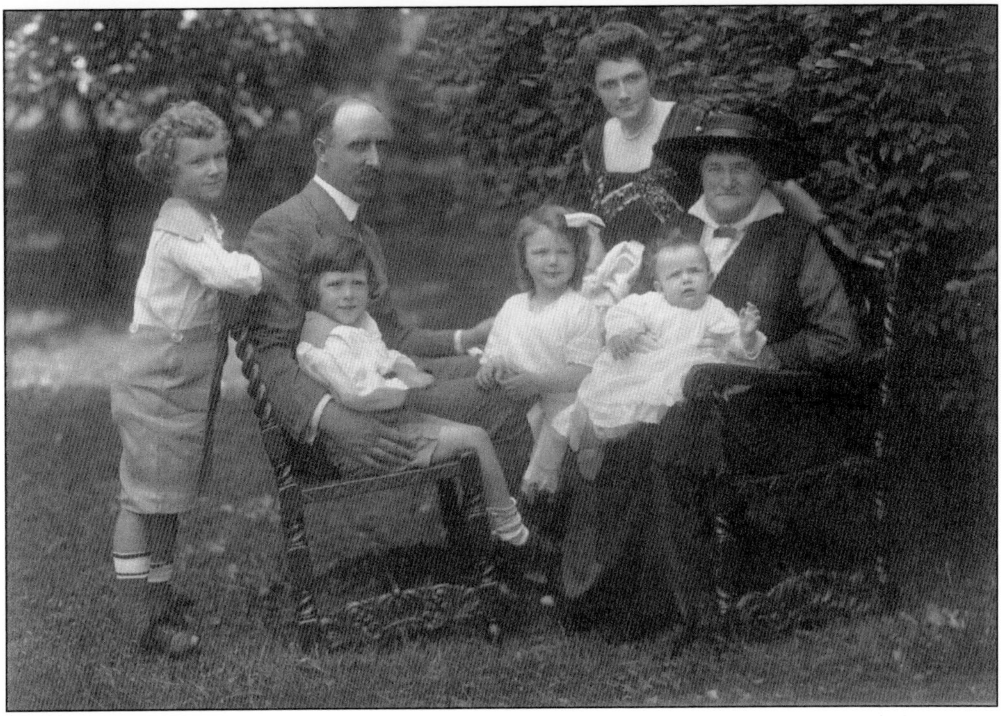

Robert Garrett is pictured above c. 1910 with his family including, from left to right, Harrison Garrett, Johnson, Katherine, Mrs. Robert Garrett, Alice, and Mrs. T. Harrison. (Courtesy of the Evergreen House Foundation, The Johns Hopkins University.)

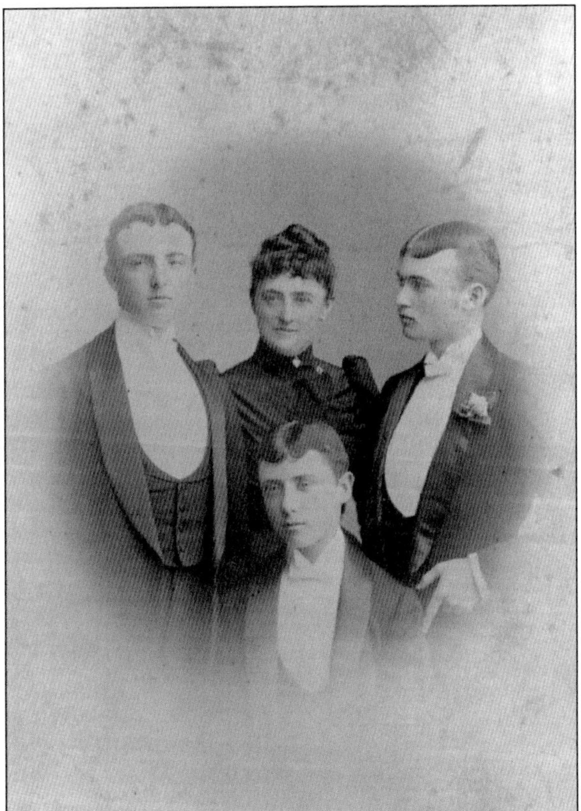

This is a photo, taken *c.* 1888, of Alice Whitridge Garrett, the wife of T. Harrison Garrett, and her sons Horatio (left), Robert (center), and John. Alice Whitridge Garrett took up residence in the town of Princeton while her sons attended college there. (Courtesy of the Evergreen House Foundation, The Johns Hopkins University.)

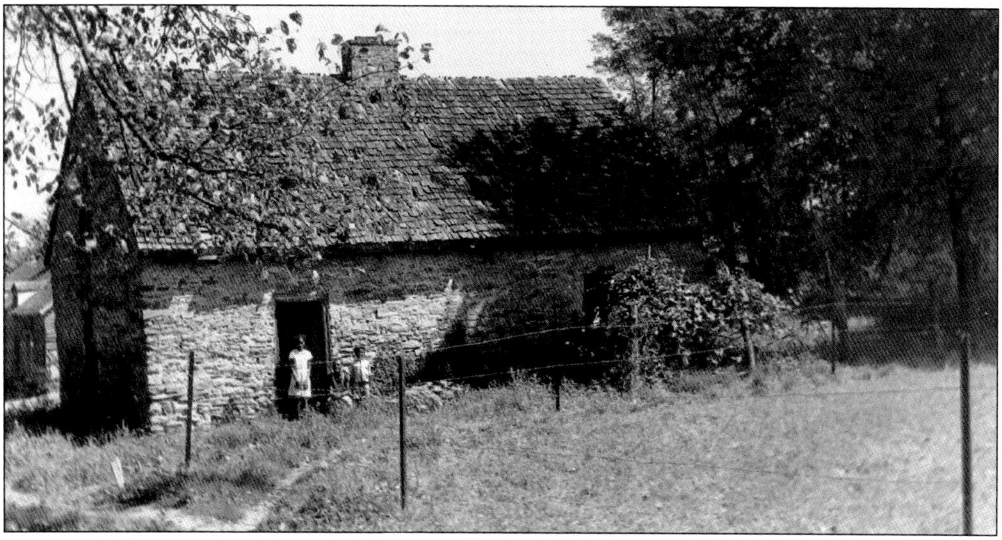

Often called "The Gateway to the South," Baltimore was the launching point of many ships going to markets in the South. From 1815 to 1860 Baltimore was the leading disembarkment point for ships carrying slaves to the Deep South. For many, suicide was a better alternative, as was infanticide, to a life of slavery. Additionally, the death rate of young children was high due to the incredible hardship of slavery and the terrible conditions that prevailed. Forty-nine percent of all deaths in the African-American community recorded between 1849 and 1850 were of children aged five and under. Slave quarters were common on the plantations that surrounded Baltimore, and in the city many of the mansions in areas such as Mt. Vernon had slave homes in the rear. In 1936, when the above photo was taken, there was still a family living in these former slave quarters. (Courtesy of the Enoch Pratt Free Library.)

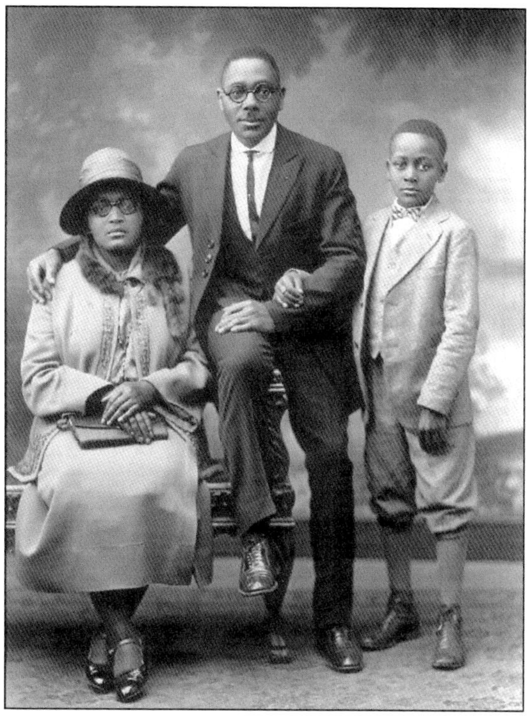

Baltimore had many upper-middle-class, African-American families. Long before the Civil War free blacks owned land and prospered in the city. This portrait shows a typical upper-middle-class family, c. 1920. (Courtesy of Nanny Jack & Co., Inc. Archives.)

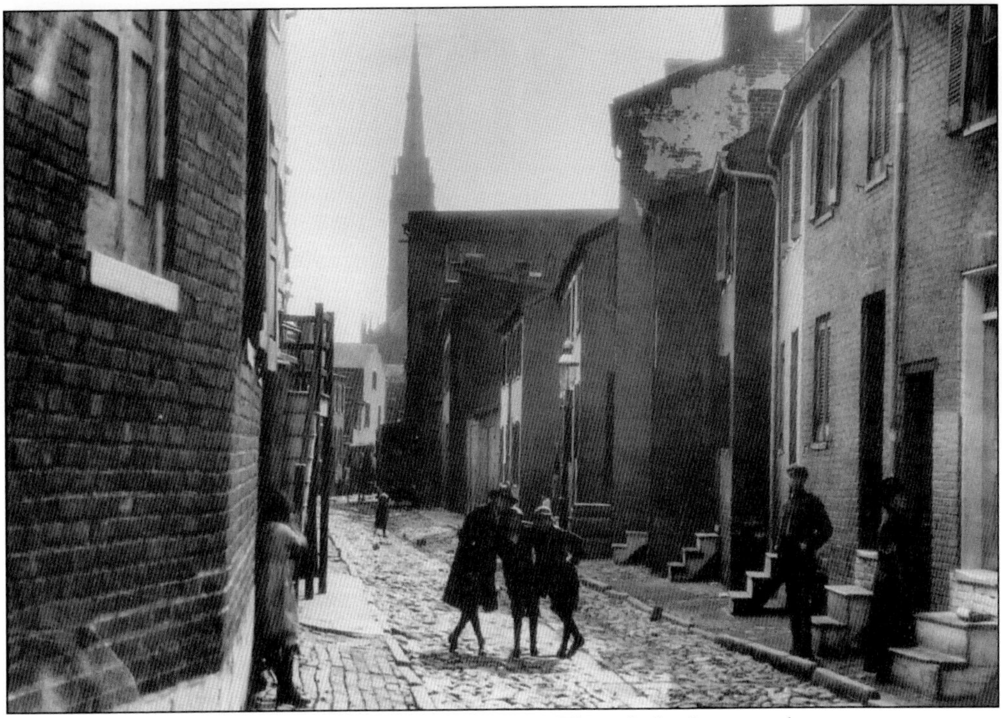

These kids playing at home on Compton Street stop to pose for the camera. This area was considered a slum in 1921. (Courtesy of the Enoch Pratt Free Library.)

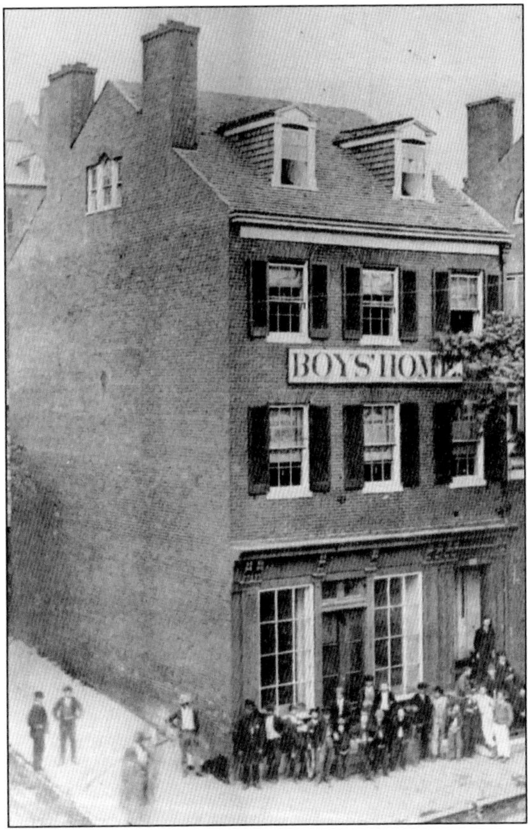

Pictured here is the first site of the Boys' Home Society of Baltimore, located at the northwest corner of Calvert and Pleasant Streets. The Boys' Home opened in 1868. A larger building was later constructed and remained at this location until 1918. The home then moved to 1219–1223 Linden Avenue. In the 1930s the home was not a truly charitable institution for the underprivileged boys it served. It was one of the agencies of the Community Fund and required, in exchange for room, board, and medical privileges, that the boys pay a portion of their weekly salaries to the facility. (Courtesy of the Enoch Pratt Free Library.)

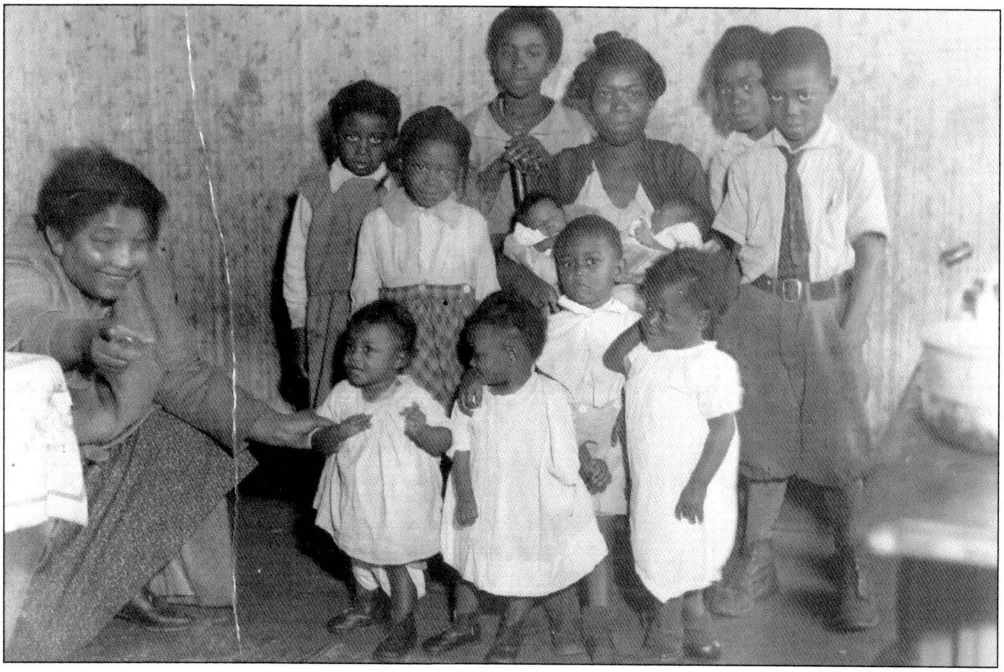

The African-American history in Baltimore, the city that brought us Benjamin Banneker, Frederick Douglass, and Thurgood Marshall, is one of both triumph and sorrow. Destitute, as many were during the Depression, this family, pictured in 1934, represented a majority of laboring city dwellers, but successful property- and business-owning African Americans lived in Baltimore before the 1830s. Several houses built in alleys in the Mount Vernon area were owned by African-American tradesmen and those employed by the neighborhood aristocracy. Affluent black families lived in more upscale housing. Prior to the Civil War, Mount Vernon Ward #11 contained the largest concentration of blacks, both free and enslaved, in the city. (Courtesy of the Enoch Pratt Free Library.)

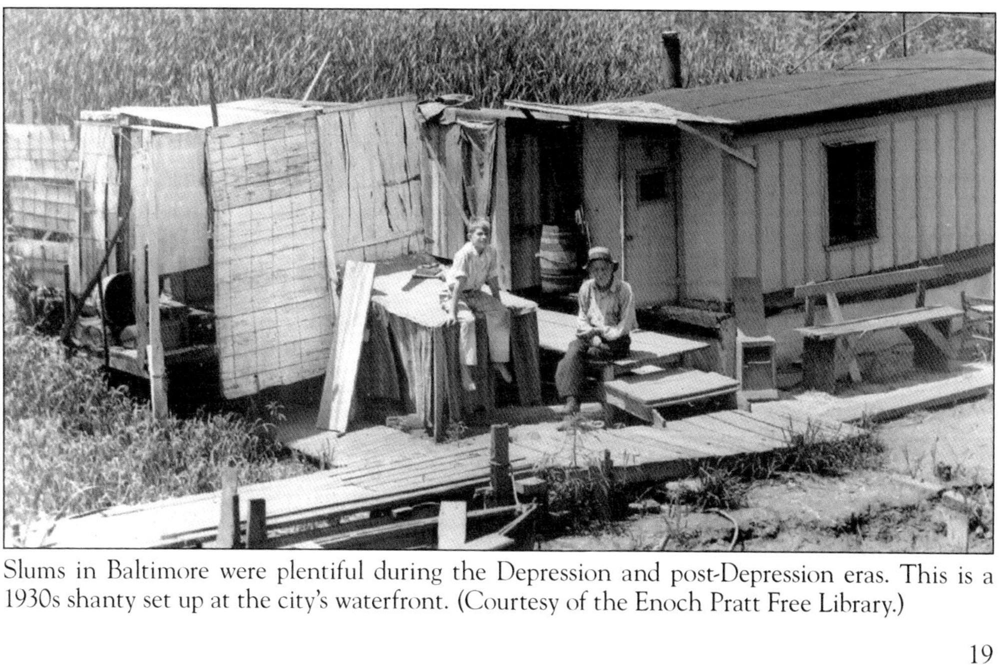

Slums in Baltimore were plentiful during the Depression and post-Depression eras. This is a 1930s shanty set up at the city's waterfront. (Courtesy of the Enoch Pratt Free Library.)

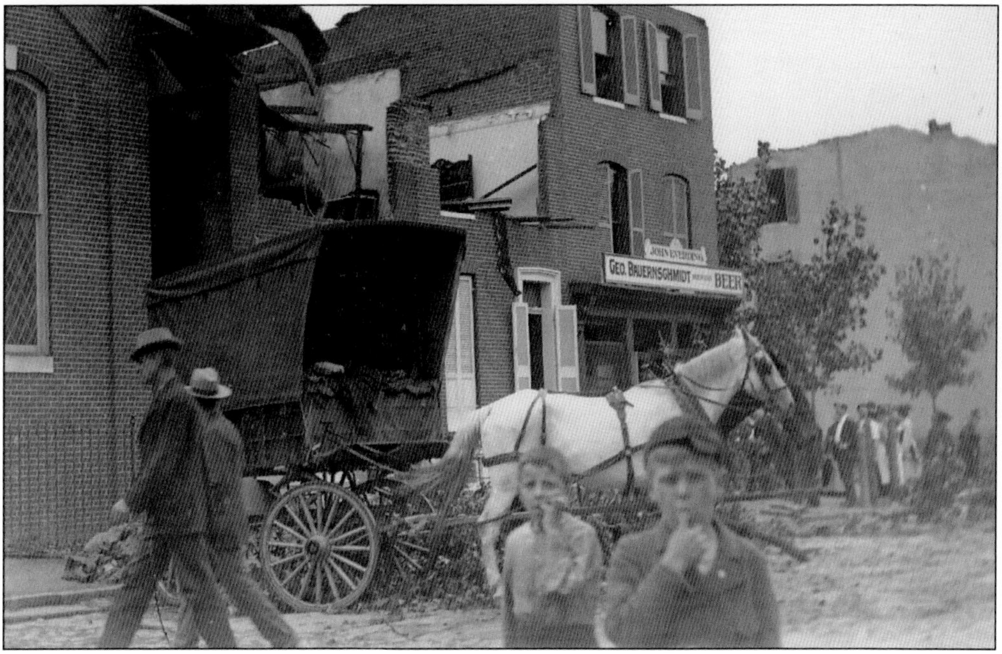

A tornado swept through Baltimore on July 20, 1902. Causing major destruction to structures in its path, the tornado tore approximately 200 roofs from houses and caused other damage in the eastern part of the city. These images, like many others of major events and disasters, were taken by the Baltimore Camera Club. (Courtesy of the Enoch Pratt Free Library.)

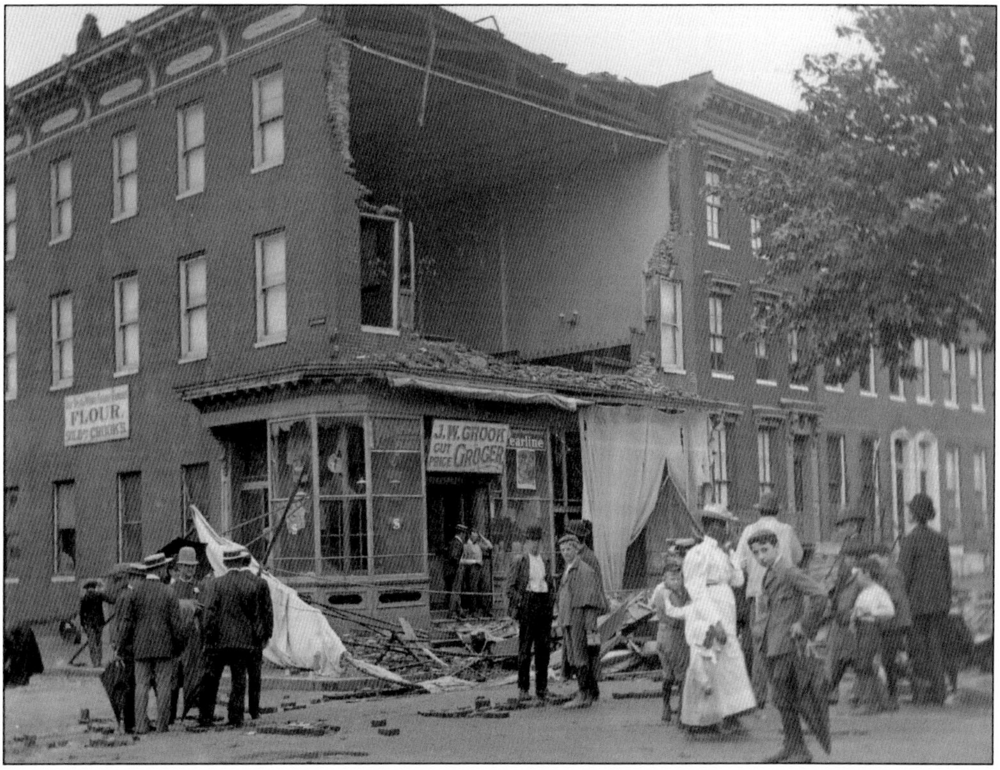

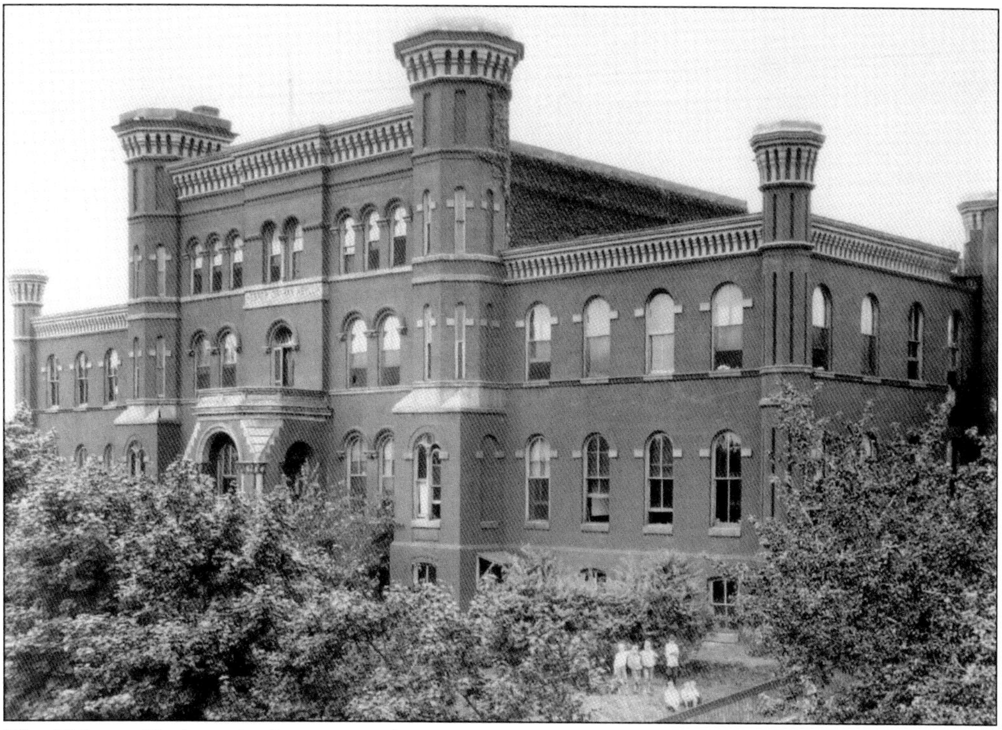

The Hebrew Orphan Asylum, created in 1872, originally occupied what had been the Baltimore County Almshouse building. The building burned down one year later and a new building was dedicated in 1876. The grounds and the second building were both gifts of Mr. and Mrs. William S. Rayner. Although the orphanage housed almost exclusively Jewish children, it did accept non-Jews "in case(s) of emergency." The building was found to be unfit for children in 1920, and the orphanage was moved to Levindale. The orphanage and some of its occupants are seen above, c. 1923. (Courtesy of the Jewish Museum of Maryland.)

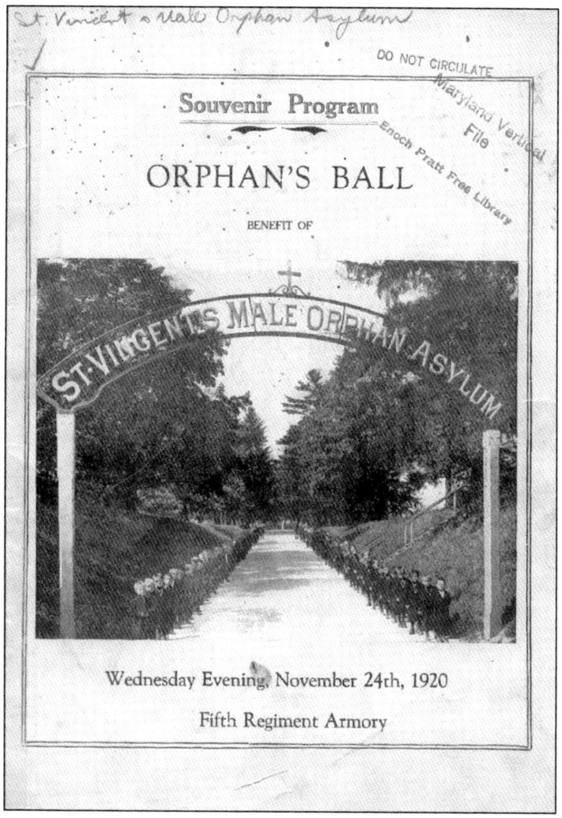

This is a booklet from a 1920 gala event that raised money for the St. Vincent's Male Orphan's Asylum. (Courtesy of the Enoch Pratt Free Library.)

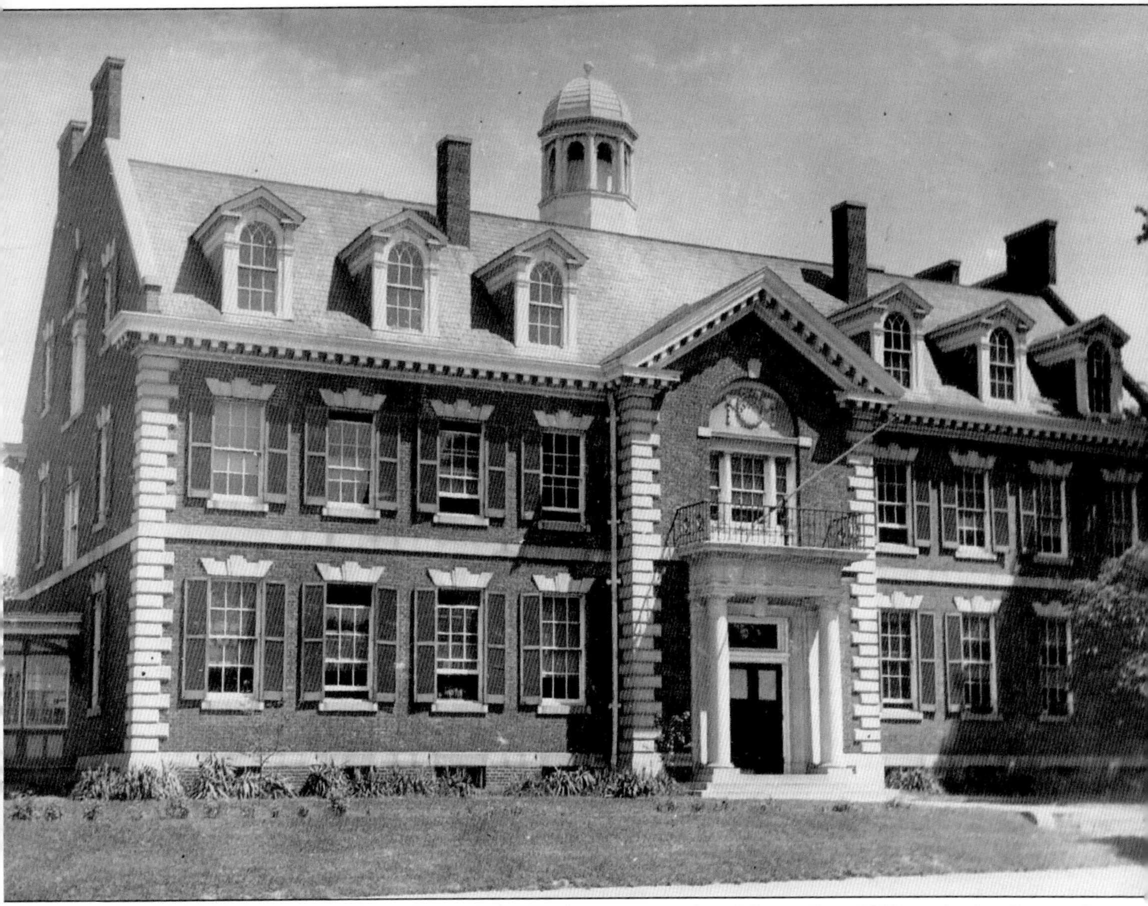

The Samuel Ready Asylum for Female Orphans opened in November 1887 with the first girls, ranging in age from 5 to 15, admitted from various places in Maryland, as well as three sisters born in Chile. Renamed Samuel Ready School in 1894 to keep the word "asylum" off the resumés of its graduates, the orphanage did not merely take in unfortunate girls and give them shelter. It provided quality education for young women and was, in many ways, ahead of its time, adopting methods of instruction quite modern for its era. This was due to the Progressive era–instruction of the school's principal, Helen Rowe, and the philanthropy of Samuel Ready. Born in Baltimore County in 1789, Ready made his wealth as a sailmaker and land speculator. He was moved by the plight of the young waifs who hung around the docks and felt that they were in more severe danger, physically and morally, than the boys. This was his motivation for creating a safe haven for the girls and giving them a brighter future. Ready wanted a place with more than other orphanages had to offer—a real home for the girls—and based his ideal for the asylum on that image. Wanting to make homeless girls into "useful women," he promoted hygiene, vocational training, and instruction to help them in motherhood and nursing. Ready drew up a charter for the school in 1864. He died in 1871, leaving his estate to the school (this was contested by his sister's family since he never married and had no children of his own) and real estate was purchased in 1882. The school remained there until 1938. (Courtesy of the Enoch Pratt Free Library.)

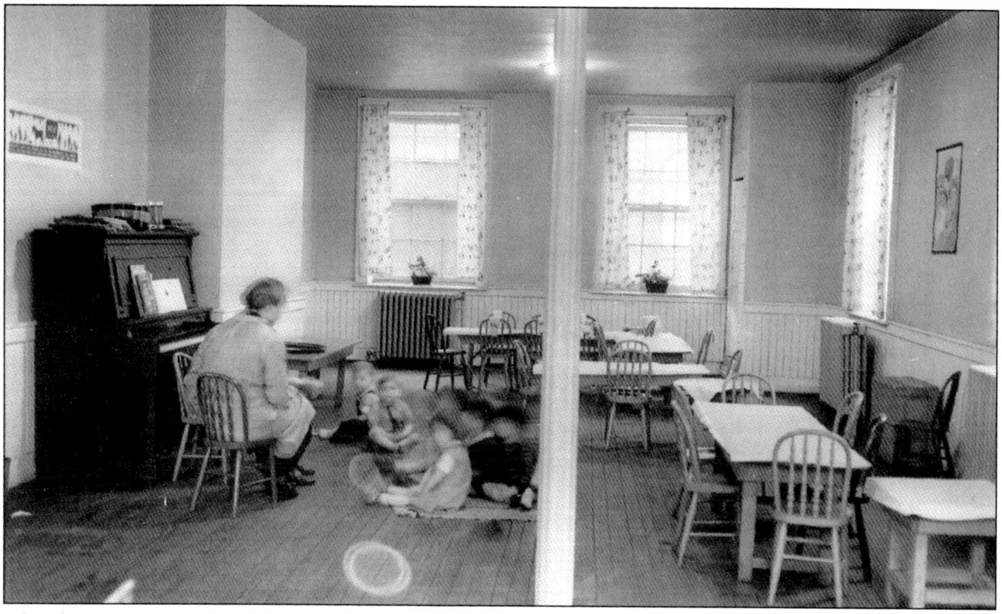

This house at Lombard and Front Streets was built by Richard and Mary Caroll Caton with money from Charles Caroll of Carollton. It was bought by the city of Baltimore in 1914, then restored and repaired. In 1937 it was used for local settlement work. This photo, taken in January 1938, shows a teacher with children in the old dining room. (Courtesy of the Enoch Pratt Free Library.)

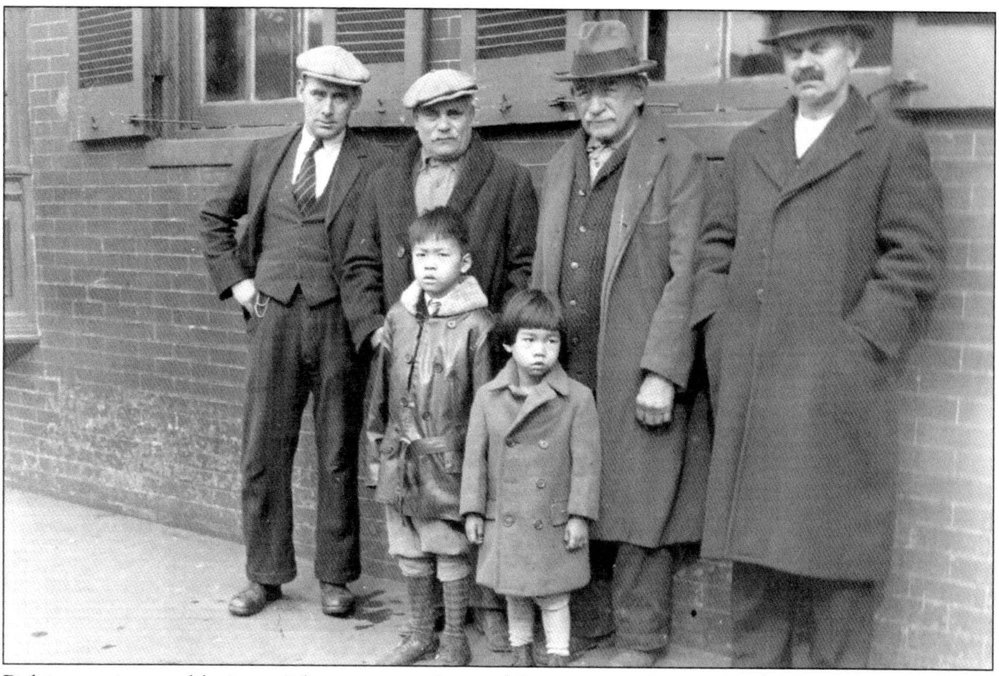

Baltimore is an old city, with many residents able to trace their roots back to colonial days. It is also a city of great ethnic diversity and a long history of immigration. These children were new immigrants when this photo was taken in the 1930s. (Courtesy of the Enoch Pratt Free Library.)

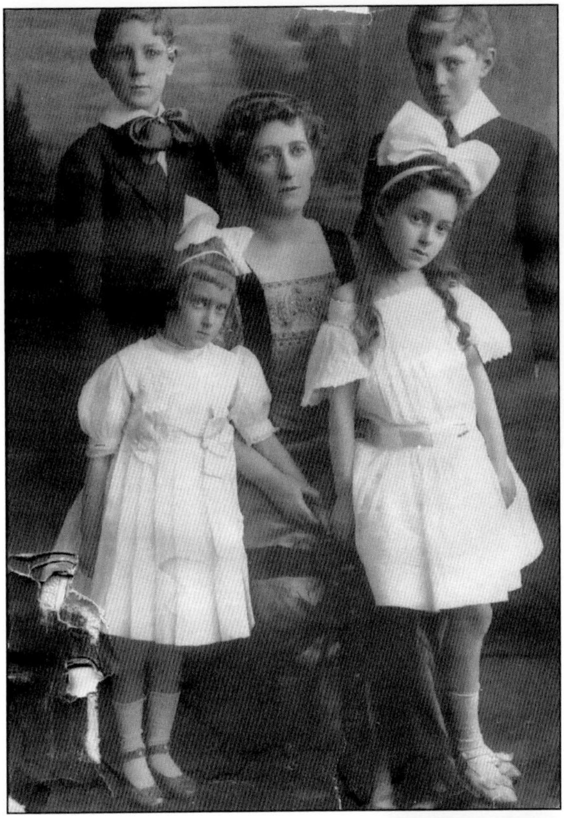

The Strauss/Kohn family has resided in Baltimore since the 1840s. Clara Strauss Kohn was born in Baltimore in 1873 and attended Western High School. Her father, Moses Strauss, came to Baltimore from Germany before the Civil War. He and his brother, Abe, died shortly after the fire of 1904 that nearly wiped them out financially. Although Moses and his wife, Caroline, were devout Jews, none of their five daughters married religious men. Clara married Benno Kohn in 1895. This was the year that, together with his brother Louis and Max Hochschild, Benno started Hochschild Kohn & Co. Clara is seen here with her four children in 1908. The boys are Martin (left) and Bernard; the girls are Carrie (left) and Eleanor. (Courtesy of Liz Moser.)

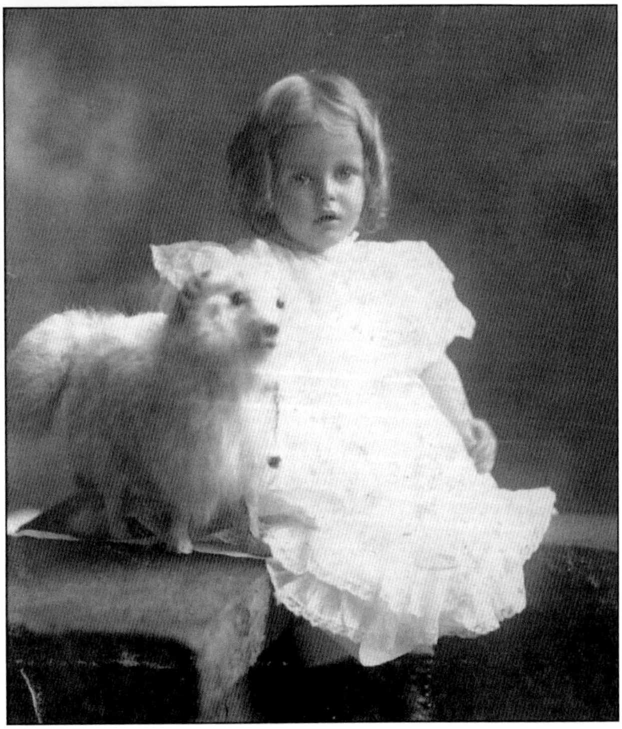

Bernard Kohn, the eldest son of Benno and Clara Kohn, is seen at right in 1897 at age two. His lovely little frills and delicate curls were typical adornment for boys of his age in this era. The family lived near Druid Hill Park on Callow Avenue. (Courtesy of Liz Moser.)

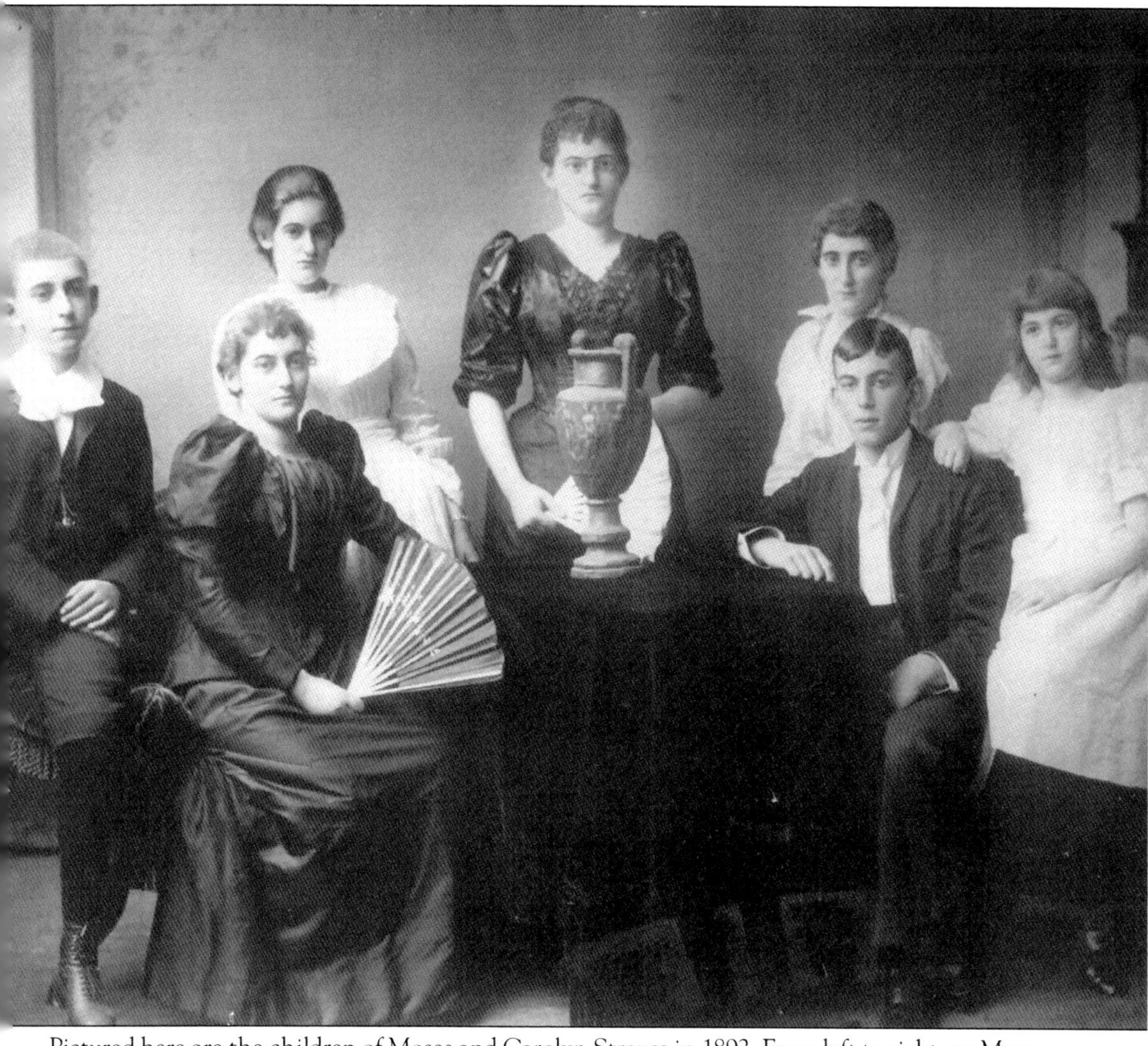

Pictured here are the children of Moses and Carolyn Strauss in 1892. From left to right are Myer, Katie, Jennie, Sophie, Clara, Laser, and Theresa, who married Louis Hutzler of the Hutzler Department Store family. (Courtesy of Liz Moser.)

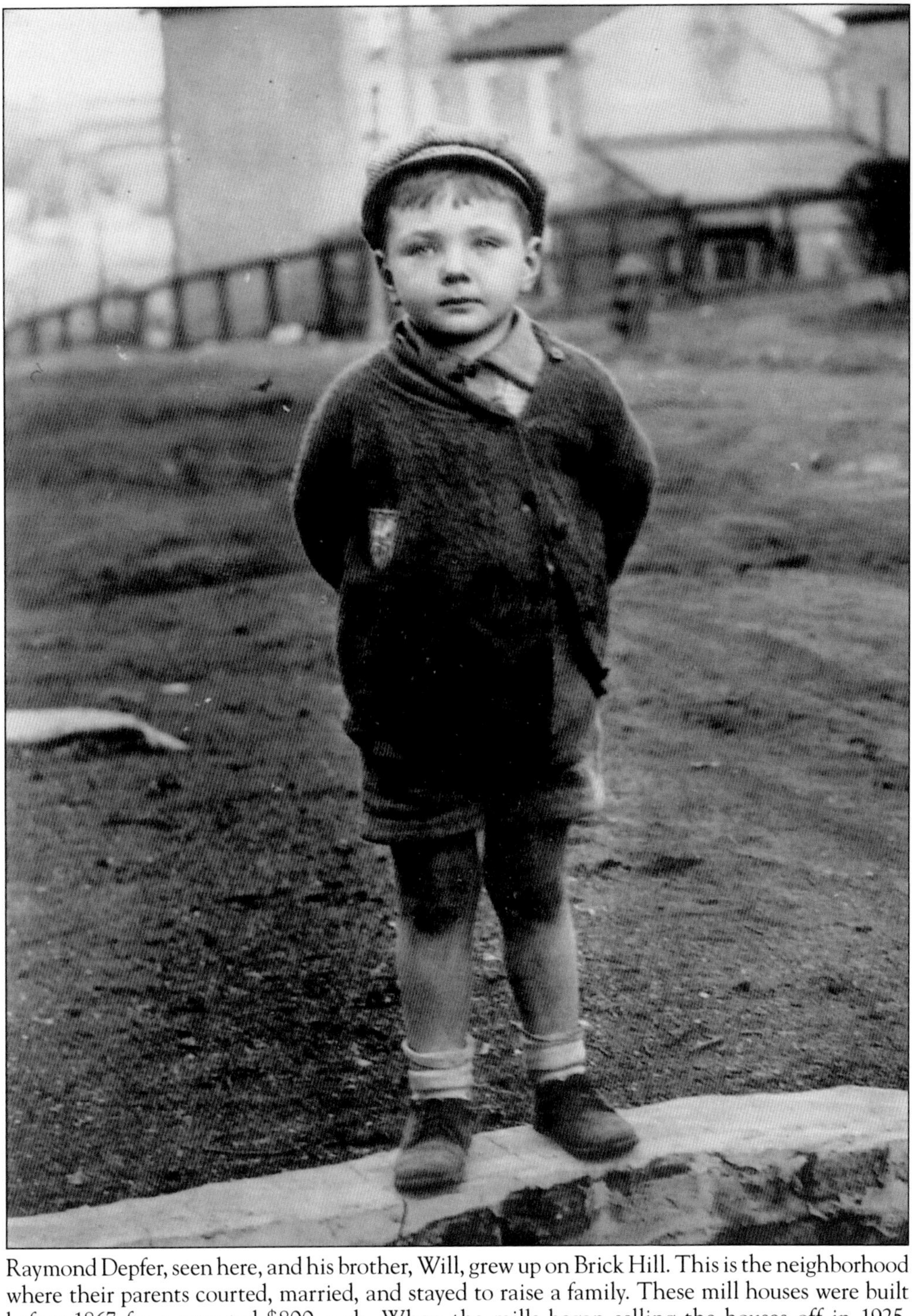

Raymond Depfer, seen here, and his brother, Will, grew up on Brick Hill. This is the neighborhood where their parents courted, married, and stayed to raise a family. These mill houses were built before 1867 for a reported $800 each. When the mills began selling the houses off in 1925, the Depfer family began to purchase them as they became available. The mill was then asking $2,500 per house. The Depfer brothers still own many of the structures here. (Courtesy of William Depfer.)

This c. 1930 photograph shows the children of mill workers. It has been said that in mill houses on Brick Hill, at one time, there were approximately 10 kids per household. There are 20 houses on the hill, meaning that approximately 200 kids were left to their own devices while their parents worked in the mills. Many of the older family members who did not work in the mills cared for the younger ones during the day. (Courtesy of William Depfer.)

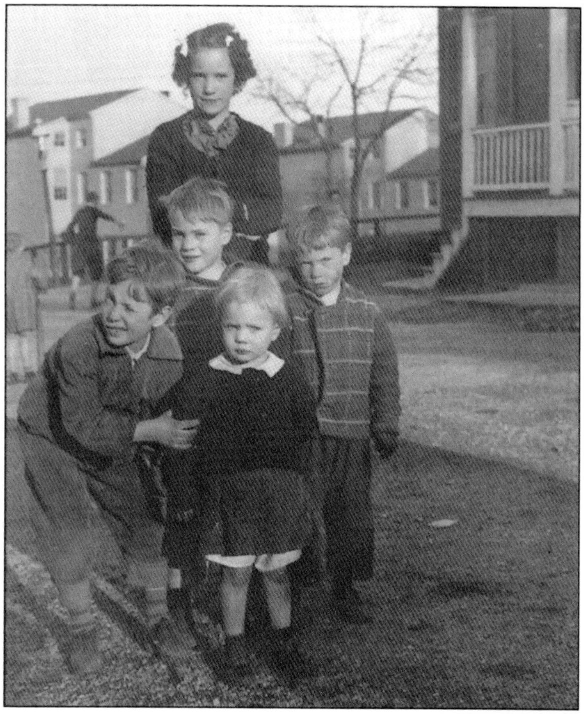

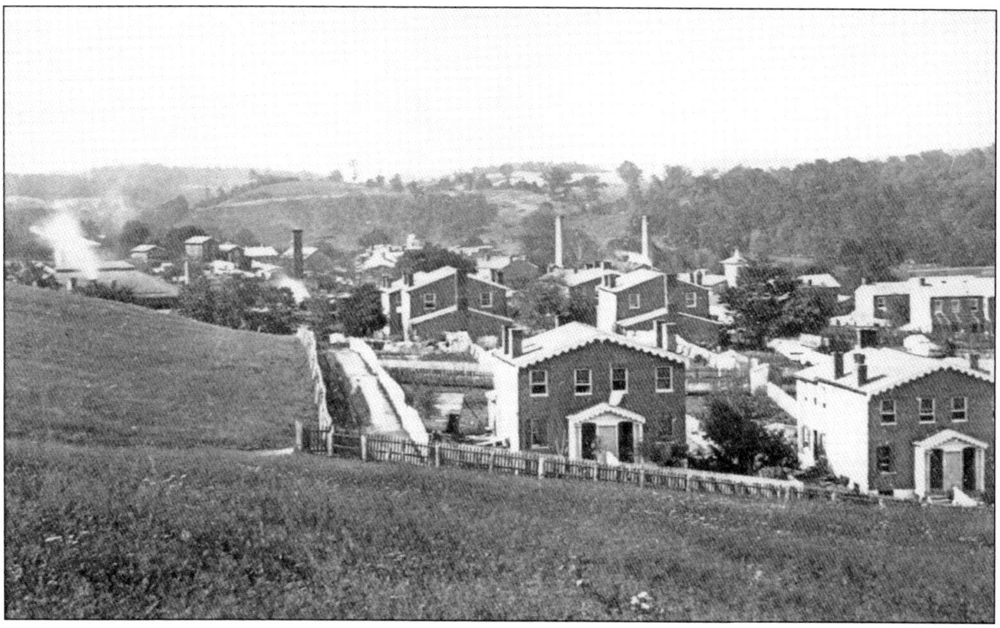

Pictured in 1867 is historic Brick Hill, which is situated in Woodberry near Hampden. The brick houses visible here were built for millworkers. It was once thought that these houses were constructed for the workers at Meadow Mill, which was built in 1877. They existed, however, 10 years prior to that, as this image demonstrates. Originally the park was groomed and the lawn kept clear, but it is now quite overgrown. The house, front left, burned down a couple of years after this photo was taken. The lot where it stood remains empty. The hill in the distant left is now called "T.V. Hill." (Courtesy of the Enoch Pratt Free Library.)

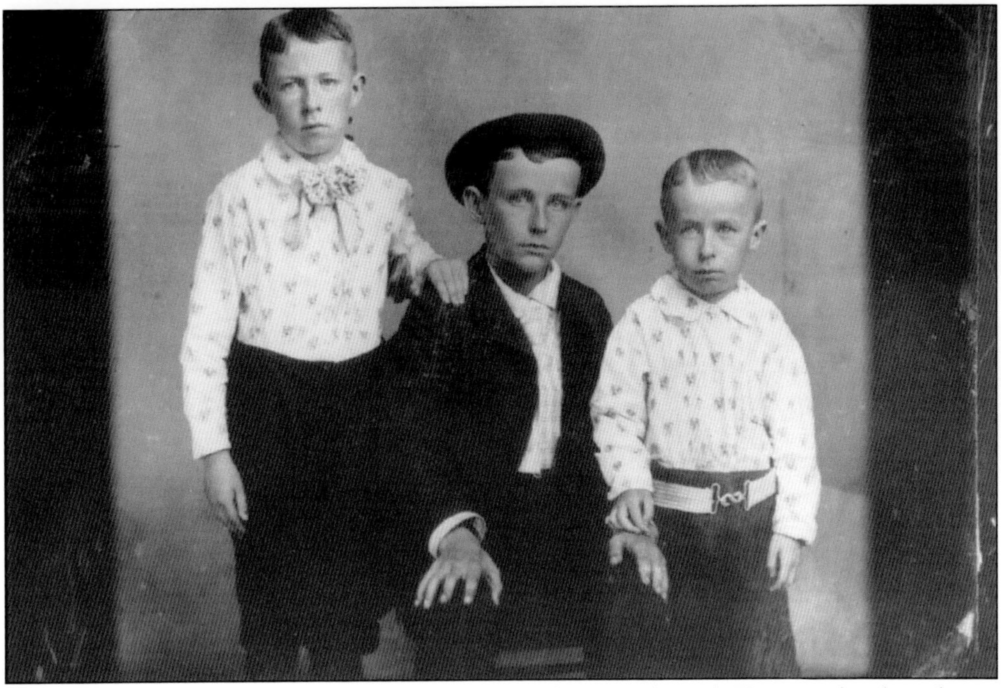

Pictured in 1887 are the Winters brothers, Peter, John Patrick, and Thomas, the three living children of Fanny and John Winters (non-surviving children had died before coming to America). At age 23, Peter, a haberdasher in 1903, went hunting and returned with a case of appendicitis. He died shortly after. John Patrick died in 1936 from a fall. (Courtesy of Denny Lynch.)

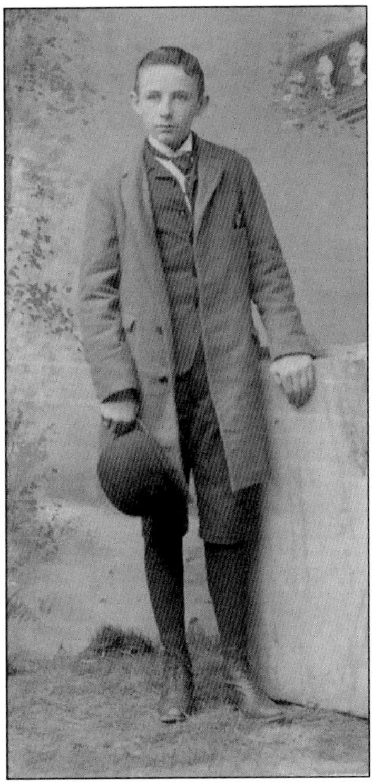

John Patrick Winters was born in County Monaghan, Ireland on April 13, 1876, and his family arrived at Ellis Island on September 14, 1880. His parents, Fanny and John, took their sons immediately to Baltimore. The family lived in Medfield where they tended horses and worked as domestics. Son Thomas was born on May 8, 1884. John died in 1886, leaving Fanny and their sons alone. Fanny managed to buy a house on what is now the 3900 block of Elm Avenue in Hampden in 1899. This house is still in the family. Until the mid- to late 20th century, Hampden, an area that is now integrated and somewhat gentrified, was a hotbed of ethnic bigotry. Settled mostly by Appalachian migrant workers, a great many of whom were illiterate and came to find employment in the mills, Hampden was a quaint neighborhood with parks and great resources for children, provided they were white and born in America. Irish immigrants found themselves the recipients of attacks. Trendy Hampden now has cafes and specialty shops, and people of different ethnicities can walk together without fear. The parks and the library in Hampden offer wonderful opportunities for all children. (Courtesy of Denny Lynch.)

Russell Winters, the son of John Patrick and Abbie (née Richardson) Winters, was born on September 4, 1900. He is seen here at approximately age two. The photographer, Armiger of Woodberry, was popular in this area at that time, and his studio was located on what was then Third Avenue, now Thirty-sixth Street. (Courtesy of Denny Lynch.)

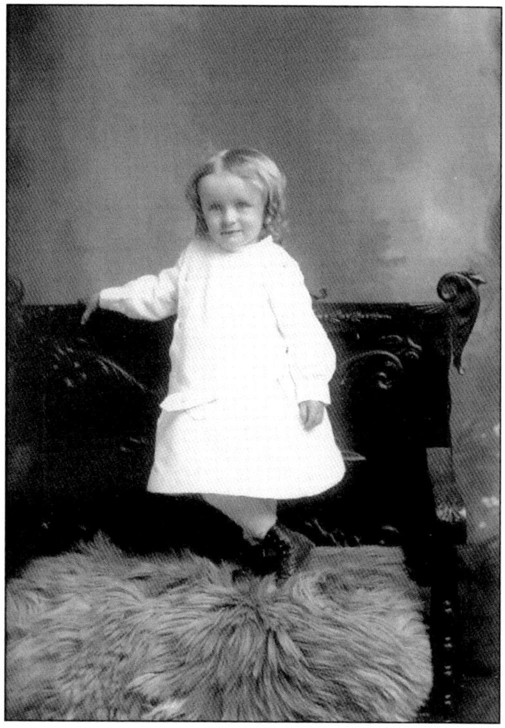

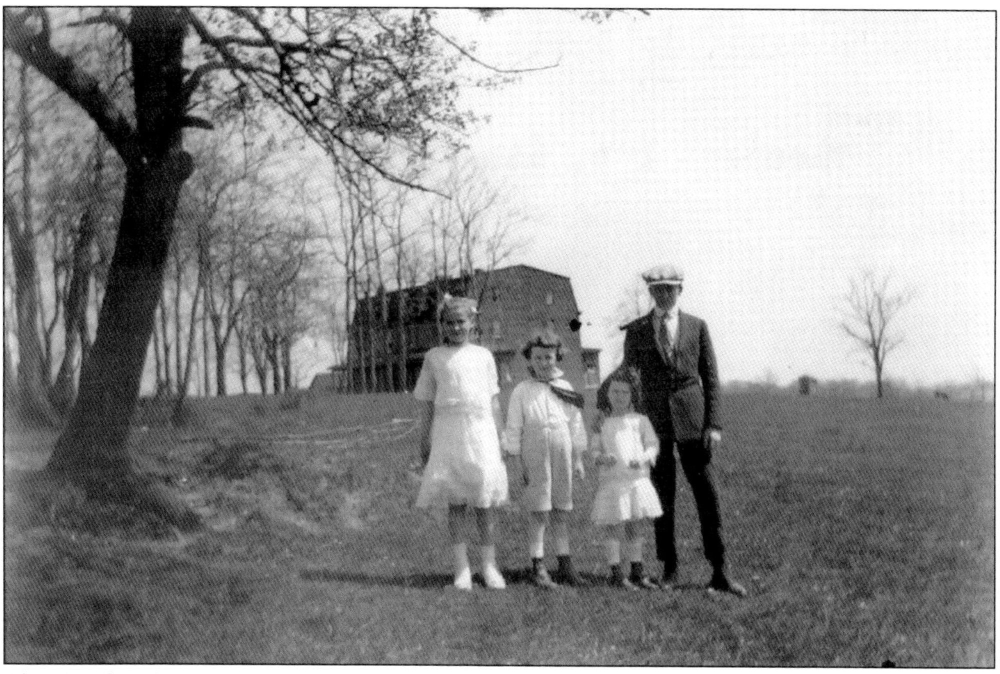

This April 1917 view was captured looking across the old field from Fanny Winters's Elm Avenue house at what was then called Hare's Hill and is now the Rotunda Shopping Center. At the time there was only the old farmhouse, visible behind the children. Pictured, from left to right, are Theresa (born 1907), James (born 1909), Ethel (born 1911), and Russell Winters. (Courtesy of Denny Lynch.)

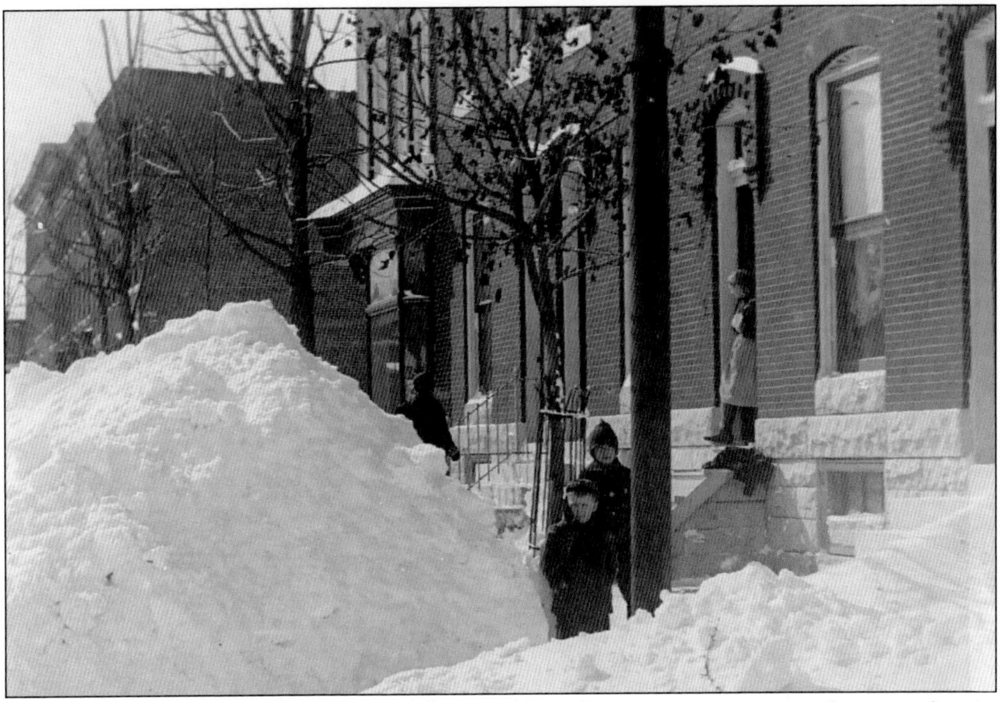

This photograph of children in front of their rowhouse home on a very snowy day was taken in 1899. (Courtesy of the Enoch Pratt Free Library.)

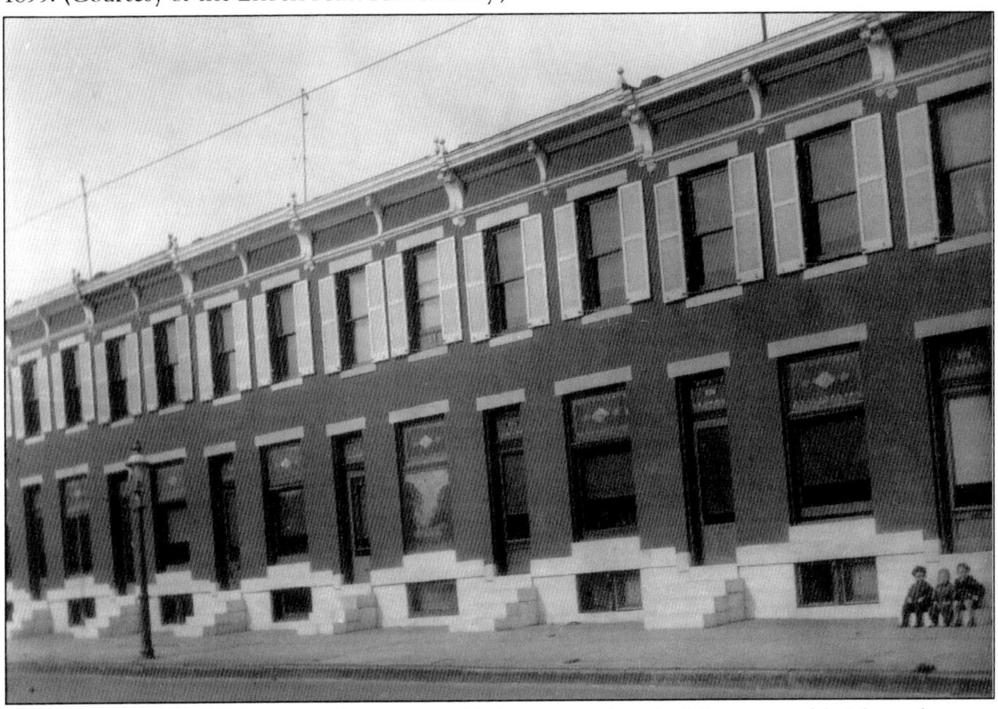

This scene on Preston Street, taken in the 1920s, shows the city's famous red brick rowhouses. Families sitting on their marble stoops is as familiar sight in Baltimore's working-class neighborhoods today as it was 100 years ago. (Courtesy of the Enoch Pratt Free Library.)

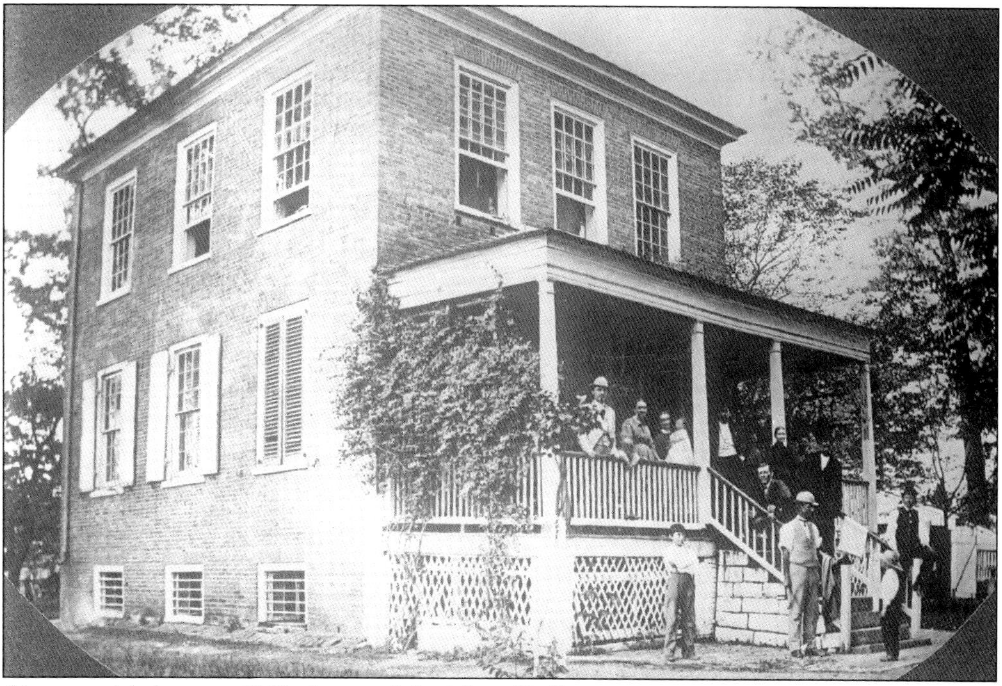

Above and below are 1868 photos of the Horn-Hoffman House at Madison and Eutaw Place on Hoffman Street, north of North Avenue. Aaron Hoffman was a wealthy pork packer in Baltimore before the Civil War, and his luxurious home was on a street named for him. The war wiped the family out and left each member to fend for his own. Grandson William Hoffman, born in 1864 in a house adjoining his grandfather's, was a politician and a horseshoer, according to newspapers of the day. Built in what was considered bucolic countryside at the time, the location where the house once stood is now in the middle of the city. (Courtesy of the Enoch Pratt Free Library.)

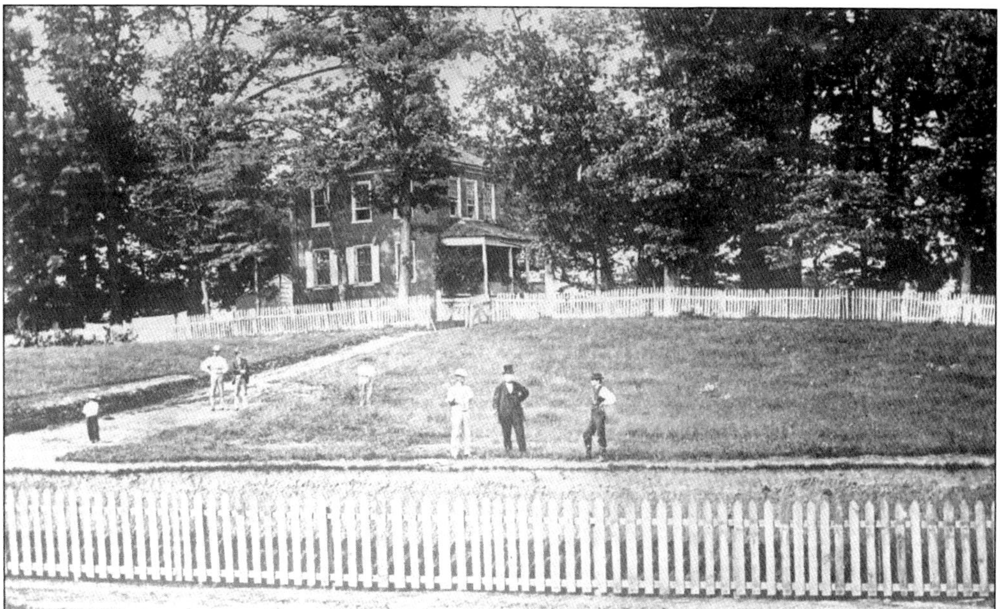

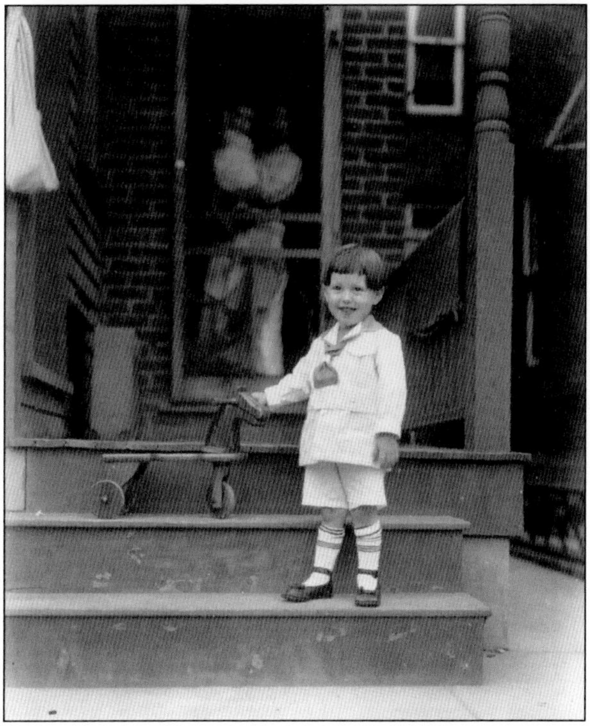

Jim Lewis (1881–1960) was a semi-professional photographer in Baltimore who was truly in love with his art. Next to his wife, Theresa, children seemed to be his favorite study. He took many photos of his own children, as well others in the neighborhood. He took many posed portraits using his "outdoor studio," i.e. his backyard. This *c.* 1918 image shows Lewis's son Jimmy, born in 1915, in front of the Lewis home. In the background, we see a mother and her baby girl, most likely Theresa with baby Estelle, who was born in 1917. (Courtesy of Jack Hennessy.)

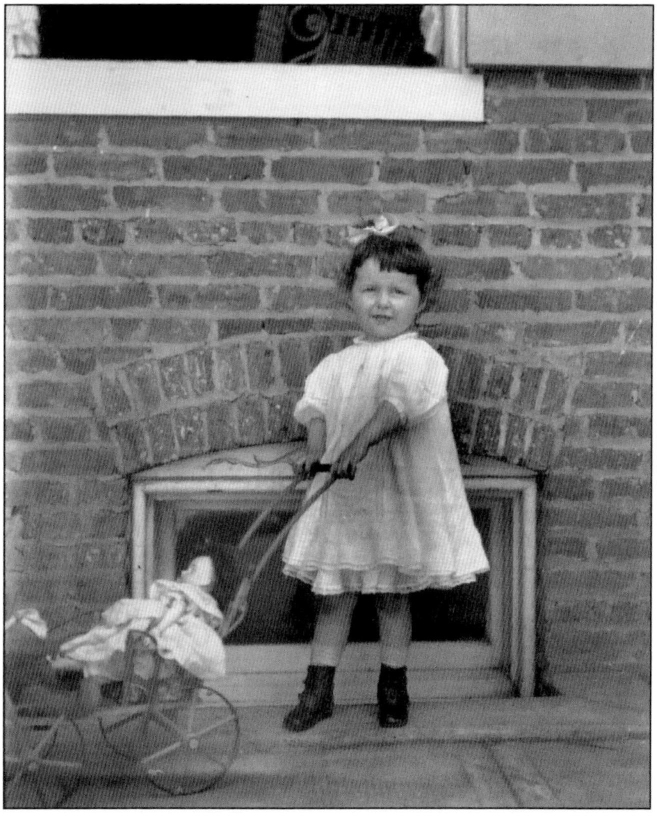

Here, Jim Lewis has taken a picture of Claire, his eldest daughter. Claire was born in 1906 and is seen here in 1909 taking her doll for a walk, most likely on or near Bank Street in Upper Fells Point. (Courtesy of Jack Hennessy.)

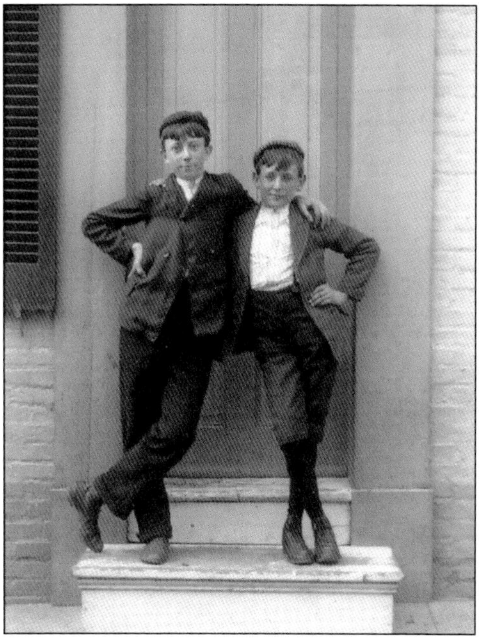

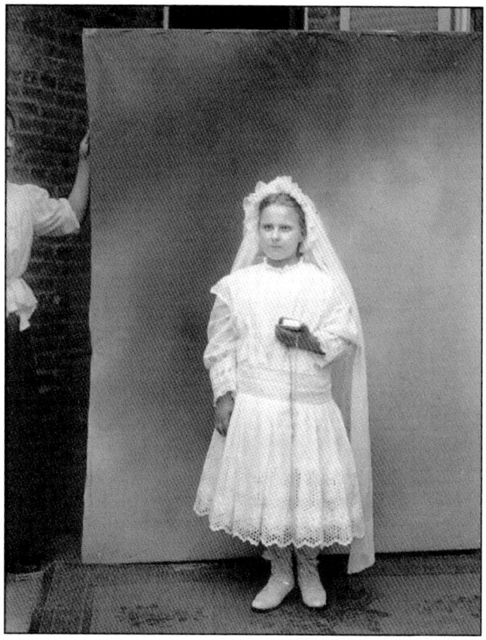

Left: These two young cards are pictured, most likely, near Fells Point, *c.* 1910. (Courtesy of Jack Hennessy.)
Right: In this photo, a little girl poses at her first communion, while Theresa Lewis holds the backdrop, usually a rug or decorative blanket. The rough edges of the photo would have been removed by a professional processor and the little girl would have appeared to be in a salon instead of outside in the garden. (Courtesy of Jack Hennessy.)

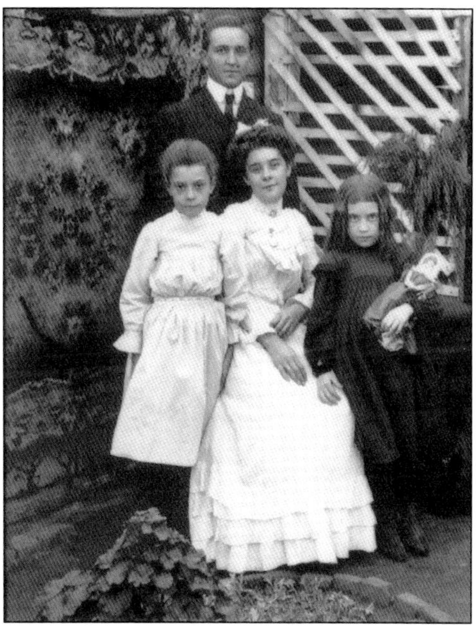

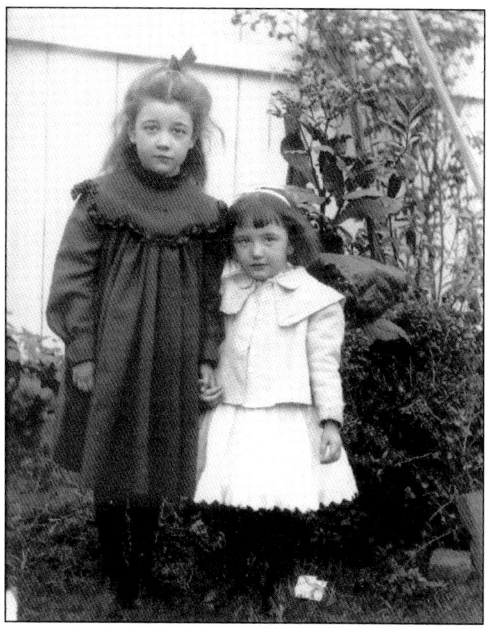

These posed Lewis photos would have been cropped by a commercial lab and given to the clients with only the background and some of the rug showing (left) and a closer crop would have been made for the girls in the garden. (Courtesy of Jack Hennessy.)

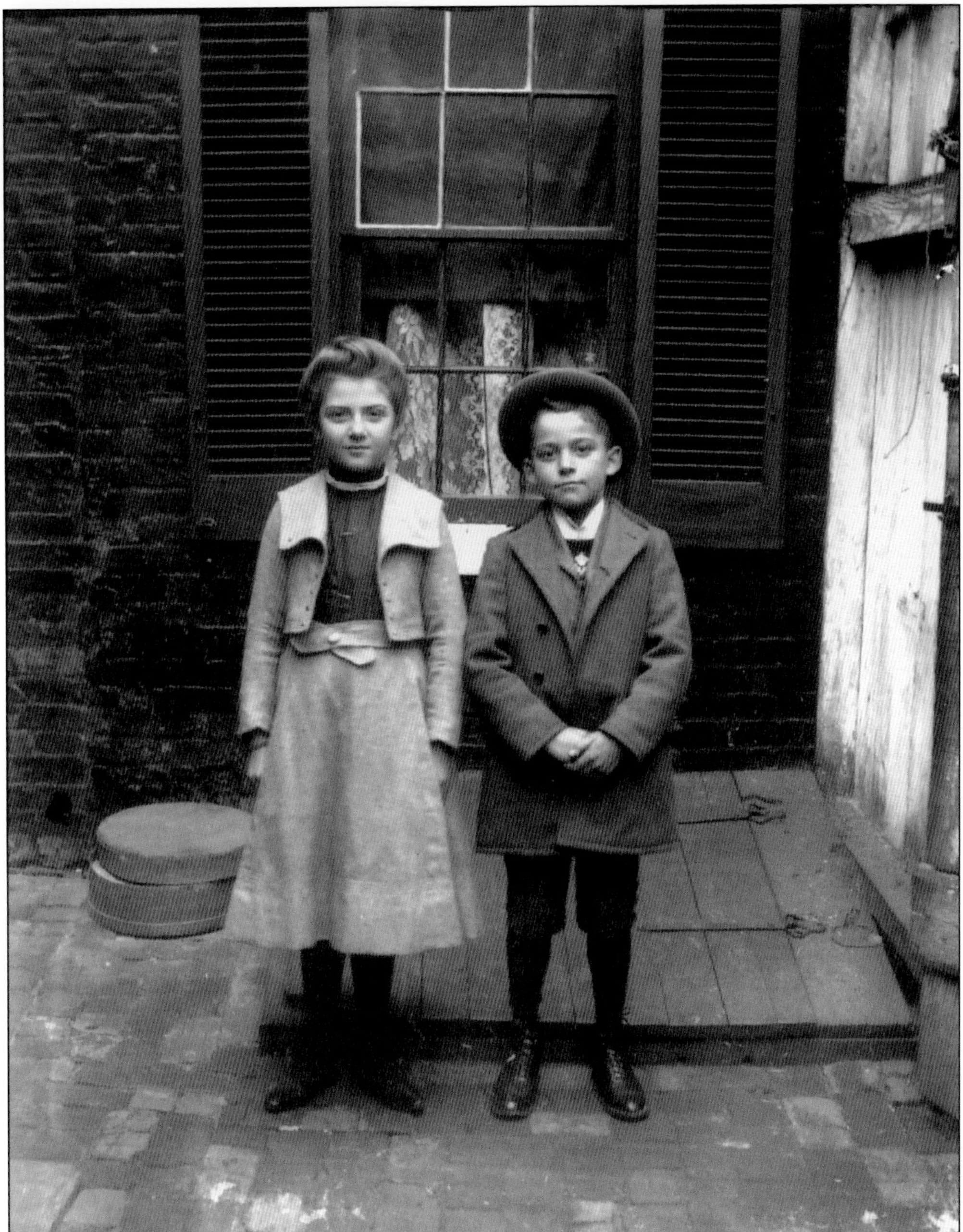

This little boy and girl, most likely brother and sister, are dressed for church or some other special occasion. They, like most of Jim Lewis's young subjects, were probably neighborhood children in upper Fells Point who captured his eye. (Courtesy of Jack Hennessy.)

Two

Children at School

When it comes to education, Baltimore has a long and complicated history. For over a century, the city has been home to some of the most elite and respected private schools in the world, one of which has been in operation for over 200 years. For those who choose and can afford costly private education, Baltimore has a superior collection of diverse schools that address the different needs of the city's elite. Parochial schools, alternative education, military academies, equestrian boarding schools—whatever a parent might want for their child, it is available here in Baltimore. In addition to standard education, several special needs schools have been a part of Baltimore for more than a century. Newer schools that offer classes for children with more recently diagnosed conditions have joined the ranks of established schools to offer a diverse group of special needs programs. Conversely, Baltimore has a long history of underfunded public schools. From the first ordinance in March 1828 to the modern day, the city's public school system has had difficulty in equipping its schools with all of the essentials. Often schools cannot afford to purchase supplies, hire sufficient staff to accommodate the student body, or maintain buildings and classrooms. Many schools not only lack an internal library, but essentials such as books, classroom space, teachers, and other educational materials. Although there are striking exceptions, the quality of education in many of Baltimore City's public schools has been considered substandard for some time. This dichotomy is only one example of the parallel worlds that have always been a part of Baltimore.

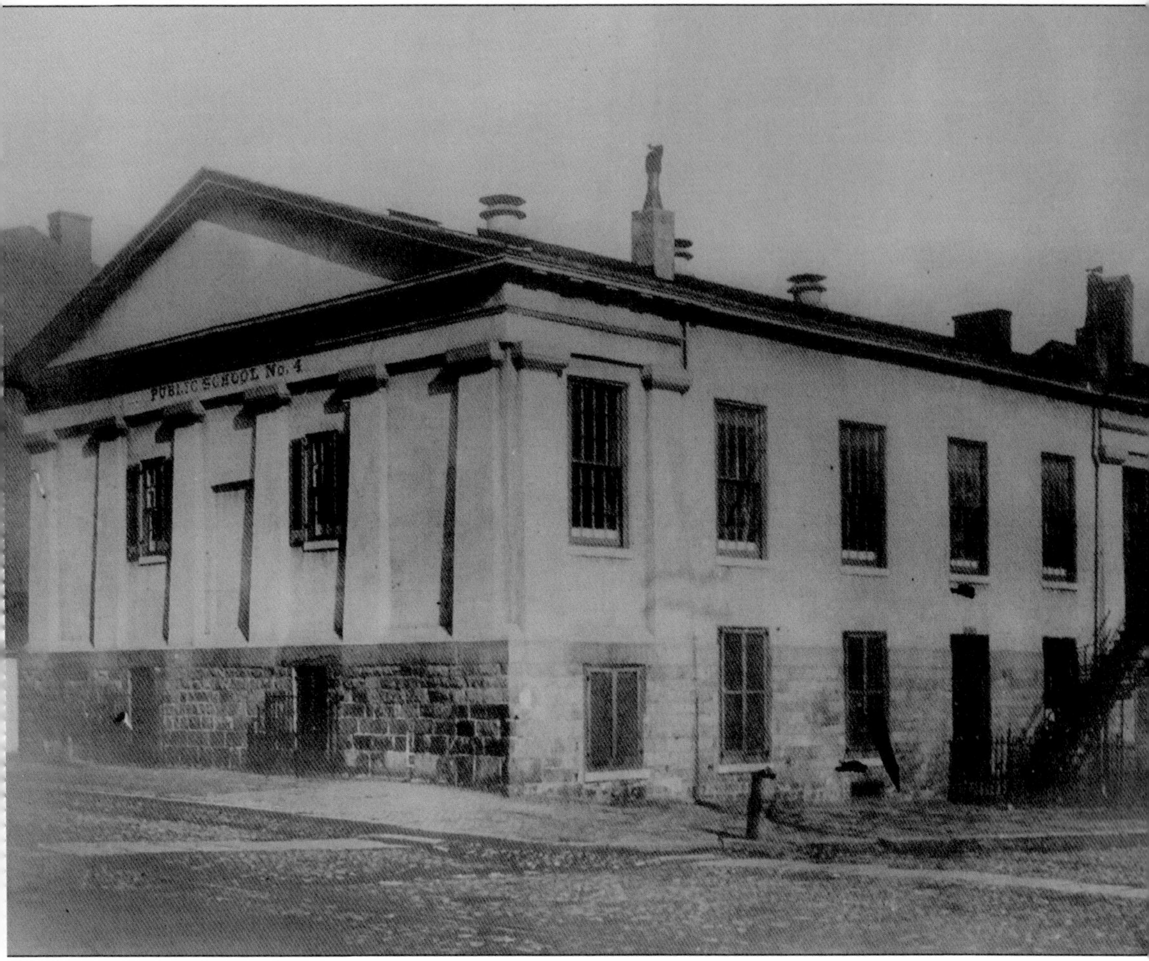

Plans to build this school were set in motion in 1832, and the construction was completed the following year. The school was used by both male and female students, although they were not taught together. (Courtesy of the Enoch Pratt Free Library.)

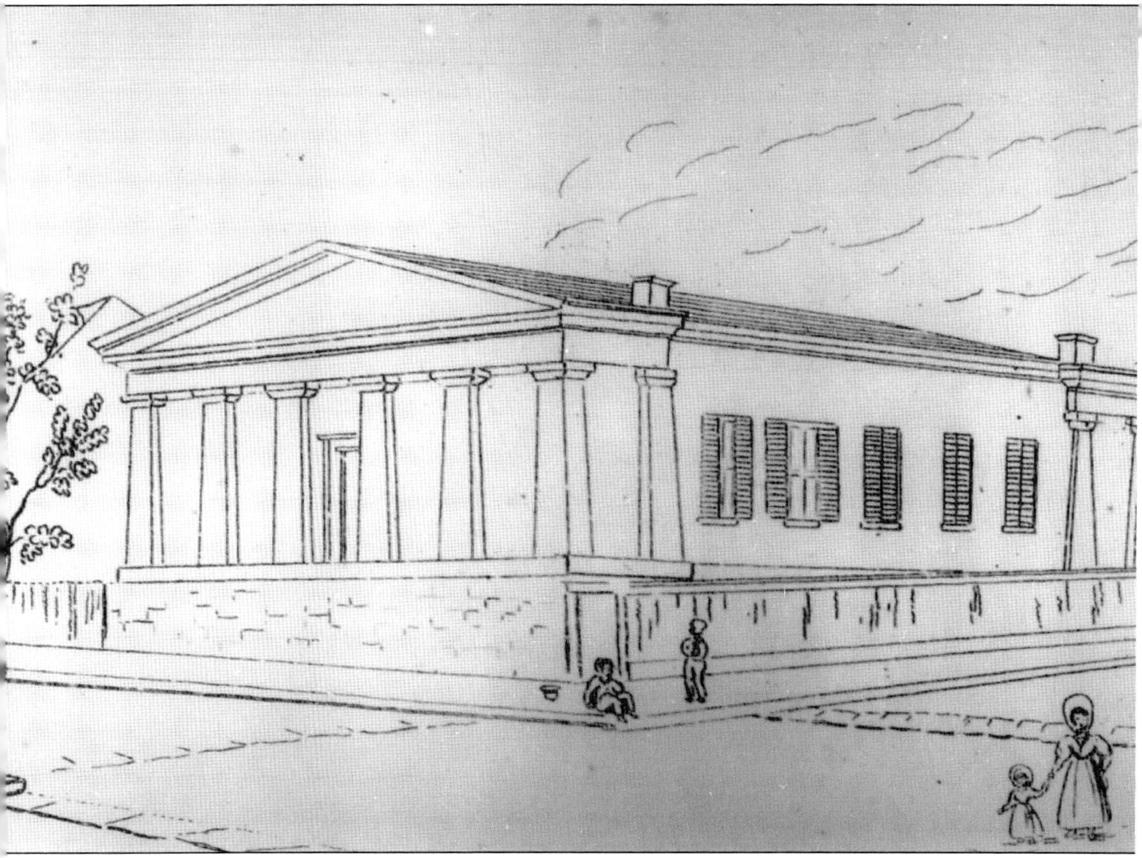

This 1832 sketch shows a plan for Public School #1. The following year a school referred to as "School #1" was erected on the northeast corner of Fayette and Greene Streets. This structure is no longer standing. The school was considered obsolete because of its size and the fact that it could not be expanded. Public School #1 was rebuilt at the same location in 1880. (Courtesy of the Enoch Pratt Free Library.)

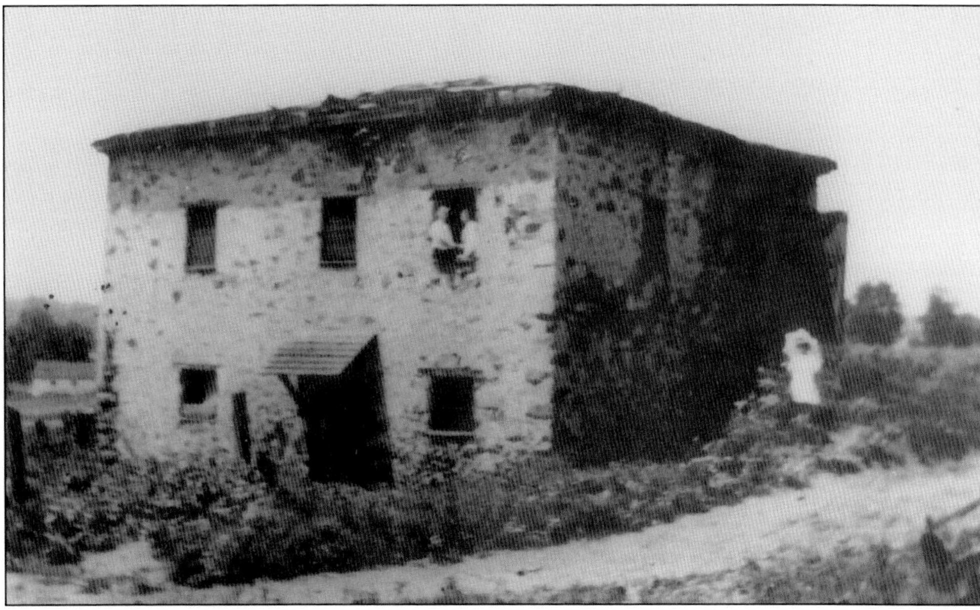

The Medfield Academy, thought to have opened *c.* 1842, was located at Falls Road and Forty-second Street in Medfield, across Falls Road from Hampden. The school had a literary society, bowling alleys, a cricket team, and a band. The Hampden Charter of 1856 called for a college, and Medfield Academy offered college courses, perhaps fulfilling this demand. It was considered an elite preparatory school in its day. John Prentiss was the school's pre–Civil War headmaster and lived in a manor near the school. Pictured above is the barn. (Courtesy of the Enoch Pratt Free Library.)

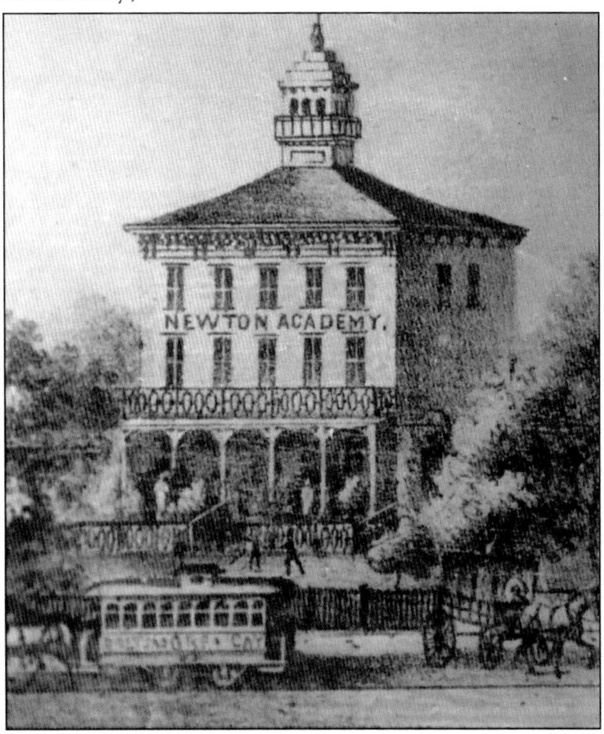

Newton Academy at 780 West Baltimore Street, just east of Carrollton Avenue, opened in 1853, and classes were taught by Dr. Thomas Lester, the owner, and his brother Samuel. Though it burned down during the Civil War, Newton was soon rebuilt. Considered an exclusive school, it had small classes. Boys who were unhappy in larger schools seemed to fare better here as the atmosphere was less disciplinarian than other schools of the era and emphasis was placed on exercise. A large outdoor play area and an indoor gymnasium were provided. The school closed in 1893, and the building was then used as an armory, later by the Maryland Medical College, and then as a theatre. Dr. Lester died in 1898. (Courtesy of the Enoch Pratt Free Library.)

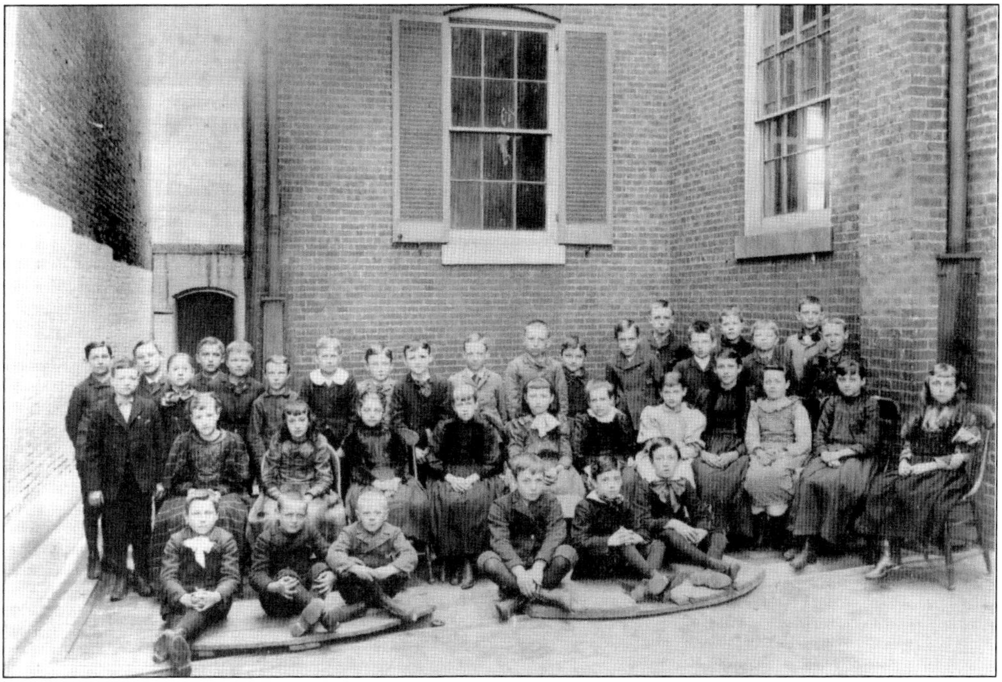

This school, referred to as School #3, was considered to be a German-English school. Located in a predominantly German neighborhood, the school's students were largely of German-Jewish heritage. The building was at Eastern and Montford. (Courtesy of the Jewish Museum of Maryland.)

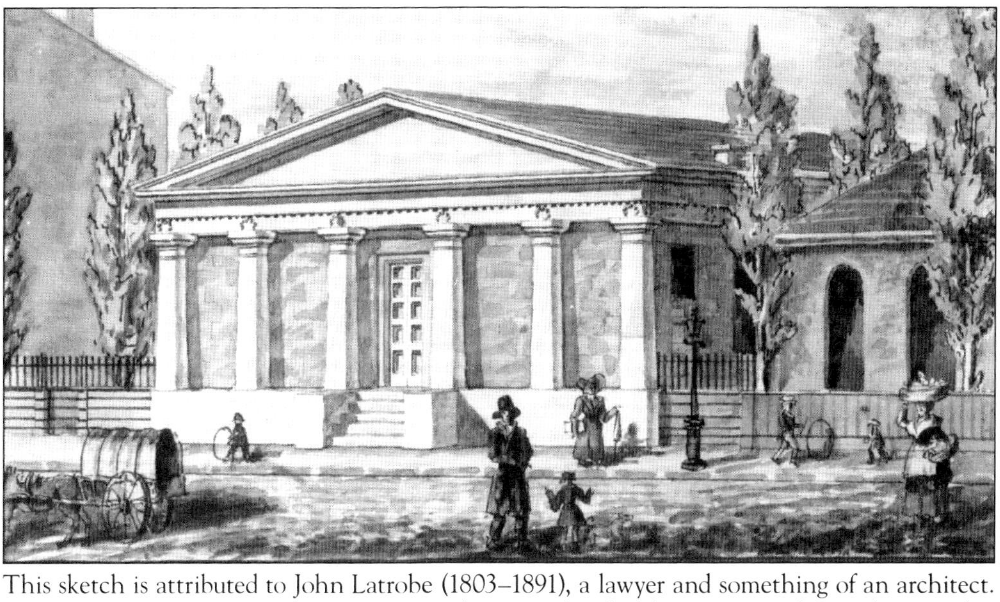

This sketch is attributed to John Latrobe (1803–1891), a lawyer and something of an architect. His grandfather was Benjamin Henry Latrobe, considered to be America's first architect. This sketch shows Public School #3, though it looks very different from the one on the top of the page. This sketch gives Aisquith Street as the school's location, not Eastern and Montford. Records show that this was a male grammar school and was on Aisquith Street prior to 1903. (Courtesy of the Enoch Pratt Free Library.)

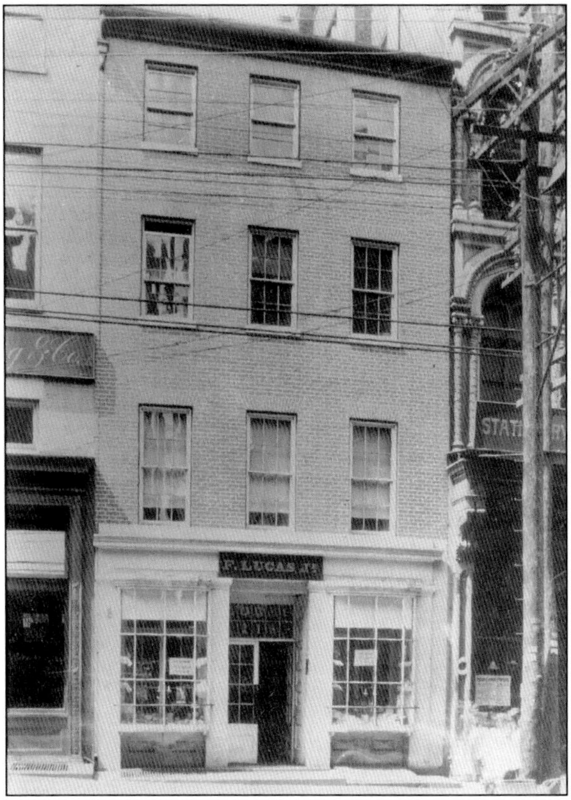

Fielding Lucas ran a book and stationers business, and his shop was said to have been designed by Robert Mills. The shop was bought from a Mr. Conrad in 1803. Lucas, once the head of the school board, was a writer of children's stories, a poet, and an illustrator, and he ran this business until his death in 1854. He was also a founder of the Maryland Historical Society and the Maryland Institute. Pictured below is a sketch of Fielding Lucas's shop prior to the fire of 1904 that destroyed it. (Courtesy of the Enoch Pratt Free Library.)

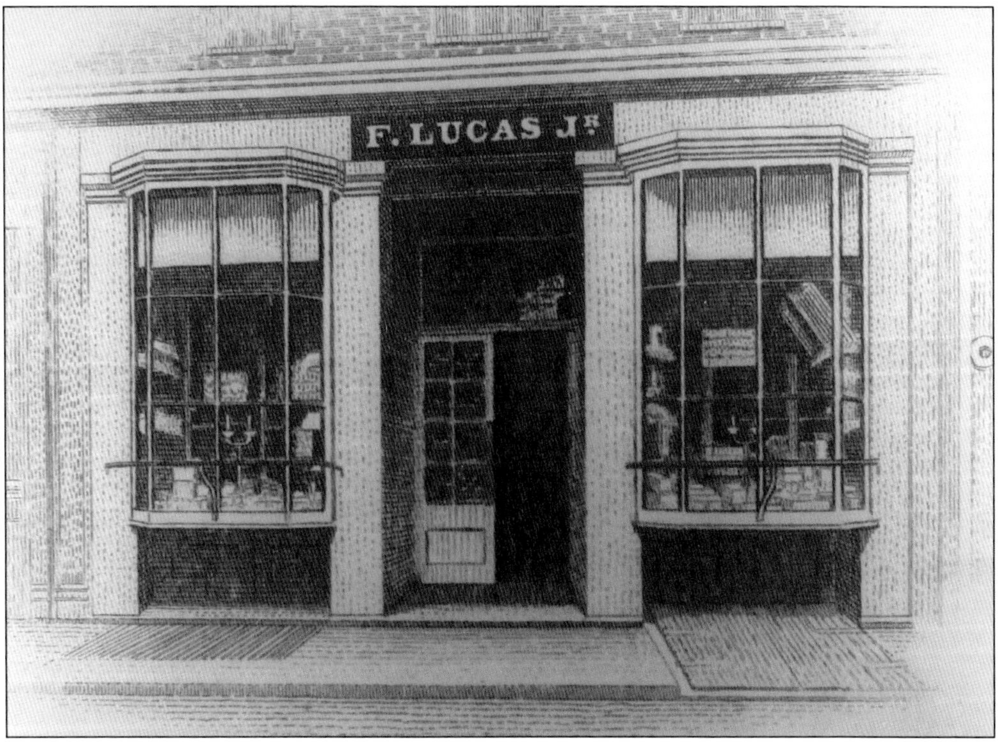

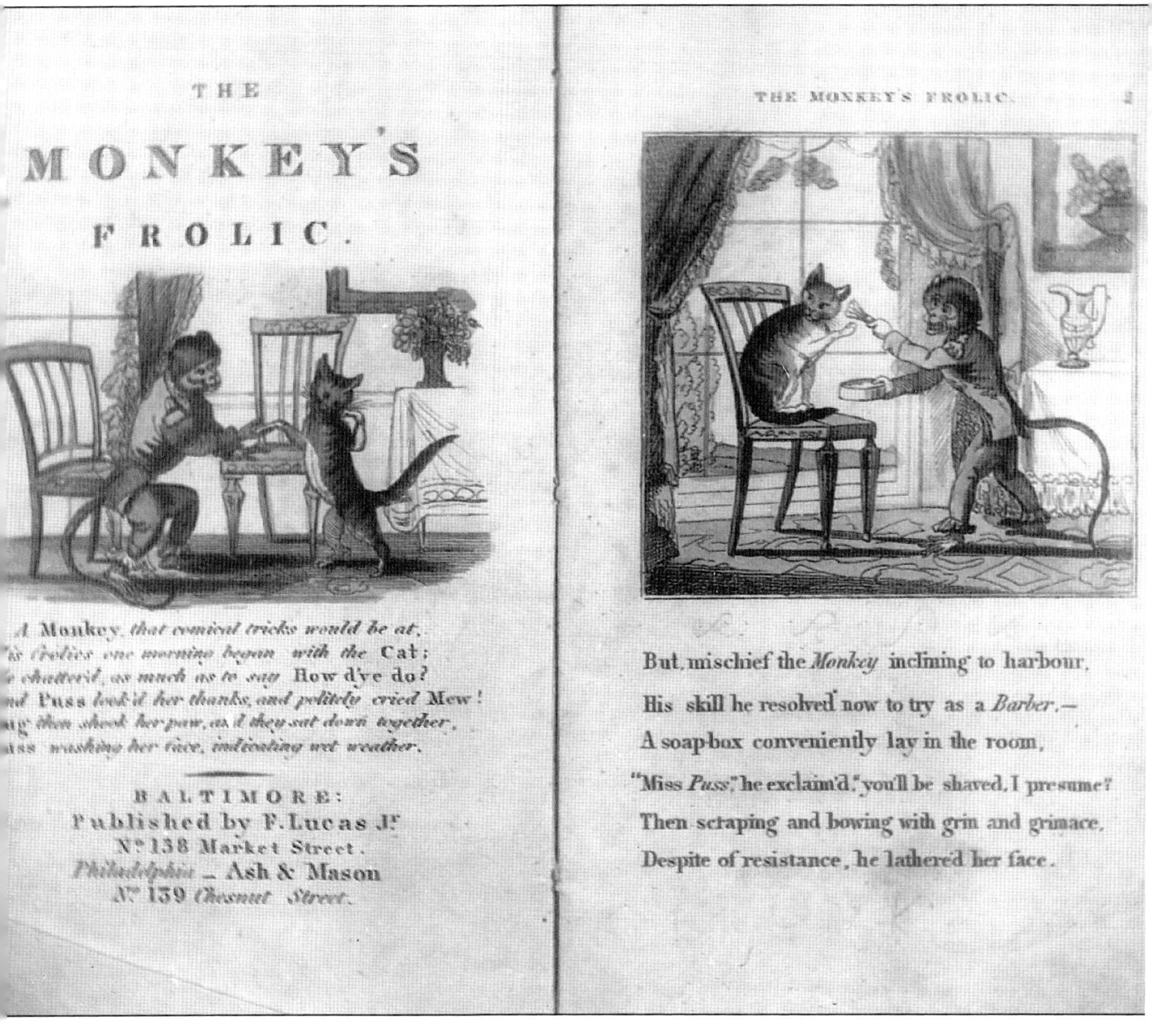

THE

MONKEY'S

FROLIC.

A Monkey, that comical tricks would be at,
is frolics one morning began with the Cat;
e chatter'd, as much as to say How d'ye do?
nd Puss look'd her thanks, and politely cried Mew!
ug then shook her paw, as if they sat down together,
uss washing her face, indicating wet weather.

BALTIMORE:
Published by F. Lucas Jr
No. 138 Market Street.
Philadelphia — Ash & Mason
No. 139 Chesnut Street.

THE MONKEY'S FROLIC. 2

But, mischief the *Monkey* inclining to harbour,
His skill he resolved now to try as a *Barber*.—
A soap-box conveniently lay in the room,
"Miss *Puss*," he exclaim'd, "you'll be shaved, I presume?"
Then scraping and bowing with grin and grimace,
Despite of resistance, he lathered her face.

Pictured here are pages from one of Lucas's stories. (Courtesy of the Enoch Pratt Free Library.)

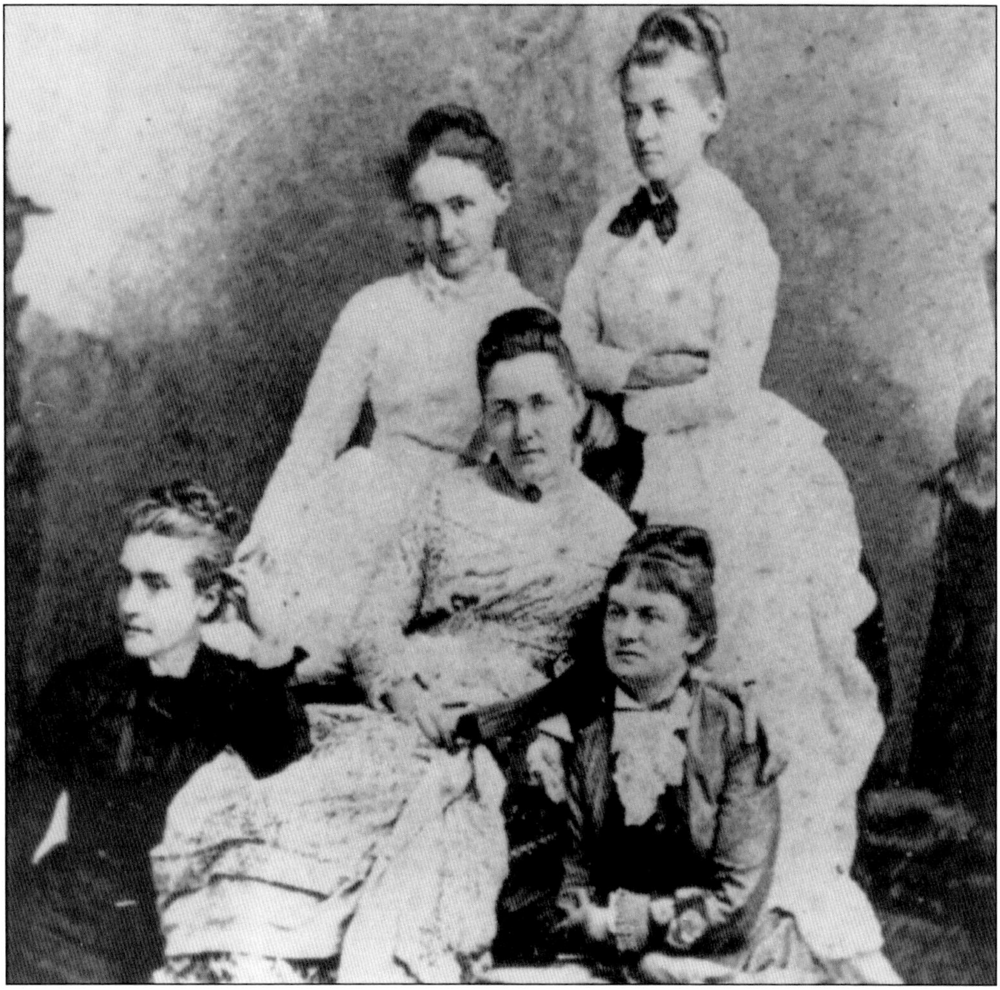

In the mid-1800s, there was little available educationally for the college-bound woman and finishing schools were in no way equal to traditional boys' schools. Nowhere could one find education for girls that was not geared towards a career in teaching or as a wife in high society. But some women sought to change this. The five founders of the Bryn Mawr School in Baltimore [from left to right, (back row) Mary "Mamie" Gwinn and Elizabeth "Bessie" King; (front row) M. Carey Thomas, Julia Rogers, and Mary Elizabeth Garrett] were strong-minded young feminists from wealthy families. Thomas and Garrett created Bryn Mawr School for Girls with the support of the other three friends, and Thomas was named dean of the newly forming Bryn Mawr college for women in the suburbs of Philadelphia. Bryn Mawr College's standards for admittance were to be so high that it influenced Thomas to also create a prep school to help young women achieve entrance. Bryn Mawr School, named after the college, was opened on September 21, 1885 at 715 North Eutaw Place, where it remained for five years. In 1890 the school moved to Cathedral and Preston Streets. Thomas and Garrett ran the school with absolute power, oversaw every detail, and made sure that their own standards of excellence were met. In addition to the school for girls, Thomas and Garrett gave hundreds of thousands of desperately needed dollars for the creation of The Johns Hopkins Medical School. The conditions of the gift were that the school meet the standards of European medical schools—even Harvard Medical School did not have exams until 1871—and that it admit women. (Courtesy of the Bryn Mawr School, Baltimore.)

It was clear from an early age that M. Carey Thomas was truly brilliant. In her Mount Vernon mansion, she was often busy inventing scientific experiments with her cousin Bessie King. She attended Cornell, one of the few American institutions where women could earn bachelor's degrees, and later, after being told she could attend classes at Hopkins only while hidden behind a screen, she convinced her family to allow her to study abroad. Thomas and Mamie Gwinn, her childhood friend and later intimate companion, found acceptance in Zurich, and Thomas received her doctorate in 1882. Although Quakers were, at the time, one of the only groups that believed in equal education for both sexes, Thomas rebelled against her parents' religion in many ways. Their irreconcilable differences of opinion included, unfortunately for all of her brilliance, Thomas's distaste for her mother's insistence on socializing with Jews and blacks. (Courtesy of the Bryn Mawr School, Baltimore.)

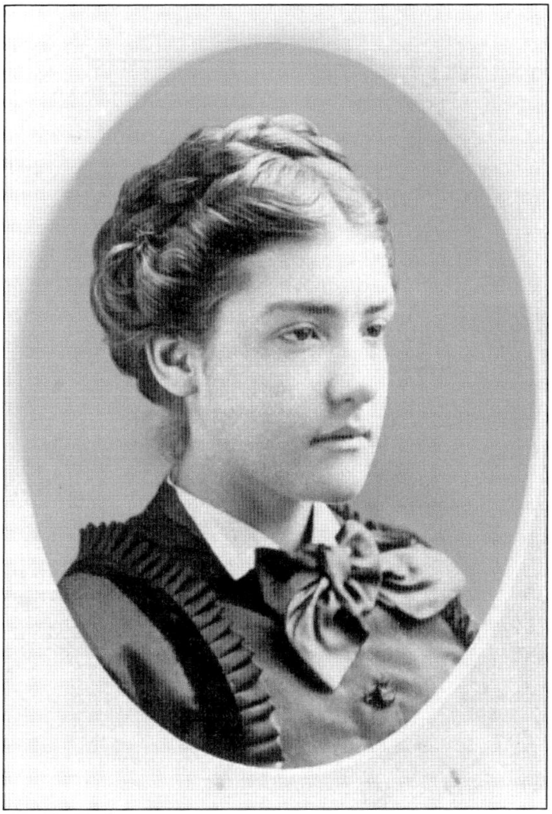

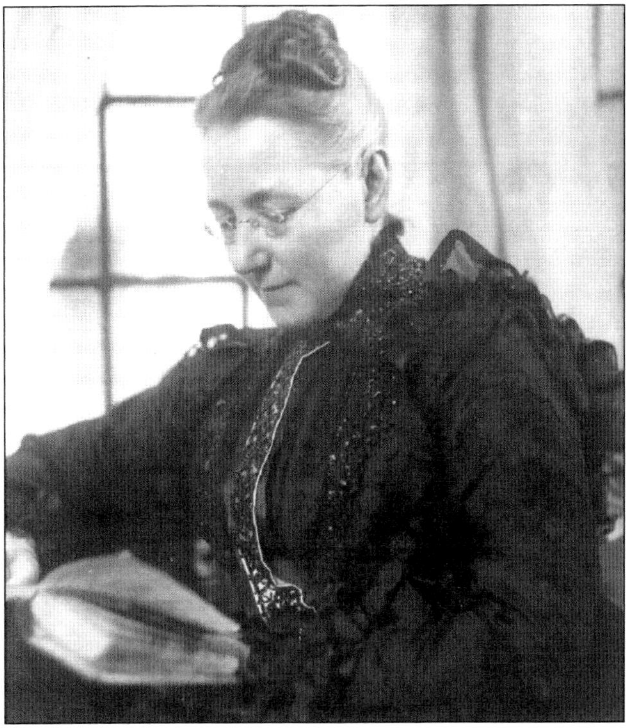

Mary Elizabeth Garrett, another child of the Baltimore social elite and Thomas's intimate companion of many years, was the daughter of John Work Garrett, the B&O railroad tycoon who played a notorious role in the railroad riots of 1877. Garrett was an assistant to her father and had a great business mind. Her father was known to have lamented that if only his daughter was a son he would have had a qualified heir to continue in the family business. (Courtesy of the Bryn Mawr School, Baltimore.)

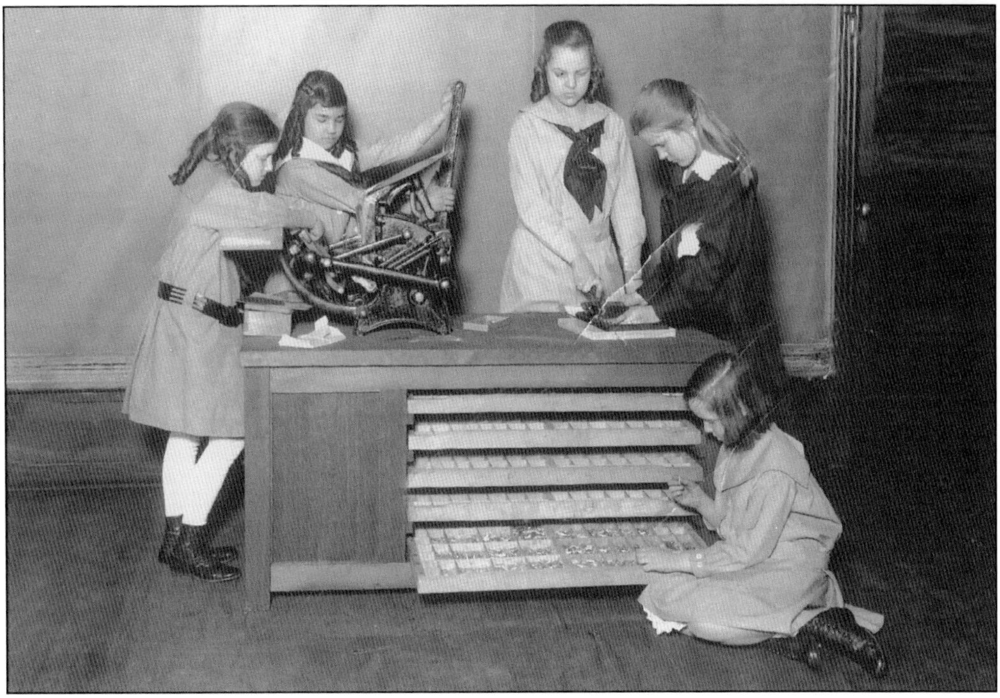

Unlike other girls' schools, Bryn Mawr taught even the youngest girls how to use the printing press (above) and how to build in the woodshop (below), c. 1895. (Courtesy of the Bryn Mawr School, Baltimore.)

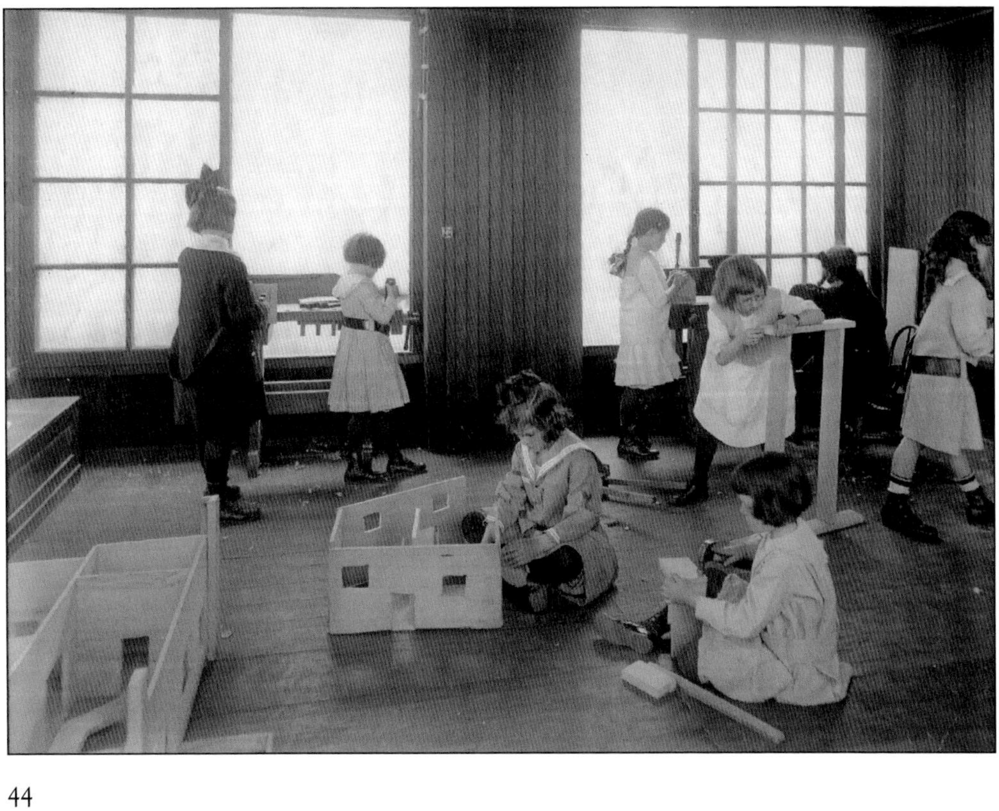

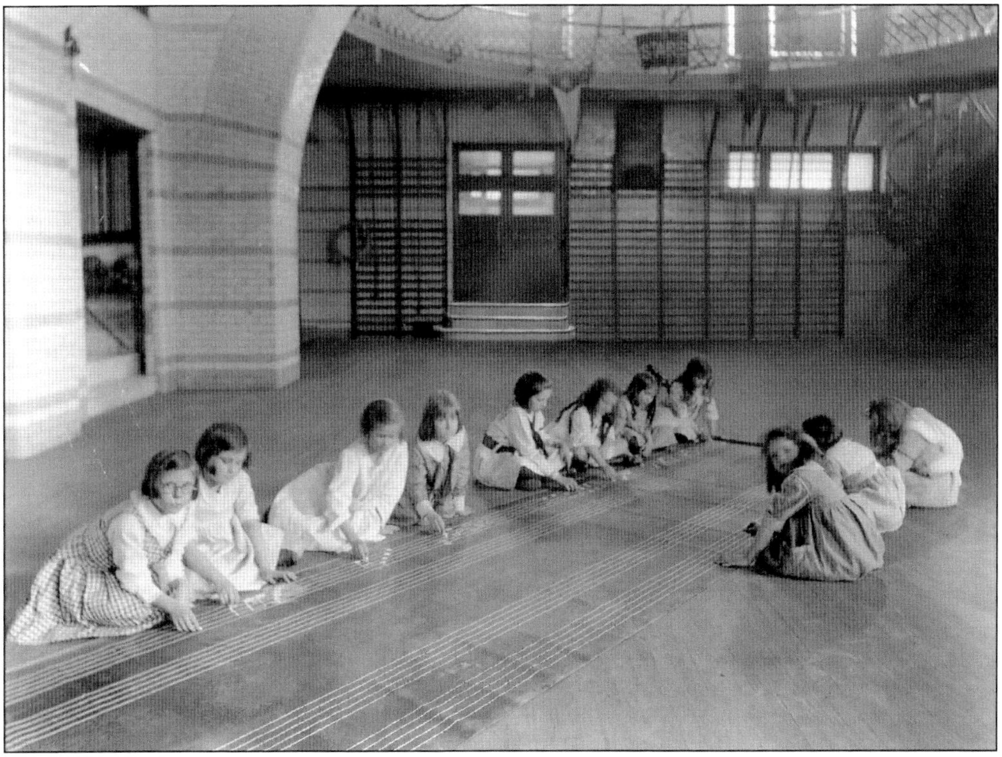

A Bryn Mawr primary school music class is pictured in the 1890s.

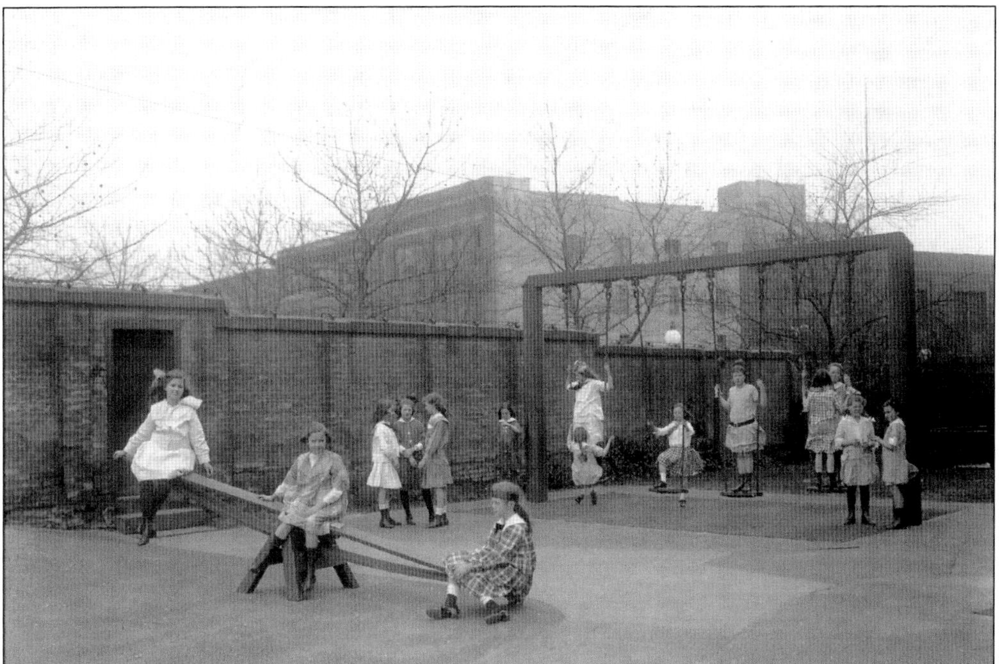

The playground at Bryn Mawr, pictured here *c.* 1895, is where students would have gym class when the weather permitted.

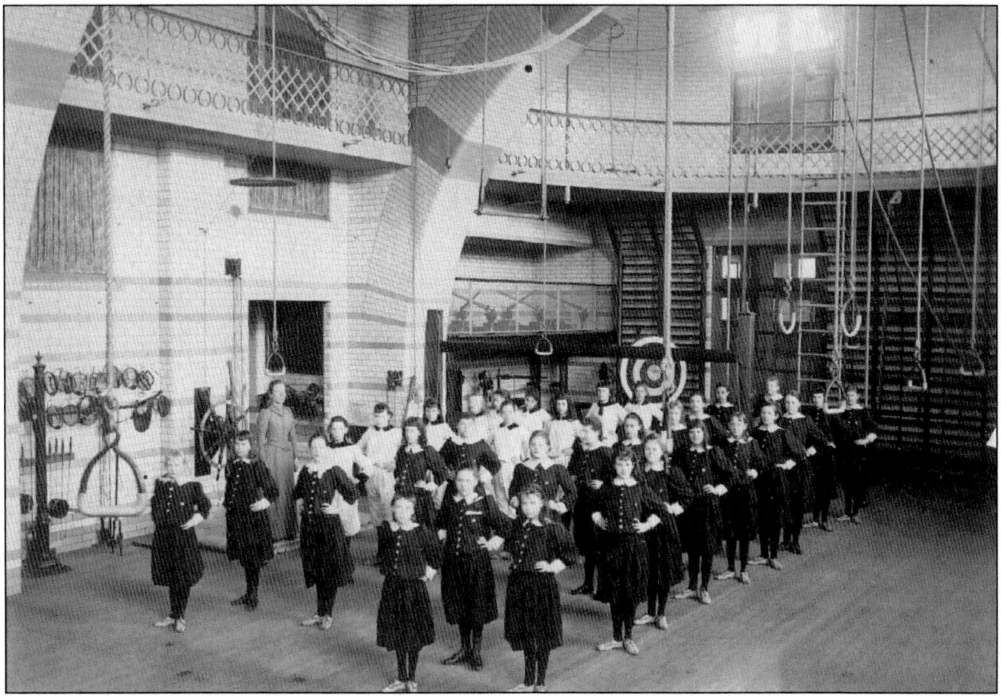

This is a gym class at the Cathedral and Preston Streets school building in the 1890s. Notice the equipment—it was considered state of the art and, at the time, certainly not for use by girls. The gymnasium was equipped with such things as the "horse," a running track, and rowing machines. The students had showers, or "needle baths," which were as unpopular then as they are today. The girls' gym costumes were taken to the dry cleaners only at the end of the year since the colors ran when washed. (Courtesy of the Bryn Mawr School, Baltimore.)

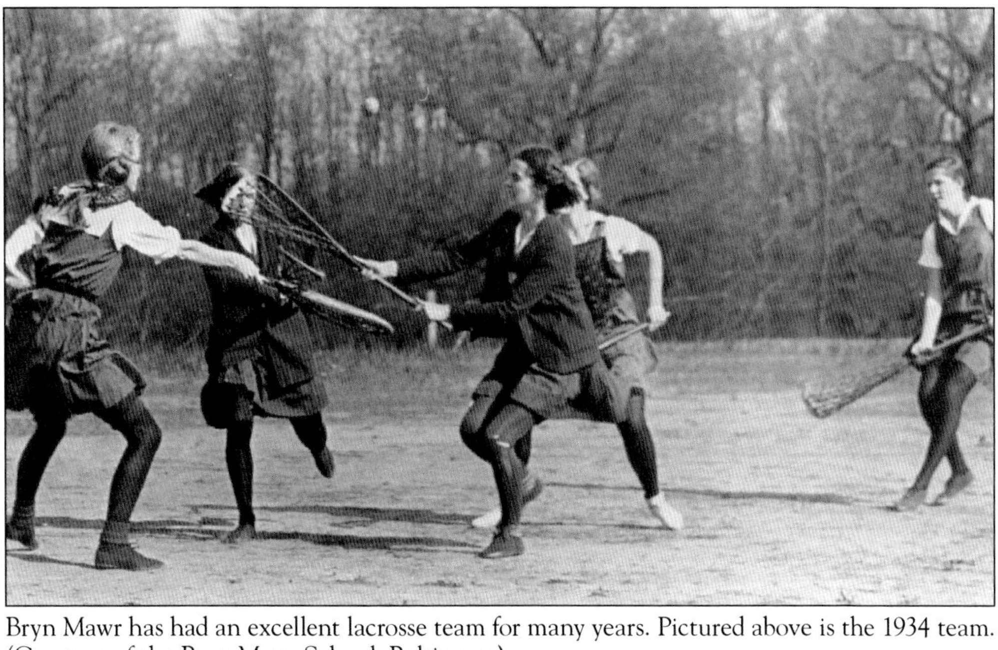

Bryn Mawr has had an excellent lacrosse team for many years. Pictured above is the 1934 team. (Courtesy of the Bryn Mawr School, Baltimore.)

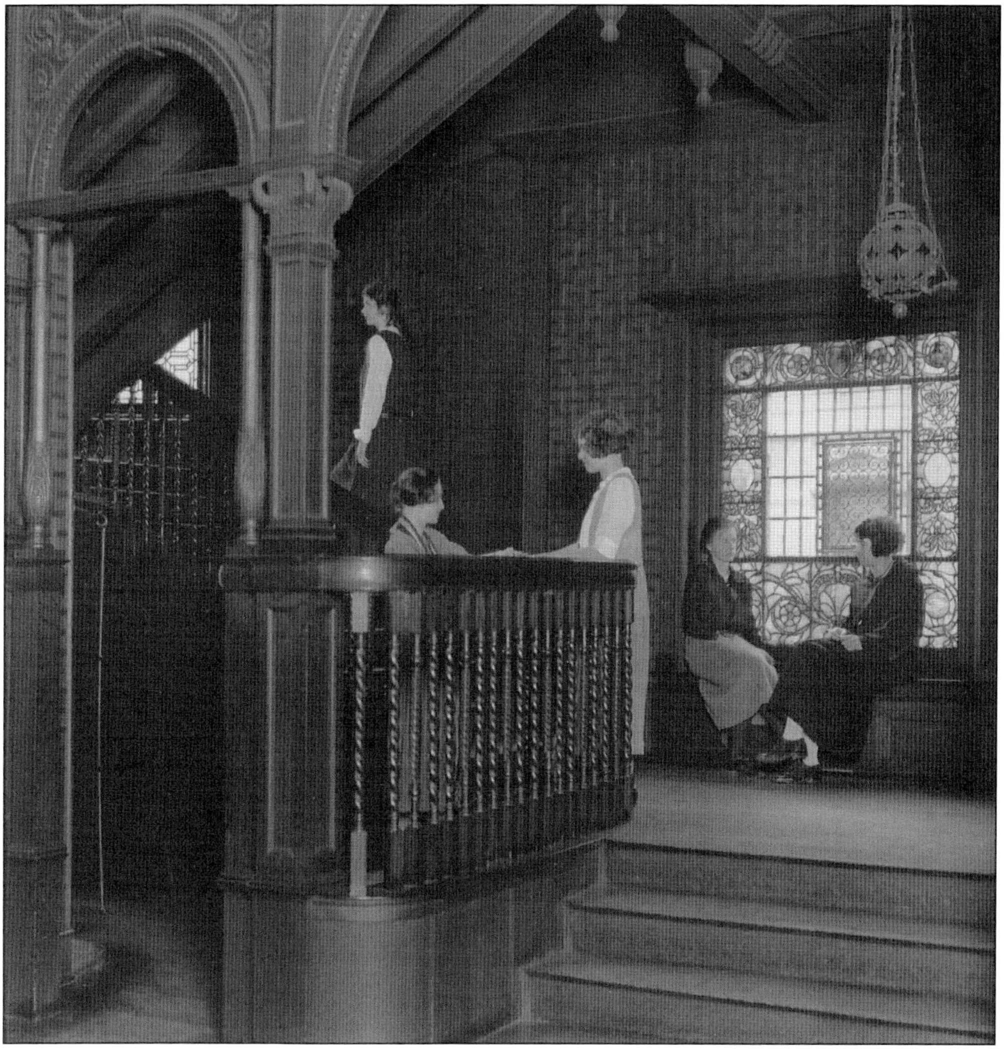

Girls' Latin School of Baltimore was founded in 1890 as a college preparatory school extension of Goucher College and was located on the campus. In a speech given in 1906, Dr. John F. Goucher quoted from a U.S. Commissioner of Education report, noting "Of all the private schools for girls in the United States which prepare exclusively or largely for the leading colleges for women, the Girls' Latin School of Baltimore represents the largest resources devoted to that purpose, enrolls the largest number who are preparing for college, and graduates each year the largest number who enter college." In 1909 Girls' Latin made a break from Goucher after the National Association of Collegiate Alumnae moved to bar from membership all colleges that had a preparatory department. The school was reorganized by Miss Nellie Maroa Wilmot and moved into a hall leased to the school by Goucher. In 1914 the school moved once again to Winan's Mansion at 1217 St. Paul Street. (The photo above and those that follow were all taken c. 1920 at that location.) Property was purchased in 1927 at 10 Club Road in Roland Park, and the school relocated for the last time. The school went into receivership in 1937 and the property sold to alumni who planned to continue running a school at the site. In 1951, Girls' Latin closed its doors forever. This was the same year that Greenwood School for Girls in Ruxton, another well-respected private school, met its end. (Courtesy of the Enoch Pratt Free Library.)

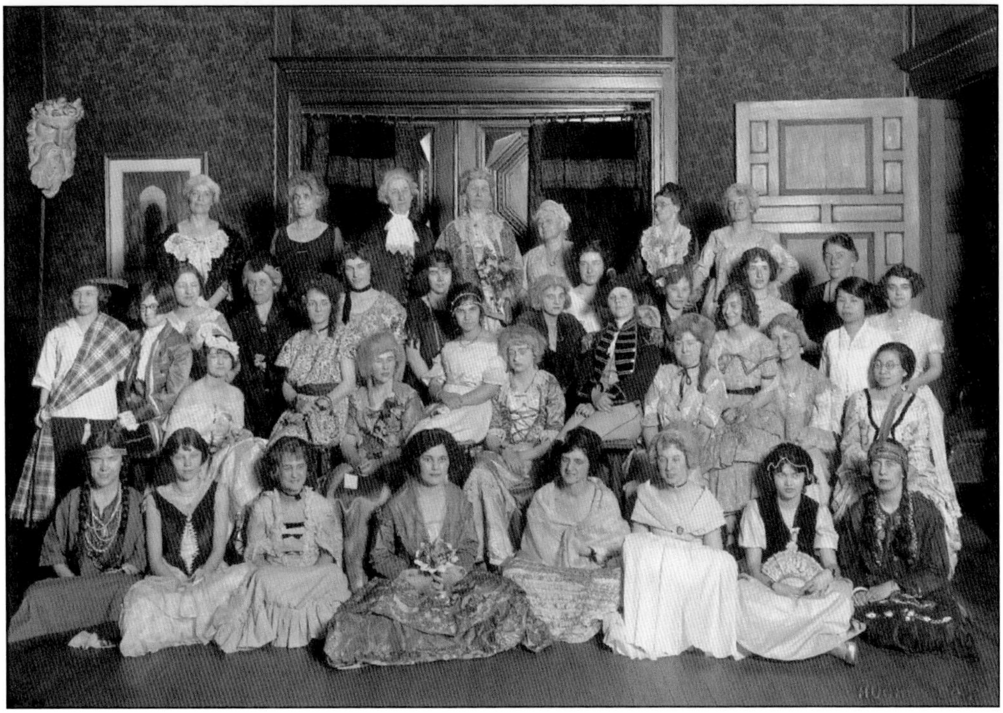

Never a place to promote exclusivity, Girls' Latin prided itself in its international and diverse student body. Many ethnicities are reflected in this group of costumed young actresses. (Courtesy of the Enoch Pratt Free Library.)

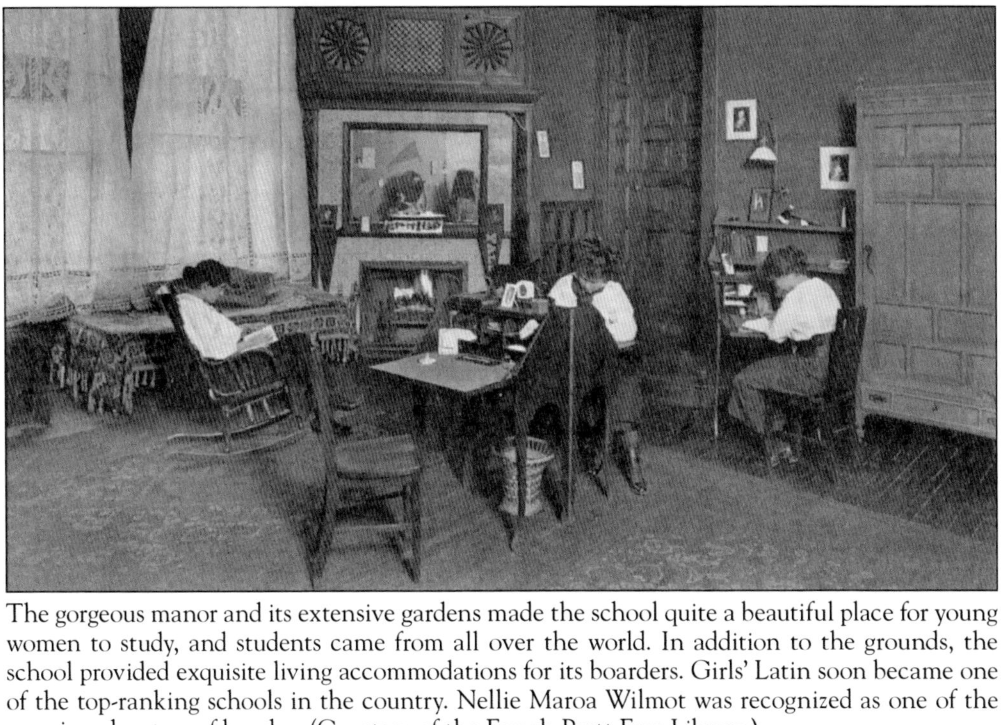

The gorgeous manor and its extensive gardens made the school quite a beautiful place for young women to study, and students came from all over the world. In addition to the grounds, the school provided exquisite living accommodations for its boarders. Girls' Latin soon became one of the top-ranking schools in the country. Nellie Maroa Wilmot was recognized as one of the premier educators of her day. (Courtesy of the Enoch Pratt Free Library.)

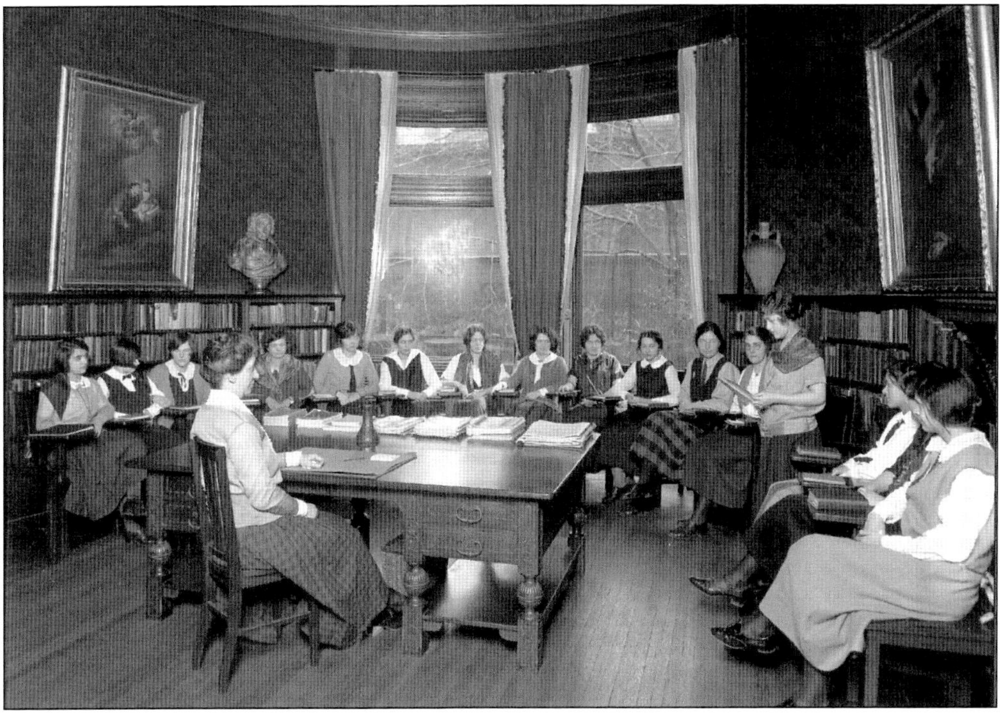

Pictured c. 1920 are a Latin class (above) and the social hall (below) at Girls' Latin. (Courtesy of the Enoch Pratt Free Library.)

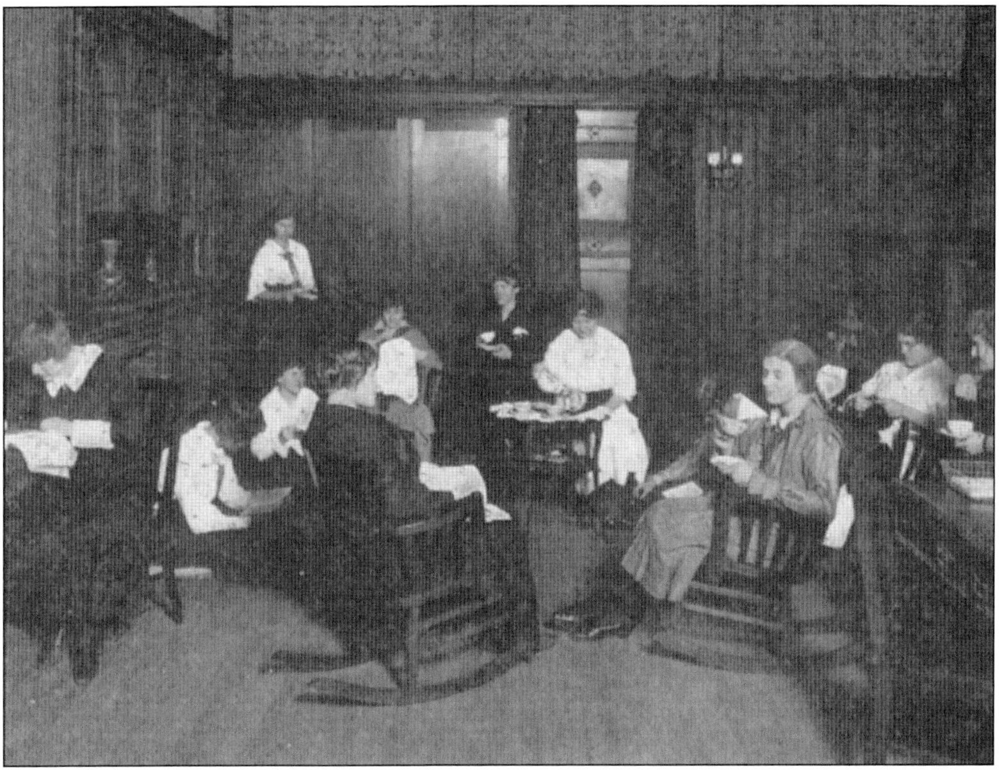

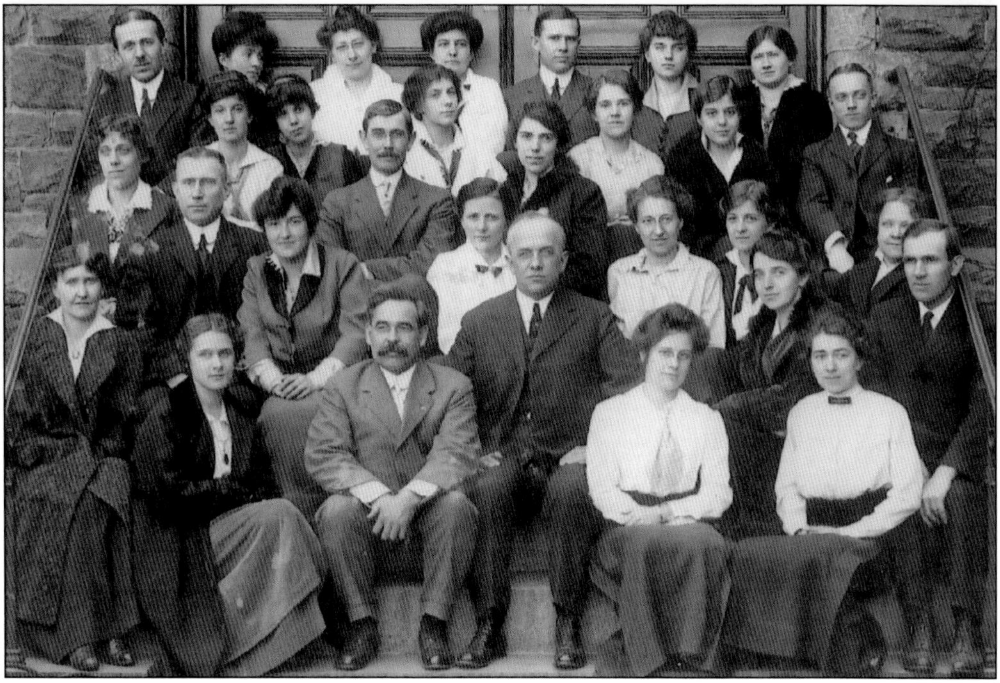

The oldest school in the city, the Friends School of Baltimore was founded in 1784 by the Baltimore Monthly Meeting of the Religious Society of Friends. Its mission was to offer children a "guarded education" that focused as strongly on promoting moral values as it did on reading and writing. The Aisquith Street Meetinghouse, then located in East Baltimore in what was referred to as Old Town, was the school's first site. In the 1840s it relocated to Lombard Street and then, in the early 1900s, to Bolton Hill. In 1925, the primary school was the first to be moved to the school's present location at 5114 North Charles Street in Homeland. By 1936 the entire student body had been relocated to the 26 acres on North Charles. Student enrollment increased from 15 to 150 between 1800 and 1900, and the school now enrolls 1,000 students. Pictured above is the faculty in 1914. (Courtesy of the Friends School of Baltimore.)

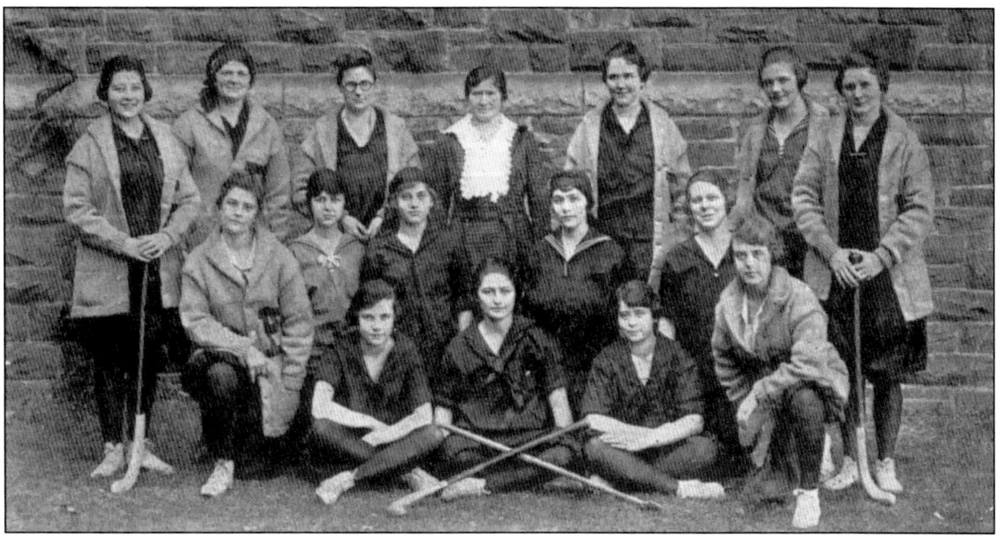

This is the 1915 girls' hockey team at Friends. (Courtesy of Liz Moser.)

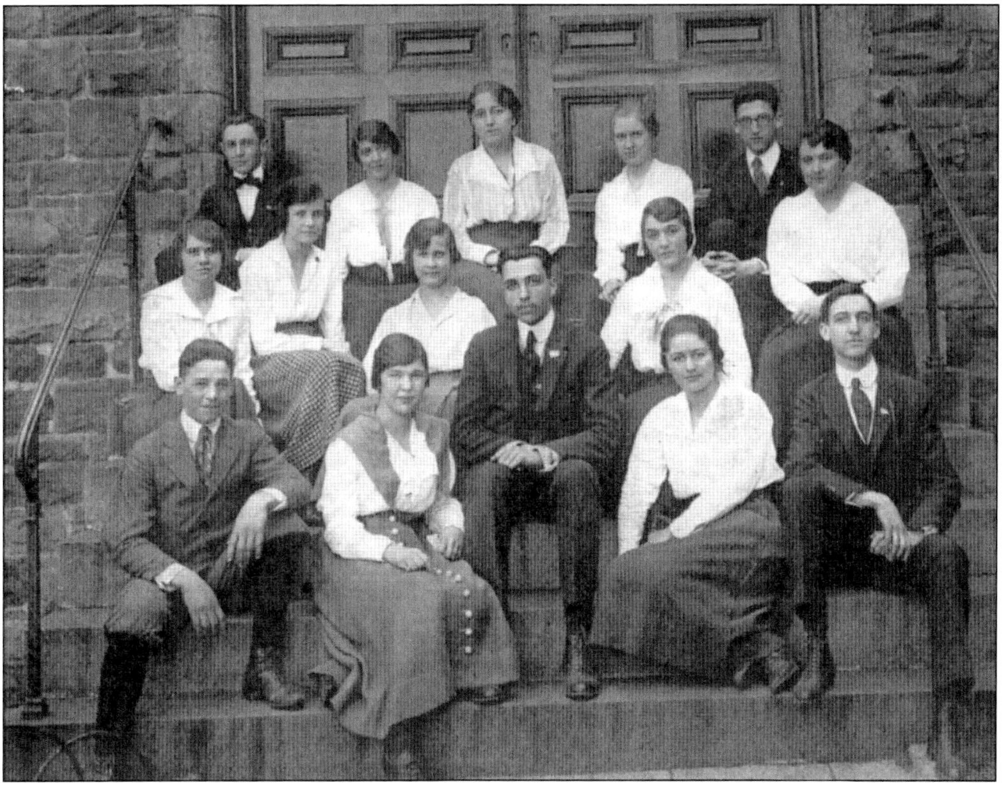

Above are the seniors of the Friends School of Baltimore graduating class of 1917. (Courtesy of Liz Moser.)

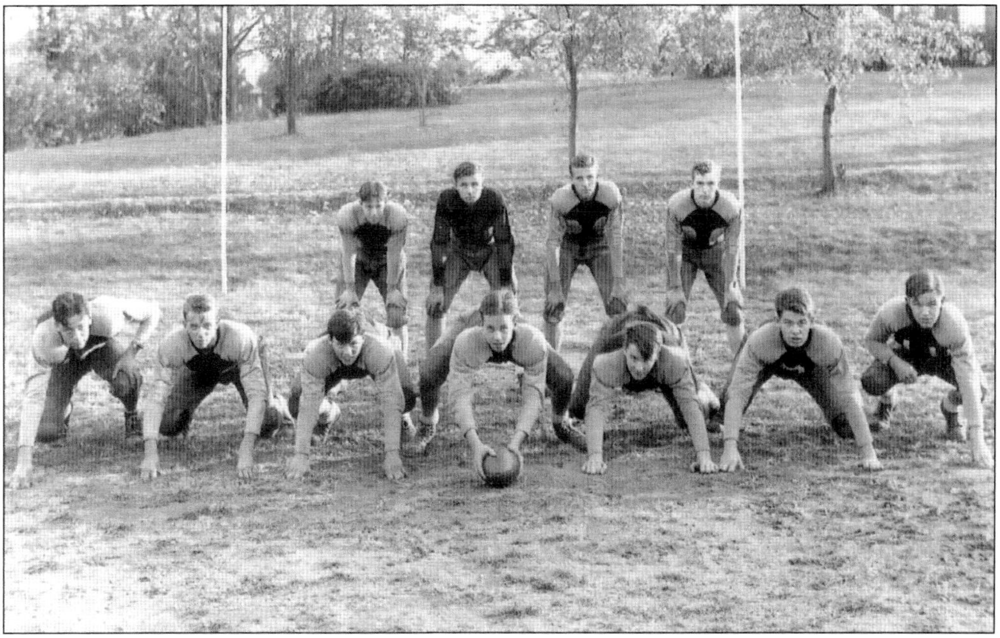

Members of the 1932 Friends football team are pictured at the Homeland campus. (Courtesy of the Friends School of Baltimore.)

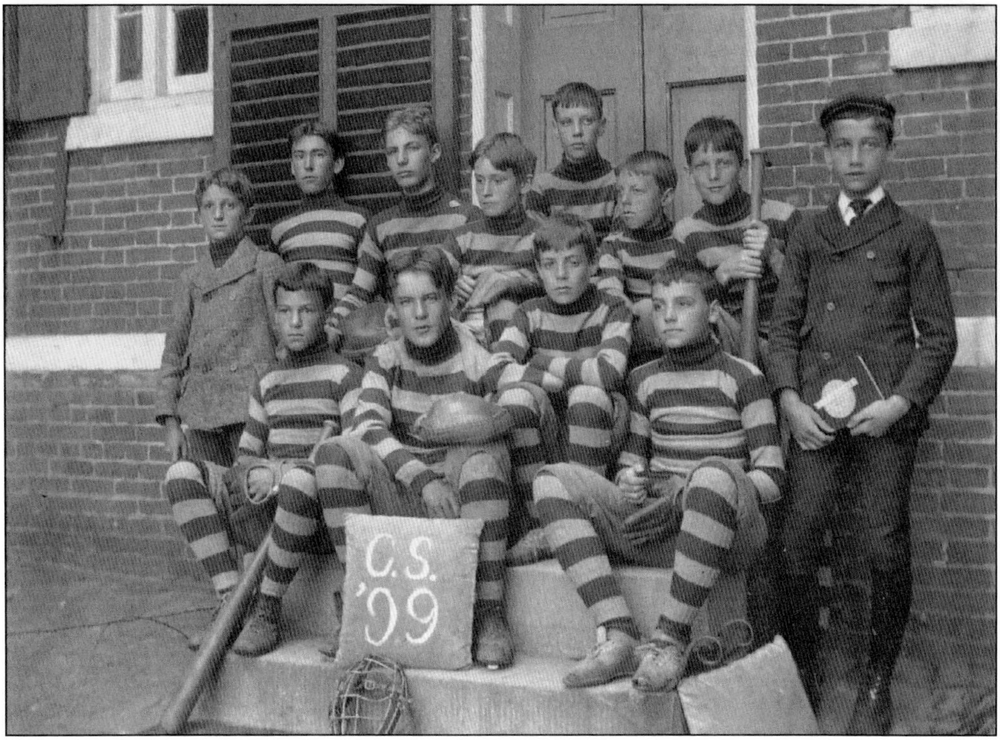

The Gilman School for Boys began as the Country School for Boys of Baltimore City in 1897. The idea for the school came from a 32-year-old Baltimore mother, Mrs. francis King Carey, who was concerned for her own child. While reform was happening in the public school system, Mrs. Carey wanted reform in the private school system and felt that a school in the country, with fresh air and a rural atmosphere, would benefit more than just a boy's mind. She enlisted a friend whose father was a judge and the three of them spoke with Dr. Daniel Coit Gilman, a pioneer in education at the time as well as president of the new Johns Hopkins University. Gilman was enthusiastic, and in January 1897, the plan was set in motion. The prospectus was immediately drawn up and officers on the committee elected. Although funds came in slowly, the decision to take over Homewood, located at the Johns Hopkins campus, was a positive move. The rent would be $1,000 per year. However, the elegant house, built by Charles Carroll almost 100 years prior, needed a great deal of work to prepare it for students, and on September 30, 1897, when the first students arrived on campus, final touches were still being made. But Johns Hopkins University was growing and, since it was clearly going to need the Homewood house for its own campus, the boys' school began to look for a more permanent location. Hopes for financing were crushed by the Baltimore fire of 1904. However, it also slowed the growth of the university. The location eventually selected for the Gilman School was a tract of land in Roland Park that had belonged to the Evans family since 1727, a farm called Vaux Hall. As the city began to grow north the Roland Park Company had it in mind to maintain the country atmosphere so the school could still expect to be considered a country school. However, the name "Country School" was not thought to be a very sophisticated name and many were concerned that, when asked at Harvard or Yale, the boys would find themselves ridiculed. In December 1910, the school was officially renamed the Gilman Country School. The main sports at Gilman during the early years were football and baseball, and pictured here is the Gilman (then Country) School baseball team of 1909. (Courtesy of the Gilman School.)

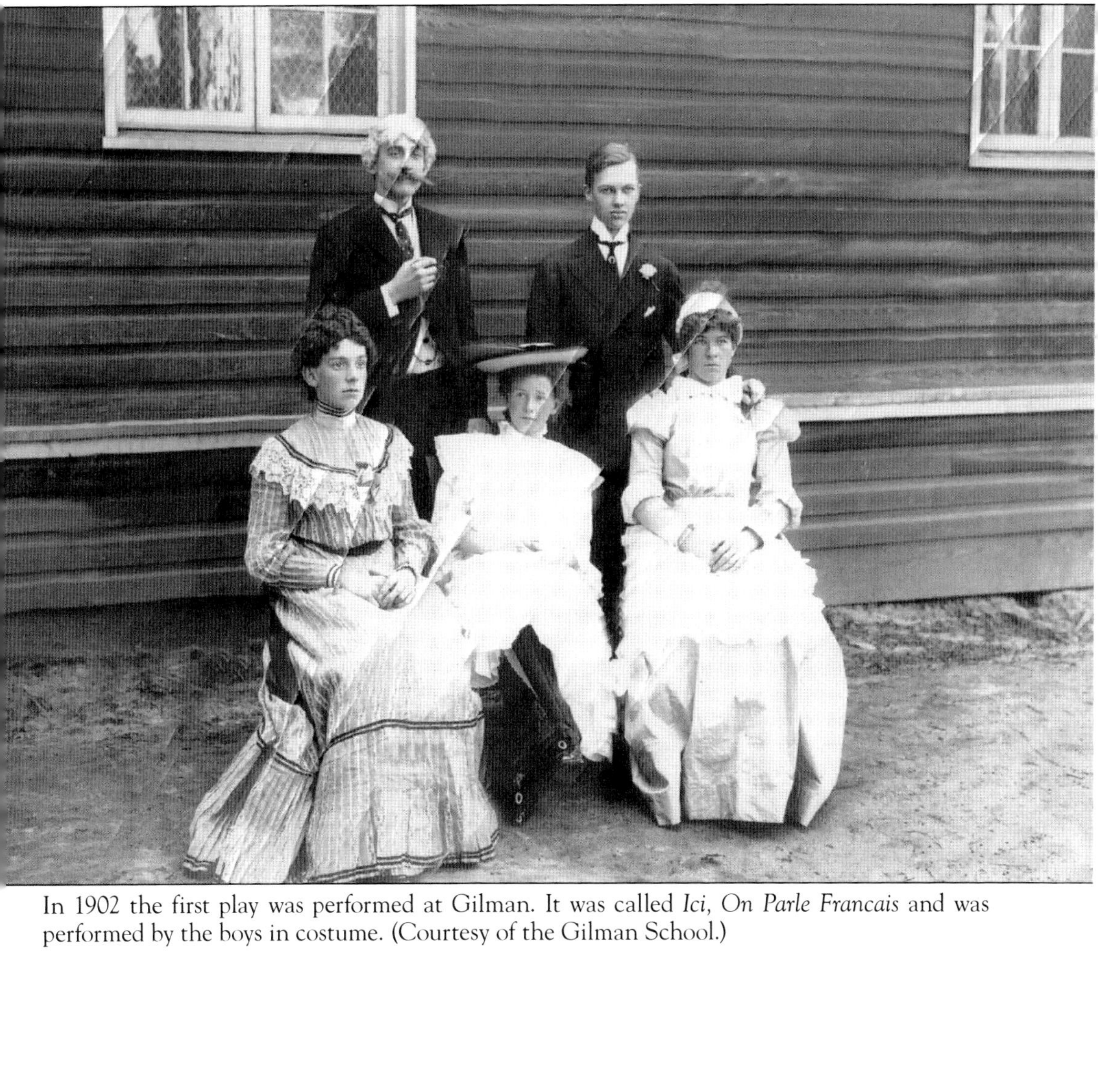

In 1902 the first play was performed at Gilman. It was called *Ici, On Parle Francais* and was performed by the boys in costume. (Courtesy of the Gilman School.)

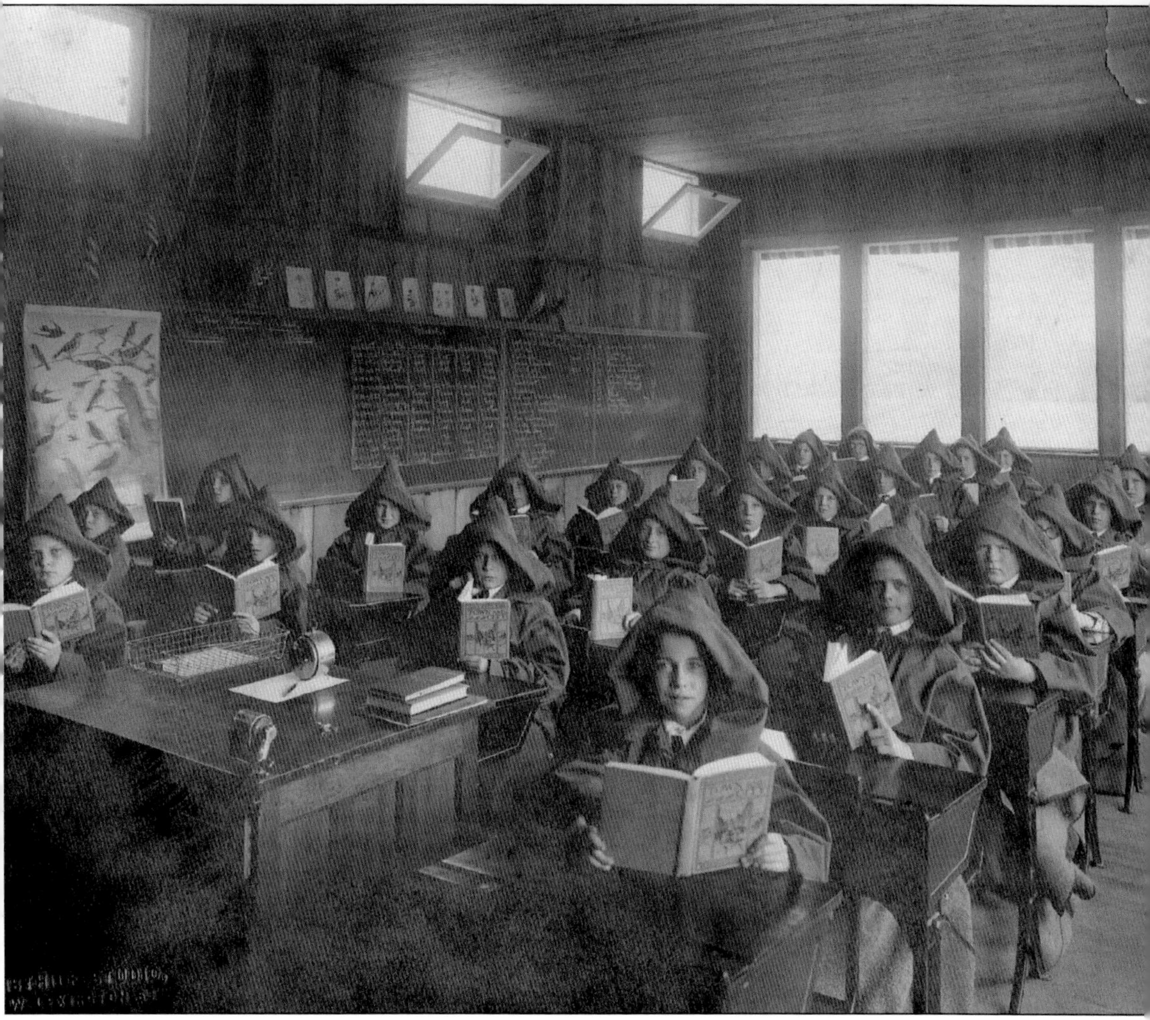

No, this is not a scene from Hogwarts School of Witchcraft and Wizardry from the Harry Potter books but an example of an open-air classroom, a program in vogue during this era at several schools in Baltimore. The open-air classroom theory was put into use at Gilman from 1911 until 1922. It was believed that fresh air would promote health, prevent the spread of contagious diseases, and allow for clearer thinking. It was thought to be so beneficial that open classrooms were used through the winter as well as the warmer months. Here, lower school boys are in class with heavy-hooded cloaks and heated soapstone for their hands and feet. They have heavy wool blankets across their legs. (Courtesy of the Gilman School.)

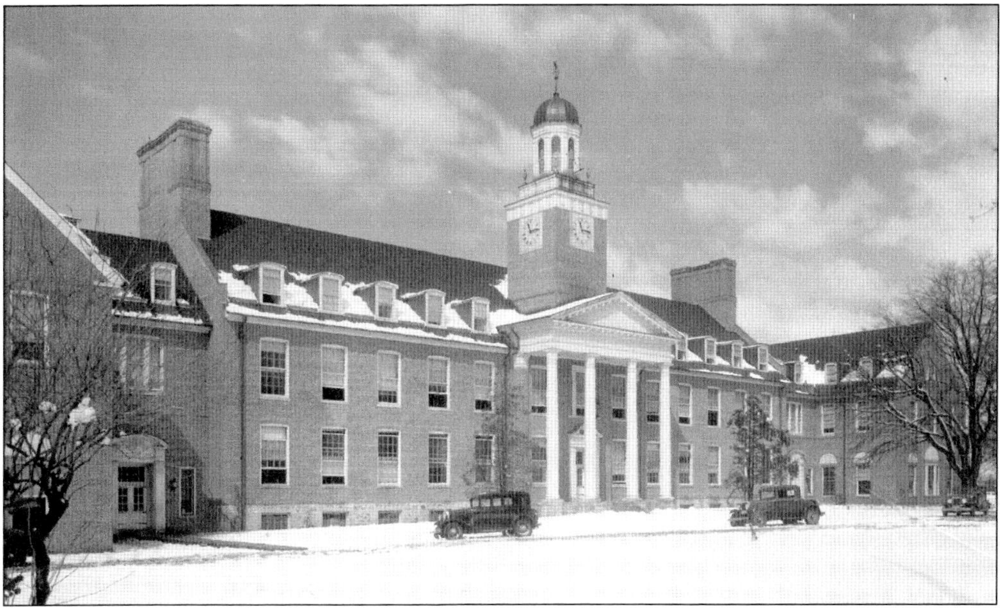

The McDonogh School, known for its militaristic style and its history of supporting the education of boys from the lower classes, was founded in 1873 for boys from Baltimore City. John McDonogh's will, the school's principle endowment, was drawn up specifically for boys who had little or no financial resources. Born in Baltimore in 1779, McDonogh moved to New Orleans at 21 and was a wealthy man by age 27. Having always shown an interest in the education of the less fortunate, he left money in his will to accomplish this in both Baltimore and his adopted city of New Orleans. McDonogh set out to create a place for city boys to have a good education and a chance at a wholesome life. At the McDonogh School, boys from families able to pay for their education were not accepted until 1922; girls were not admitted until 1975. The original school burned to the ground in 1928. Only McDonogh's zeal for religion seems to have been tantamount to his passion for philanthropy. Pictured above is McDonogh in 1929; below are cadets in 1937. (Courtesy of the Enoch Pratt Free Library.)

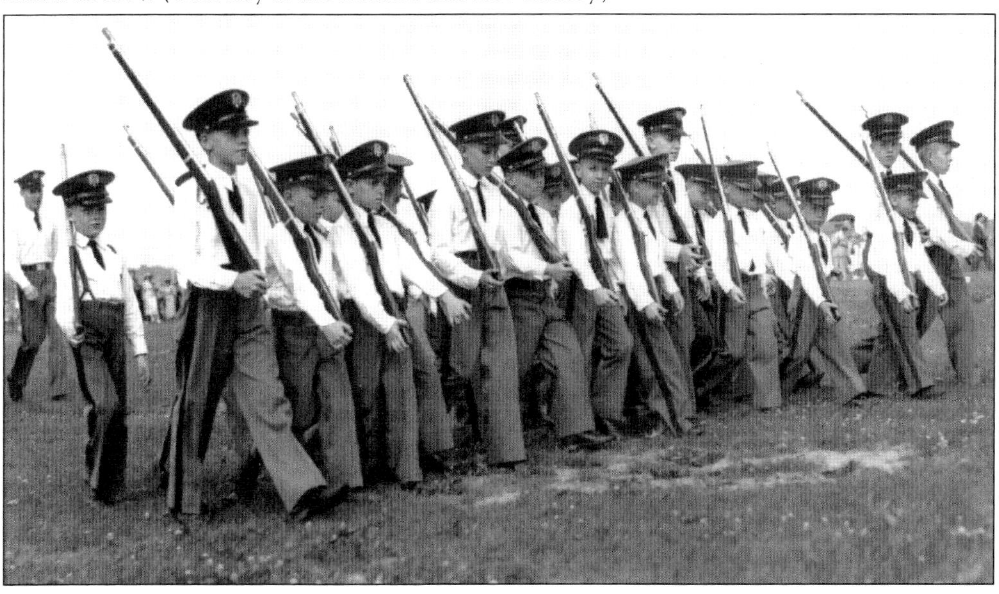

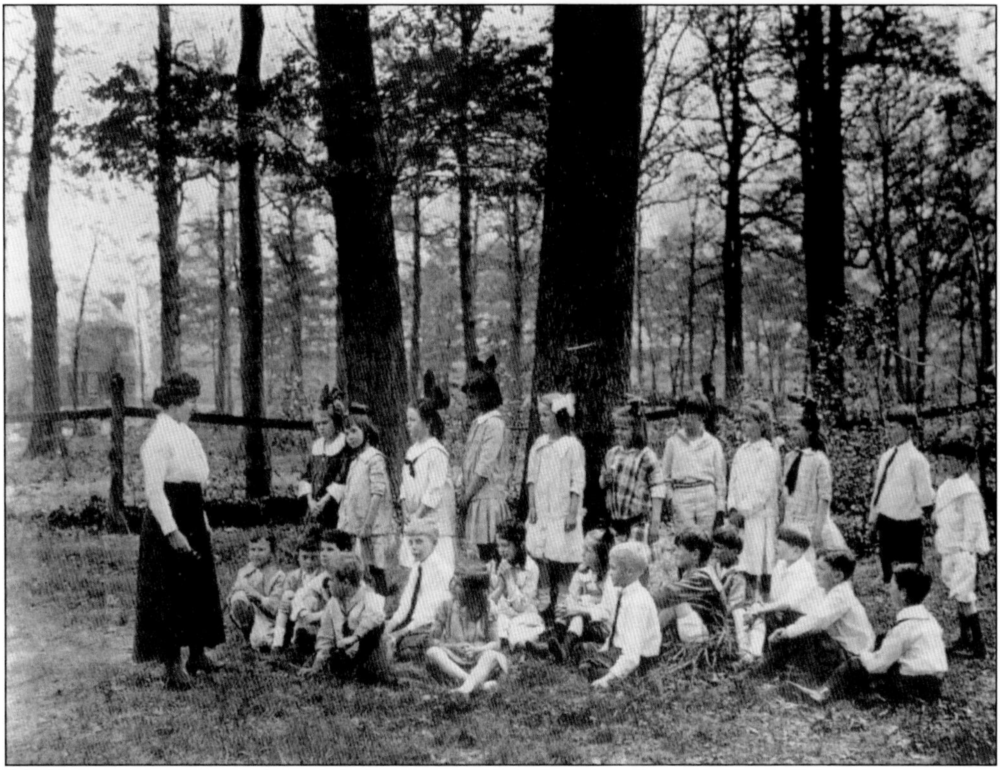

The neighborhood of Roland Park was established in 1891 by the Roland Park Company. Edward H. Bouton, who headed the group, envisioned sweeping streets, wide plots, and an English aesthetic. He, in fact, used English capital to develop the perfect countryside setting—close to the city yet very suburban. Roland Park was designed to have its own power, water, volunteer fire department, bakery, post office, grocery stores, and churches. By 1901 the area was expanding and a school was needed. Gilman, then the Country School for Boys, was still at Homewood; Calvert and Bryn Mawr were in town; and Friends, which had been around for over 100 years at that time, was on Park Avenue. There was a school in Roland Park in 1894, on what is now Keswick Road, that was run by two sisters, Katherine and Adelaide Howard, who moved their school to Hawthorne Road in 1899. It was then taken over by Miss Corinne Jackson and Miss Bertha Chapman, and later sponsored by the Roland Park Company, who moved it to what is now 4608 Roland Avenue, a house called "The Poplars," which still stands. The school was called Roland Park Country School. Bouton hired high-quality staff, and the school went from a small neighborhood school to a first-rate college preparatory institution in a very short time. The primary school offered French and science, using the Montessori method of teaching. In 1905 principal Bertha Chapman instituted a college preparatory curriculum. Bouton and his company remained the school's sponsor until 1908 when it was incorporated as a non-profit under Maryland law. In 1916 the school moved to 817 West University Parkway, where it remained—despite a fire that destroyed 75 percent of the school in 1947—until 1980. It is now located at 5204 Roland Avenue in Roland Park. This photograph appears to show a natural science class, *c.* 1910. Although Roland Park Country School is a school for girls, the primary classes, at different times, have allowed boys. (Courtesy of Roland Park Country School.)

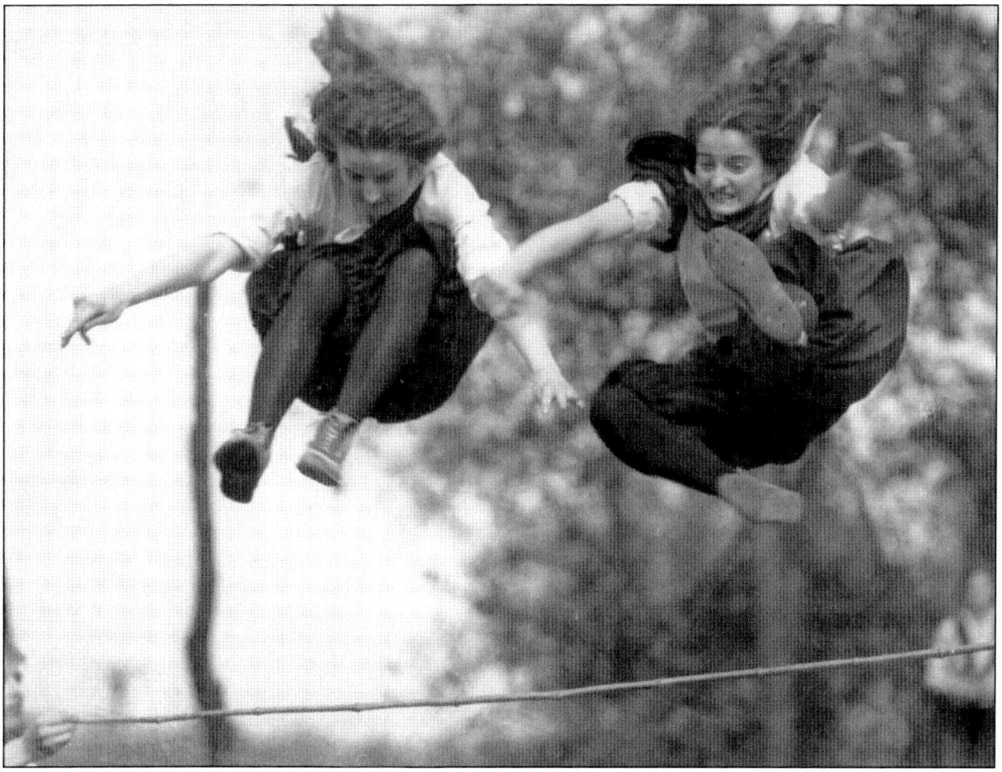

Sports have formally been a part of Roland Park Country School since World War I. The basketball rivalry between Roland Park Country School and Bryn Mawr has been in existence since 1917. Here we see two high jumpers, c. 1920, making their jumps despite the constraints of their cumbersome gym clothes. (Courtesy of the Roland Park Country School.)

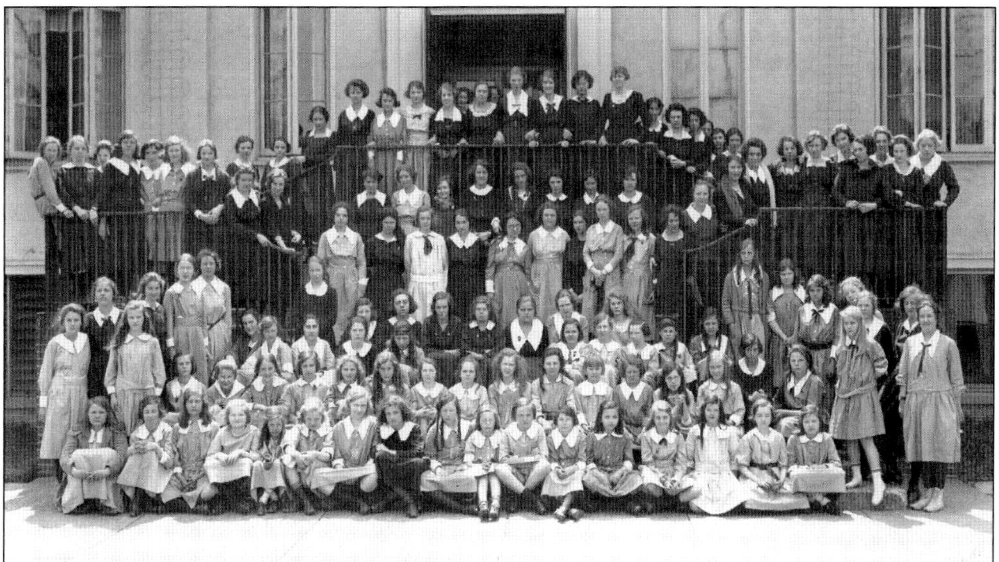

This is the school staff and student body in 1921, the year that Roland Park Country School's student government was formed. (Courtesy of the Roland Park Country School.)

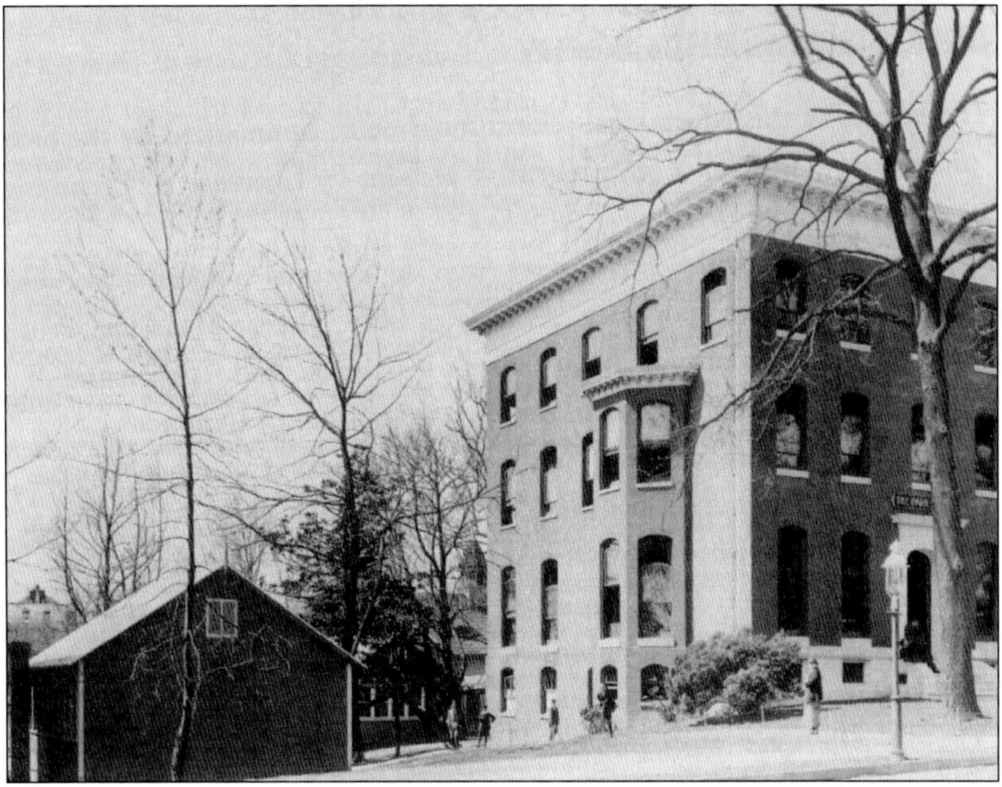

Superior education and non-discrimination were the desires of the founders of the Park School of Baltimore. In 1912, three school board commissioners were dismissed and two others resigned due to the differences of opinion between the board and Mayor James Preston—the board members' more innovative approach to education was not to the mayor's liking. One of these former commissioners was a college professor who believed that education should not stop in the classroom but should continue throughout life. Another was a Jewish man whose children were kept from attending the private schools of Baltimore. This ethnic discrimination, coupled with the desire to create a better form of education, was the impetus for the development of a new school. The idealism of its founders made the Park School of Baltimore a unique endeavor, meant to override ethnic, racial, and social exclusion, while creating an institution of high-quality education following the ideals of philosopher John Dewey. Although anti-discrimination language was in the school's charter, there was nothing formalizing integration until 1950. The first African-American student was admitted in 1954. Some of the more famous graduates include Edward Witten (Class of 1968), winner of the Field's Medal, the "Nobel Prize" for math; MacArthur Award–winning choreographer/director Martha Clarke (Class of 1962); and Alan Guttmacher (Class of 1915), a leader in reproductive rights for women and the president of Planned Parenthood. This 1917 photograph shows the school's first location near Druid Hill Park at Auchentoroly Terrace, formerly Orem Mansion. Adjacent to the main building is Park's version of the open-air classroom, which was started in 1916. By the end of 1918 the school had moved to Liberty Heights. In 1959 the school moved to its present location on Old Court Road. (Courtesy of the Park School of Baltimore.)

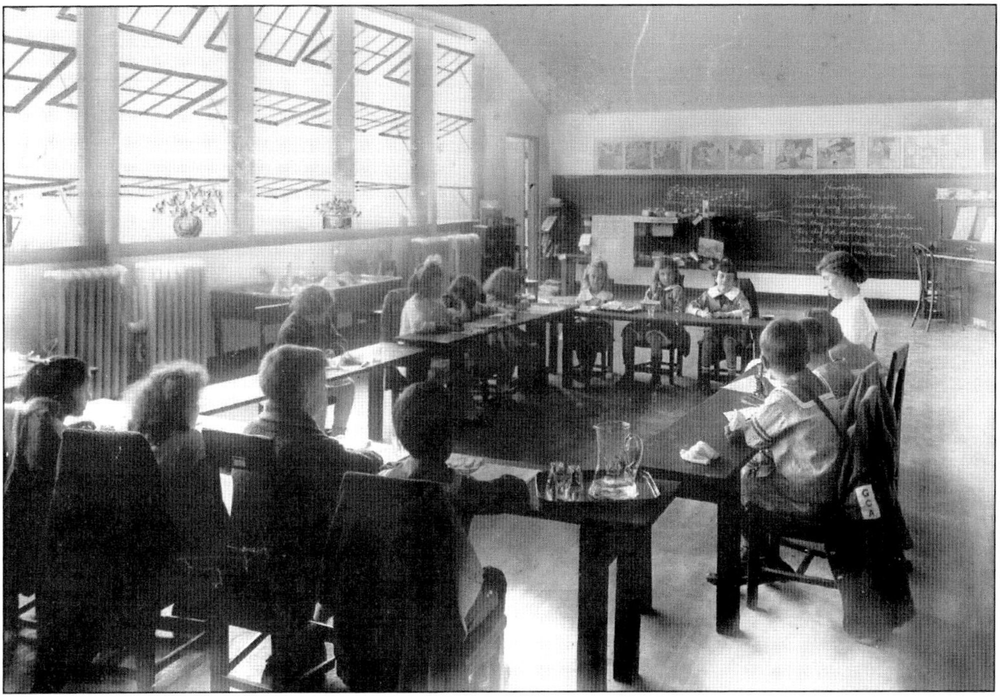

First graders in 1917 enjoy their lunch at the new Liberty Heights location. (Courtesy of the Park School of Baltimore.)

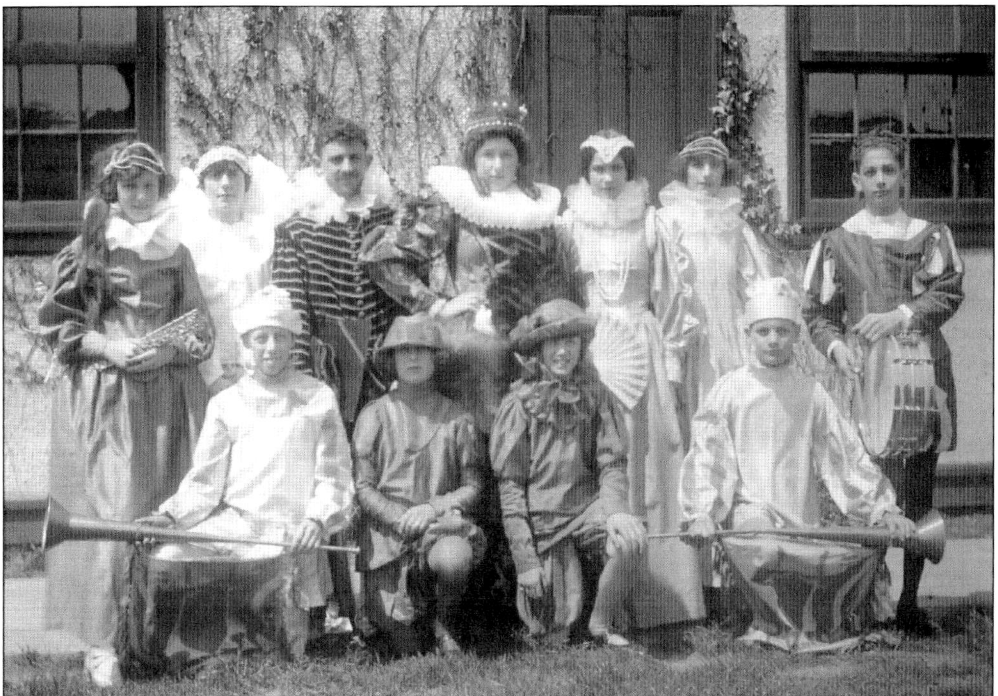

Performers at Park School's May Day celebration are pictured here in 1924. (Courtesy of the Park School of Baltimore.)

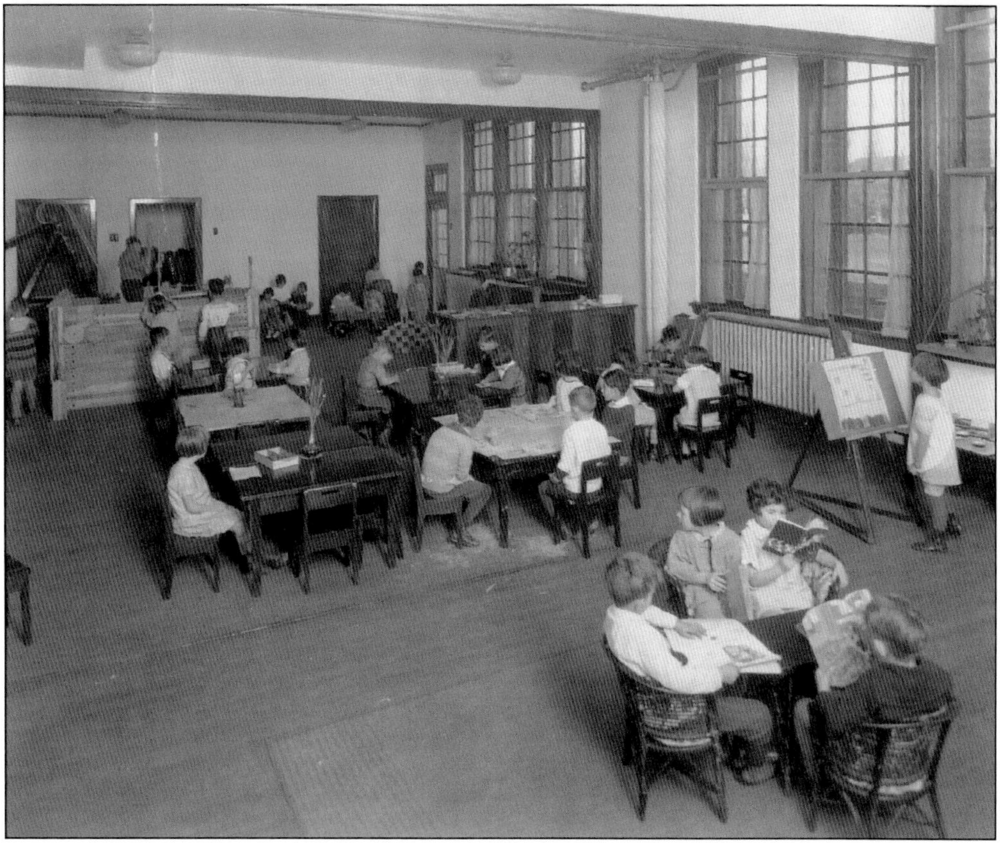

The Ordinance of March 1, 1828 stated that 12 schools would be established in Baltimore, 6 for boys and 6 for girls, but did not offer any means for financially supporting this endeavor. Therefore, the Commissioners of Public Schools decided that they would do what they considered the minimum—a school for each sex in the eastern and western parts of the city. Thus decided, they chose instructors and pursued venues. The commissioners were aware, even then, of the effects that adequate comfort would have on education. They noted "it is important, not only for the instructor, and most beneficial to the economical employment of his time and talents, but to the health and improvement of the pupils that the room should be large, light and well ventilated." After the strike of 1877, city authorities looked for a way to undermine the actions of the unsatisfied underclass, considering the possibilities that education might have as a way of defusing social tensions. In 1884 Baltimore established its first vocational school, the Manual Training School for Boys. By the 1890s Baltimore was a very unsanitary place with open sewage and festering garbage in the streets. The city's classrooms were considered by many to be unhealthy for children. The State Board of Health declared the air in schools filthy and "impregnated with foetid poison," a far cry from the plans of the original commission to make the classroom a healthy place. In 1898 the new city charter allowed for education professionals to replace the officials then in power. Pictured here is a primary class at School #14, located at Lincoln and Wilson, c. 1910. (Courtesy of the Enoch Pratt Free Library.)

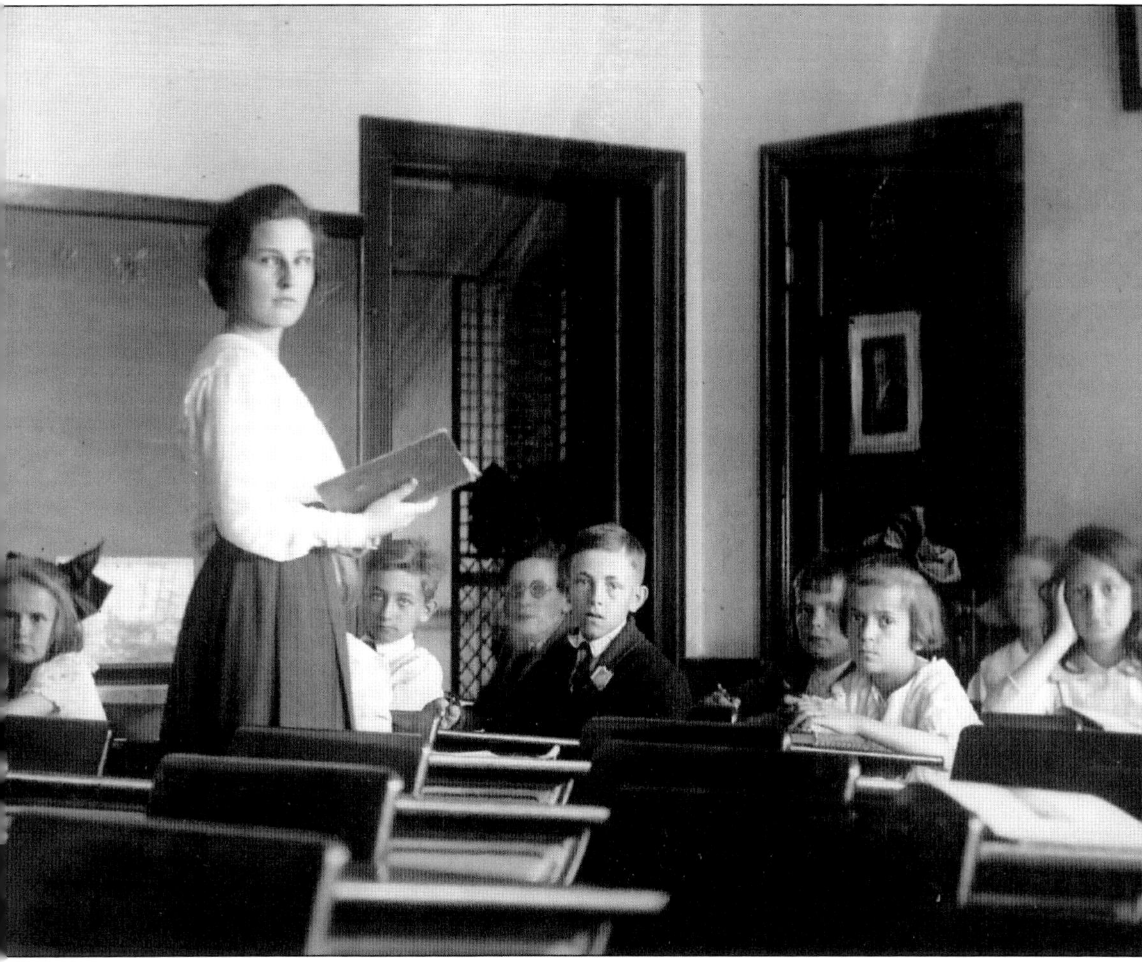

What is today known as Franklin Square High School at Lexington and Stricker Streets was built in 1961. It may have replaced the older school by the same name that is seen here *c.* 1910. It obviously was not only used as a high school since these children are primary school students. Western High School, formerly at Paca near Fayette, and Eastern High School, formerly at Front and Pitt Streets, both no longer in their original locations, have offered education for girls since 1844. Western High School added mild physical education to the curriculum in 1866 and Eastern High School added photography and telegraphy to the curriculum, which were the first vocational courses that were not geared exclusively towards the teaching profession. In 1876 preparatory classes were added, and by 1880, many classes were eliminated because parents felt that so many courses were injuring the health of the girls. It was considered to be too much of a strain for the girls' delicate natures. (Courtesy of the Enoch Pratt Free Library.)

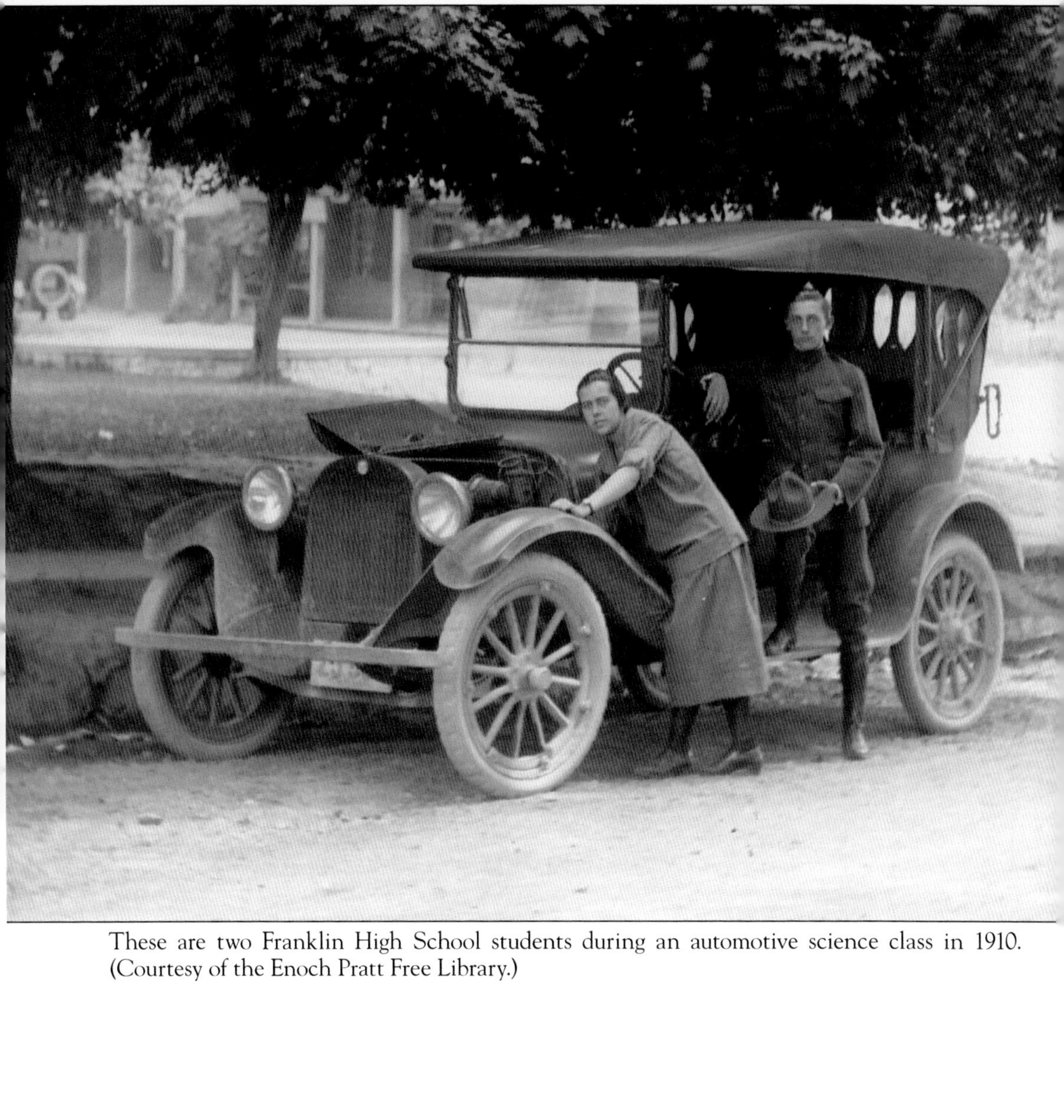

These are two Franklin High School students during an automotive science class in 1910. (Courtesy of the Enoch Pratt Free Library.)

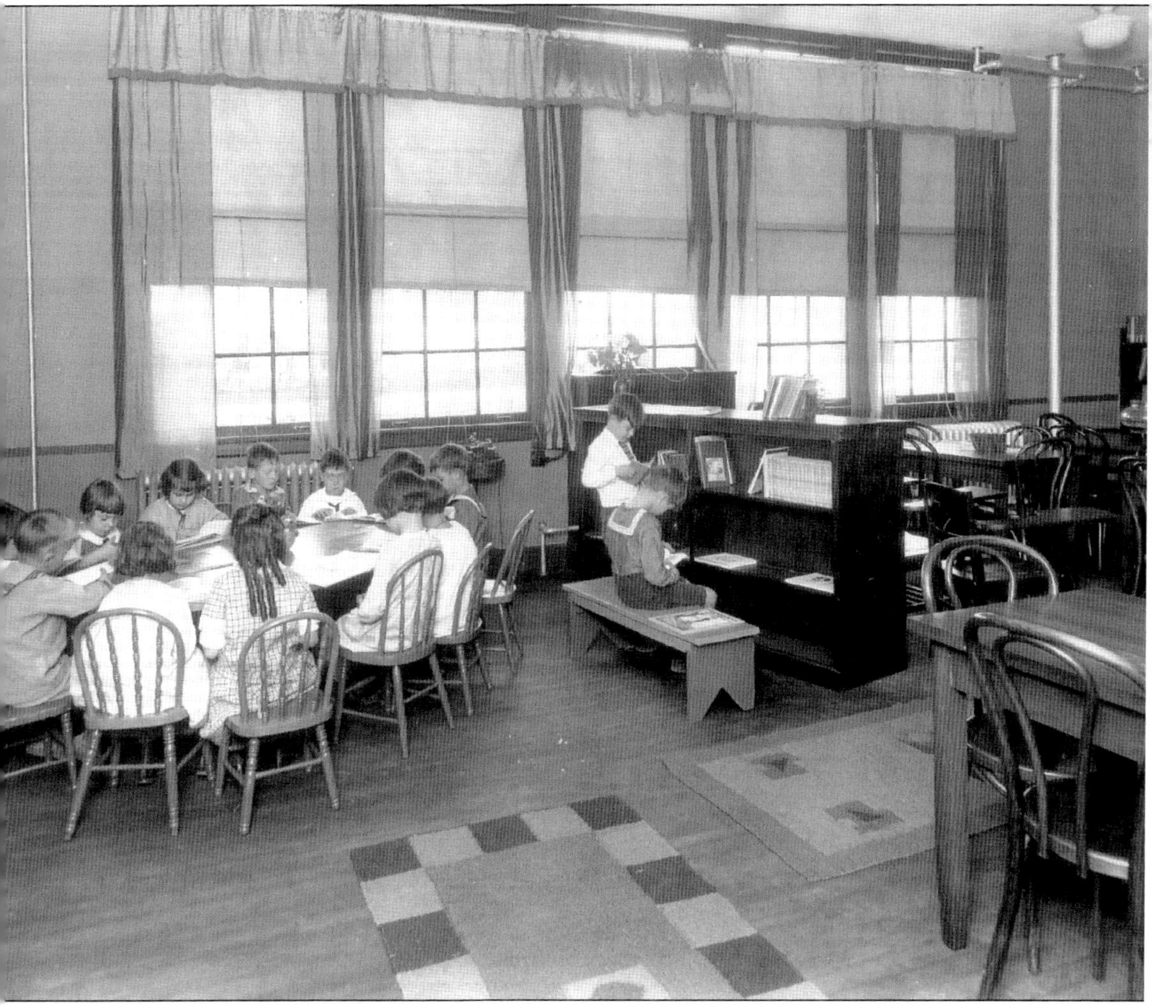

A primary public school classroom (location unknown) is pictured here in the 1920s. (Courtesy of the Enoch Pratt Free Library.)

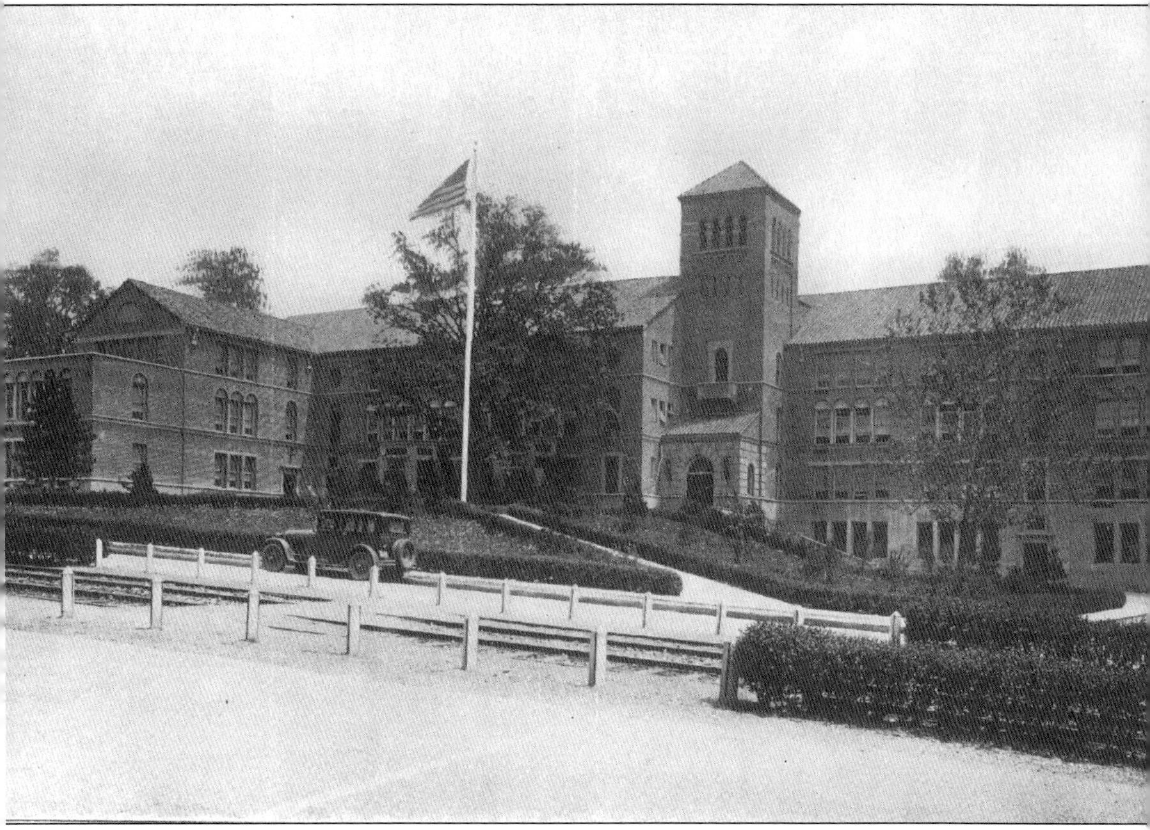

Although the history of Baltimore's public schools, and the present state of the school system, does not always inspire great confidence, it must be mentioned that there are true exceptions. Roland Park School (School #233), formerly "Todd's Academy" at Roland Avenue and St. John's Road and then located at Roland Avenue and Linden in 1924, has become a Blue Ribbon School, winning state science competitions and math competitions against some of the most elite schools in the country. In the 1913 catalogue from Roland Park Public School, we find many of the same concerns expressed today by those involved in public schools. To quote the catalog, "In some other sections of our country where the operations of public school systems are not so hampered by short-sighted financial considerations on the part of the public, those children who are sent to private schools, generally speaking, are not able to keep up with the standards of public schools." This 1929 photograph shows the exterior of the school in its present location. (Courtesy of Roland Park School.)

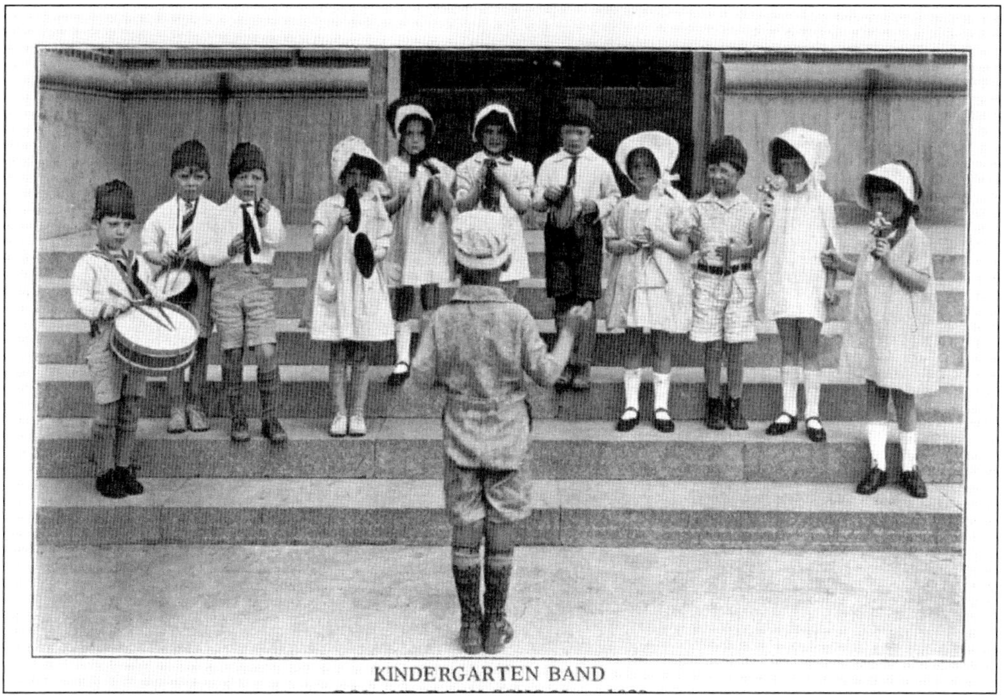

The members of the kindergarten band of Roland Park Public School pose on the steps of the school in 1928. (Courtesy of Roland Park School.)

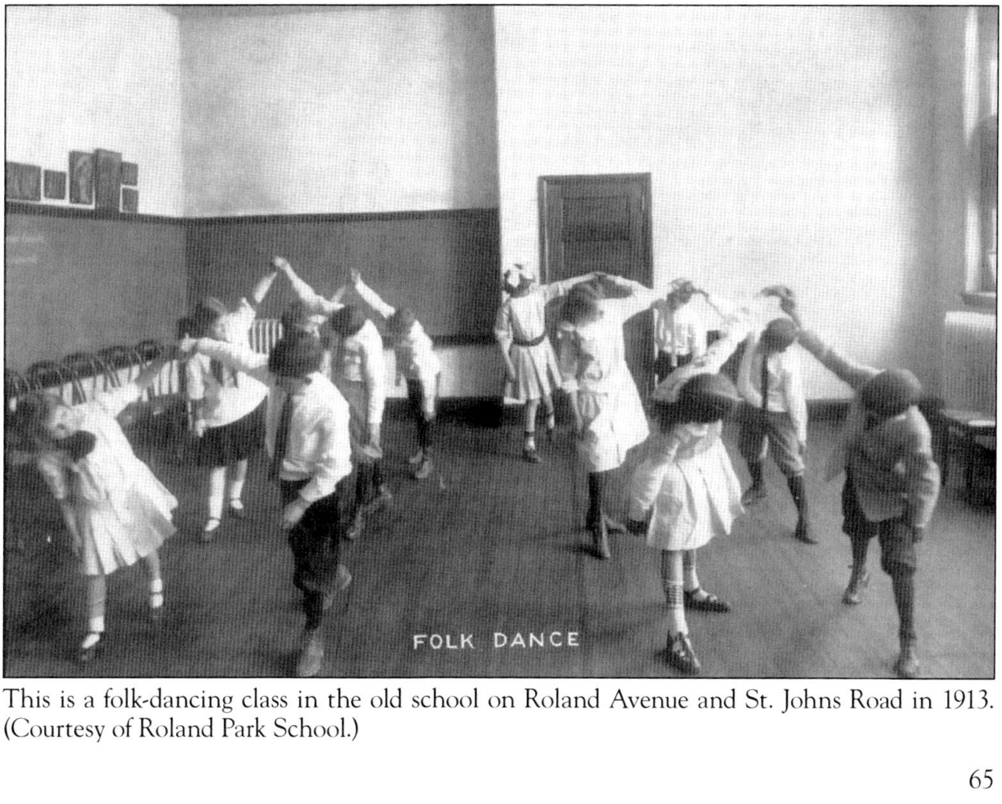

This is a folk-dancing class in the old school on Roland Avenue and St. Johns Road in 1913. (Courtesy of Roland Park School.)

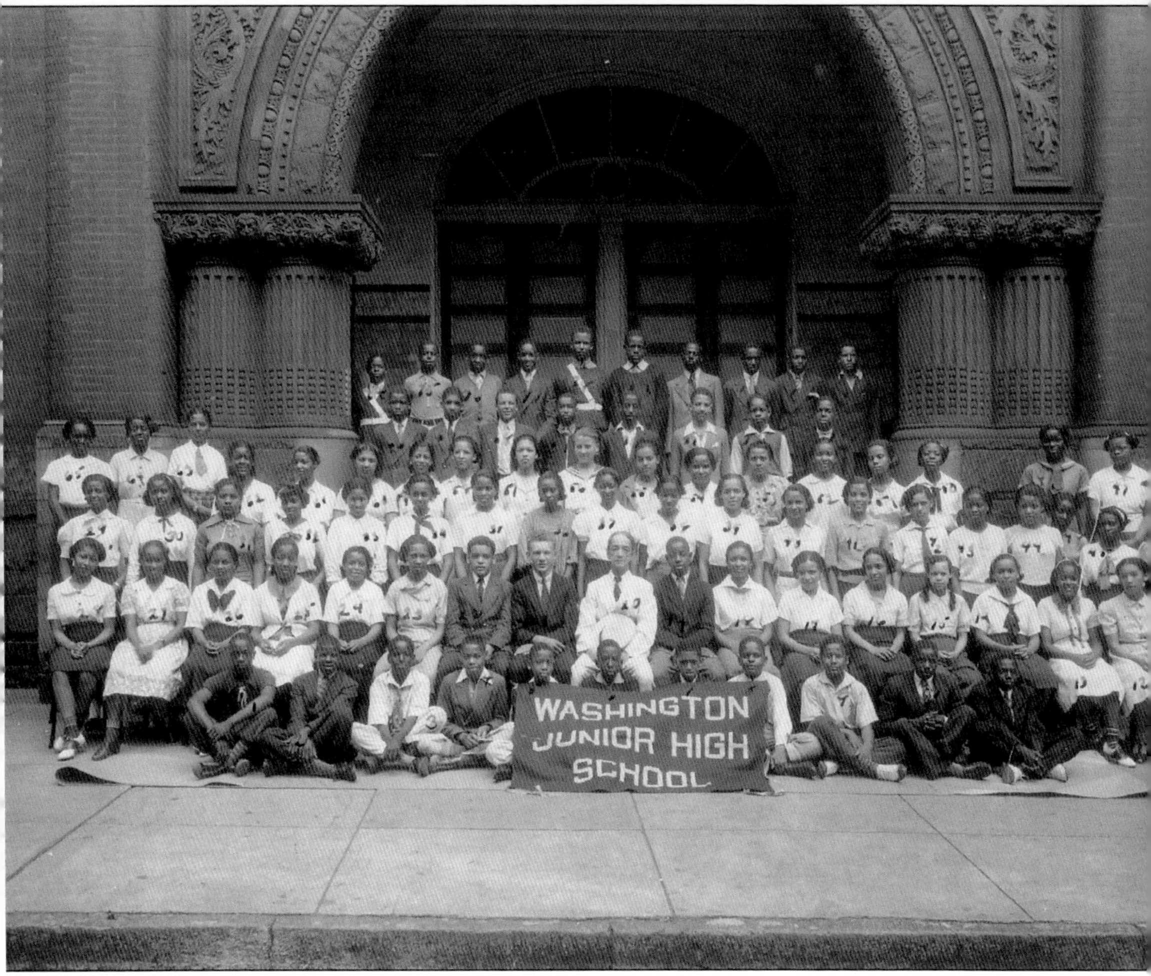

Booker T. Washington Junior High School, shown here with the class of 1937, is still open and at 1300 McCulloh Street in west Baltimore. Seated on the ground in the front row directly in front of the principal is Ellis Larkins. Larkins was considered something of a prodigy and later became a well-respected pianist, making his New York debut at age 19. His many appearances on stage include a performance for Eleanor Roosevelt at Frederick Douglass High School in Baltimore and a concert with Leonard Bernstein and Ella Fitzgerald at New York City's Carnegie Hall. (Courtesy of Nanny Jack & Co., Inc. Archives.)

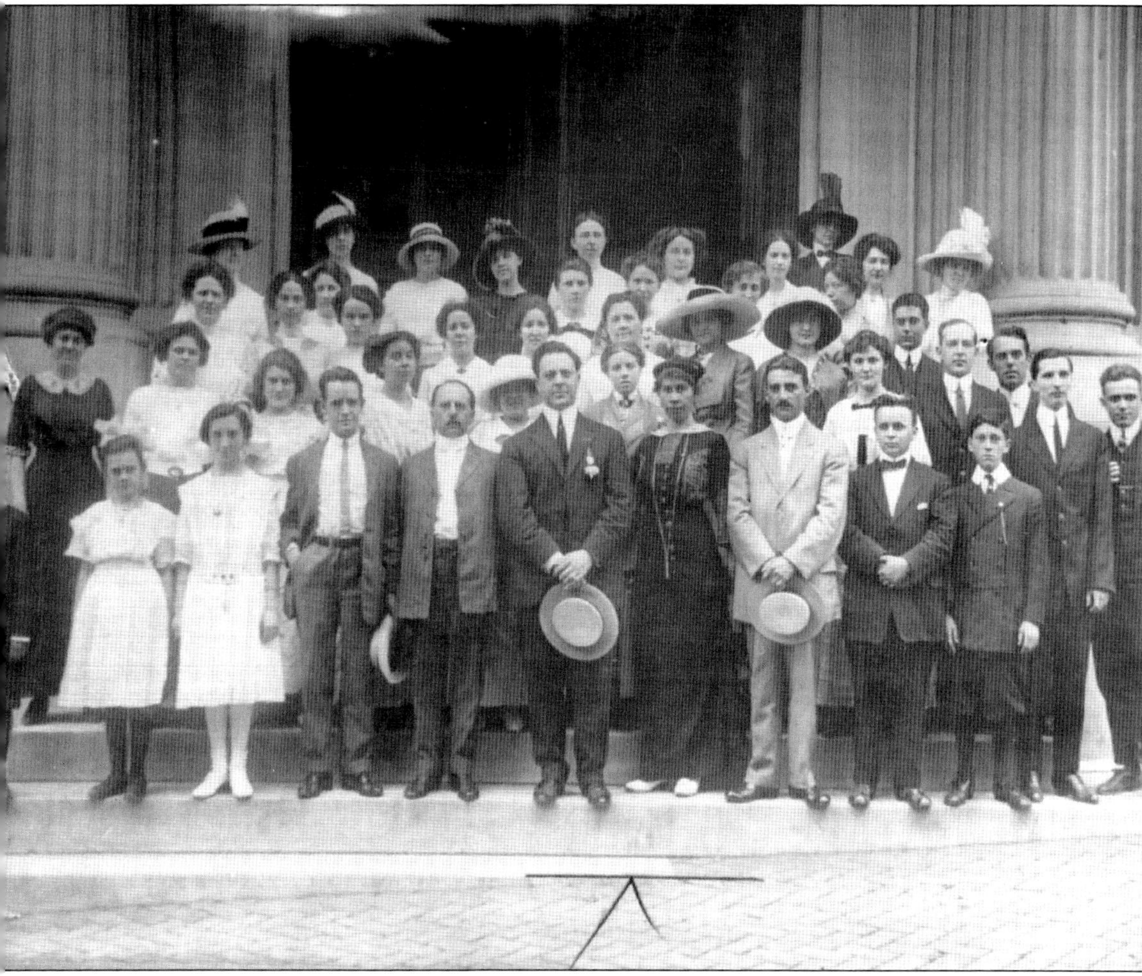

In 1866 the Peabody Institute was dedicated. George Peabody, born in 1795, achieved great wealth as a banker in Baltimore and founded this cultural center, which included a library, an art gallery, and a music academy. Peabody died in 1869. Pictured here is the first summer school class and faculty in 1911. (Courtesy of the Enoch Pratt Free Library.)

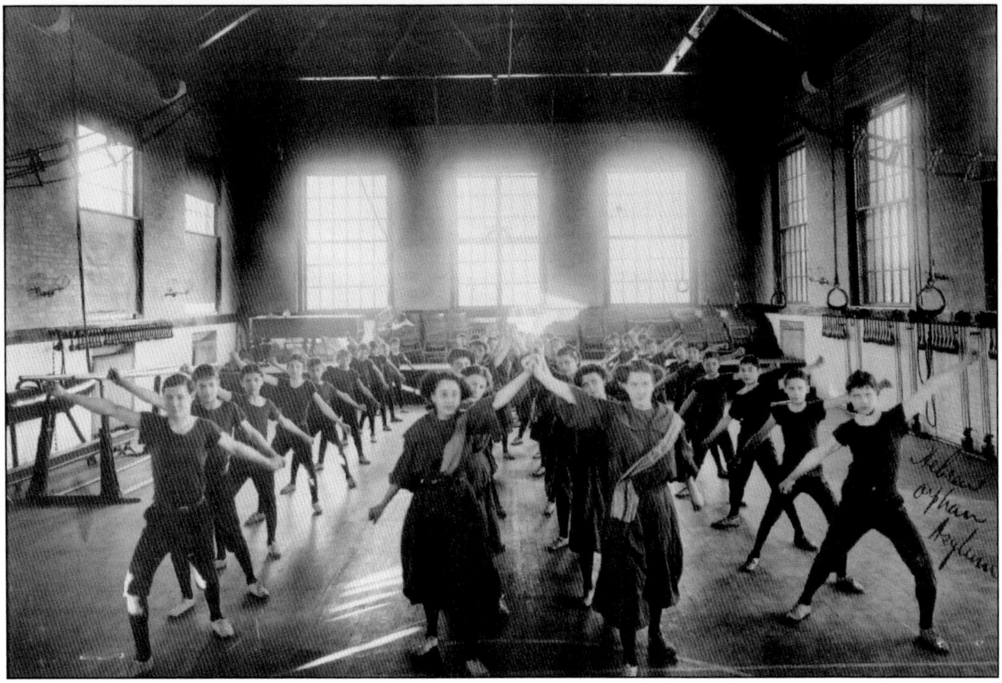

This photo shows the gymnasium at the Hebrew Orphan's Asylum, *c.* 1911. It seems unusual that there would be a co-ed gym class; however, in this photo and others from this series, the children appear to be preparing for some type of performance. (Courtesy of the Jewish Museum of Maryland.)

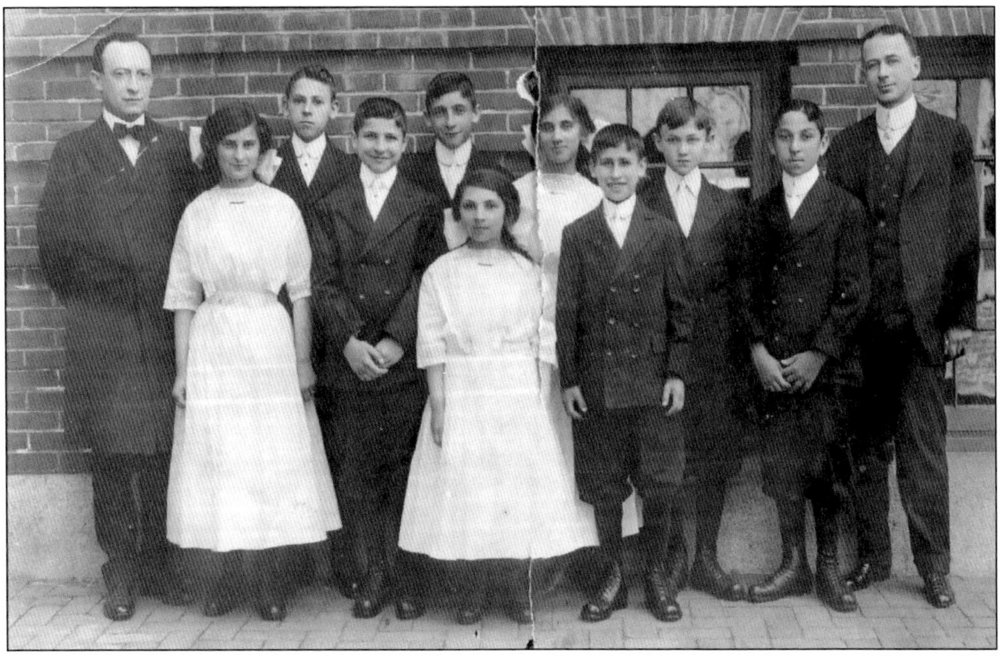

In attempts to Americanize customs, bar mitzvahs and bat mitzvahs were often called "confirmations" by non-Orthodox Jews. Here is a confirmation class from the Hebrew Orphan Asylum, *c.* 1914. (Courtesy of the Jewish Museum of Maryland.)

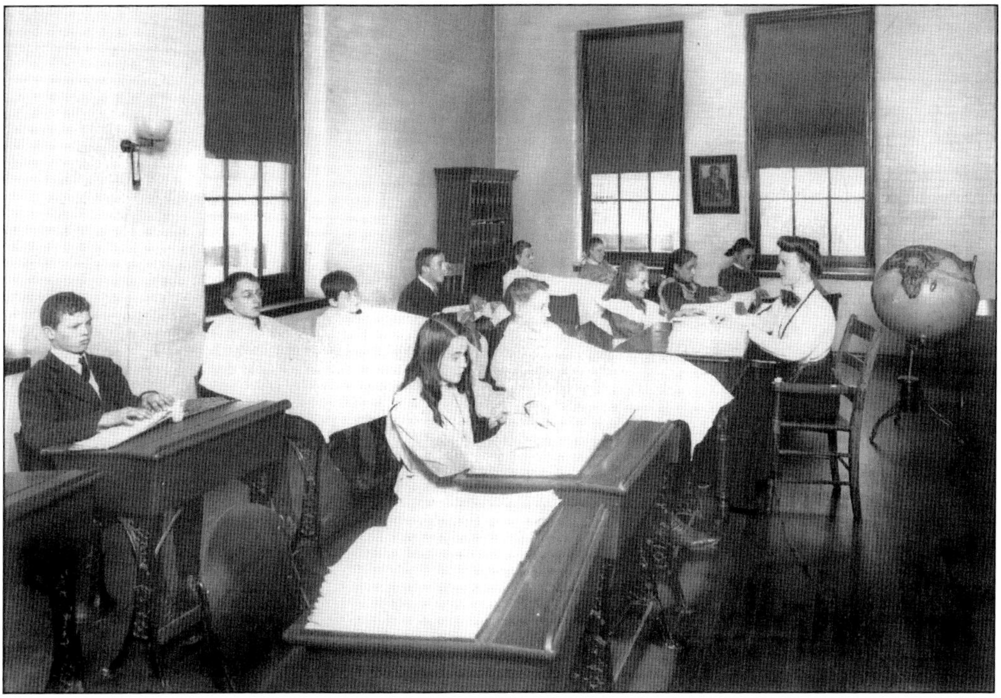

Prior to the founding of the Maryland School for the Blind 1853, children in Baltimore who were visually impaired were sent to a facility in Pennsylvania. The Maryland School for the Blind (called the Maryland Institution for the Instruction of the Blind until 1886) is and was a state-aided private school. Hoping to create a place where young people could learn with special assistance, Benjamin Newcomer, John McJilton, William Baker, Jacob Cohen Jr, John Glenn Jr., and Smith Hollins became the school's first board of directors. In this 1880 photograph, partially-sighted children learn to read Braille. The cloth over the books helped students learn without looking at the pages. (Courtesy of the Maryland School for the Blind.)

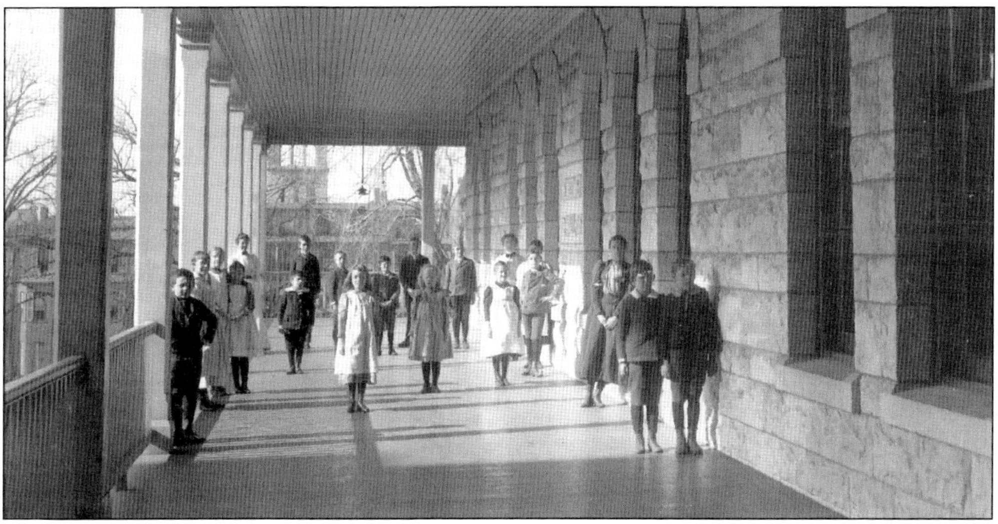

This eerie photo, c. 1906, shows primary school students on the porch of old Newcomer Hall at the former campus of the Maryland School for the Blind on North Avenue. (Courtesy of the Maryland School for the Blind.)

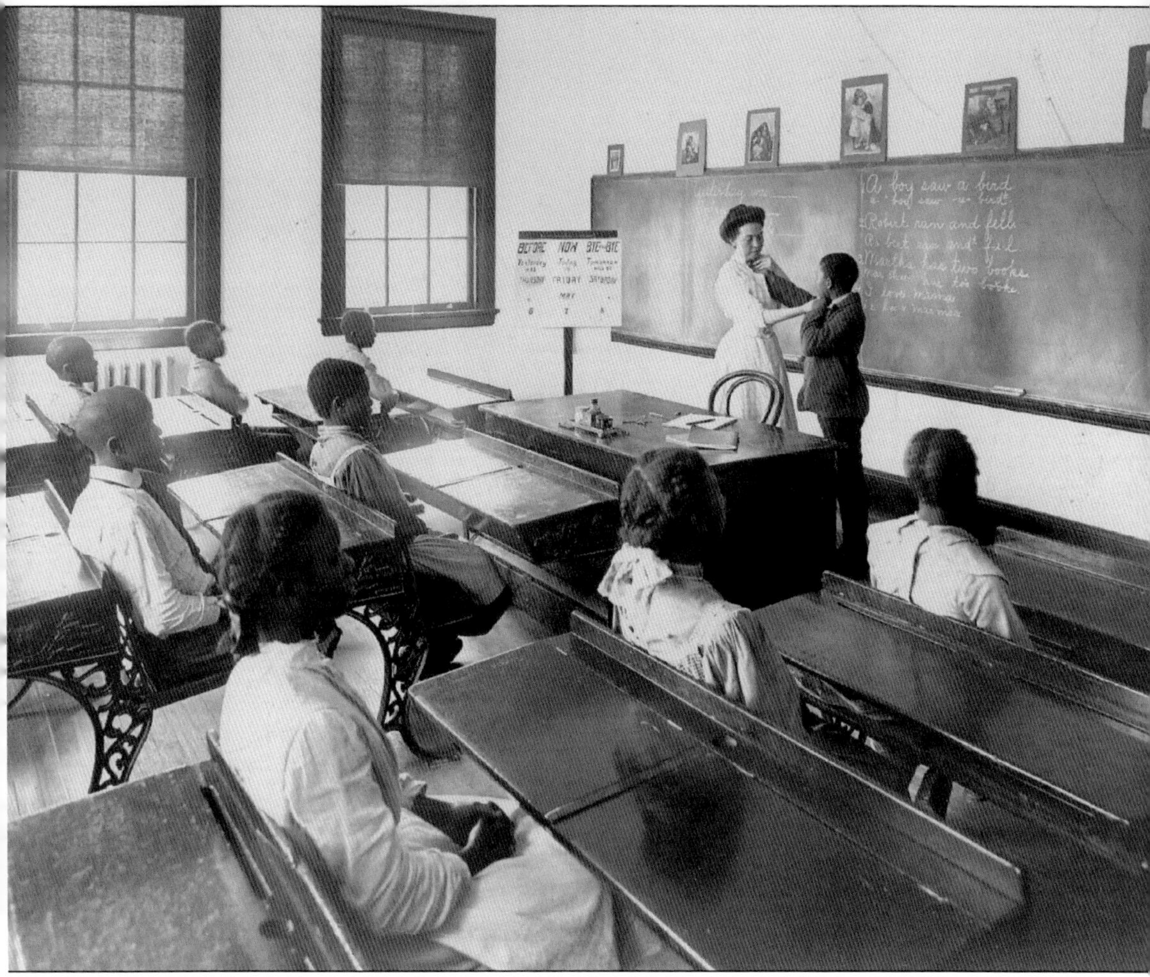

Originally located on West Saratoga Street, the Maryland School for the Blind served only white children until 1872, at which time it began providing assistance to African-American children as well. This c. 1872 class, including children with both vision and hearing difficulties, is being taught Tadoma, the language of Helen Keller. Although the school was not fully integrated until 1961, children of both races shared classes and dining areas prior to the Supreme Court ruling of 1953. In 1868 the school moved to what was then called Boundary Avenue, now North Avenue. The school purchased property north of the city on Taylor, east of Harford Road and, taking first the black students in 1907 and then the white students in 1911, moved to its present location. (Courtesy of the Maryland School for the Blind.)

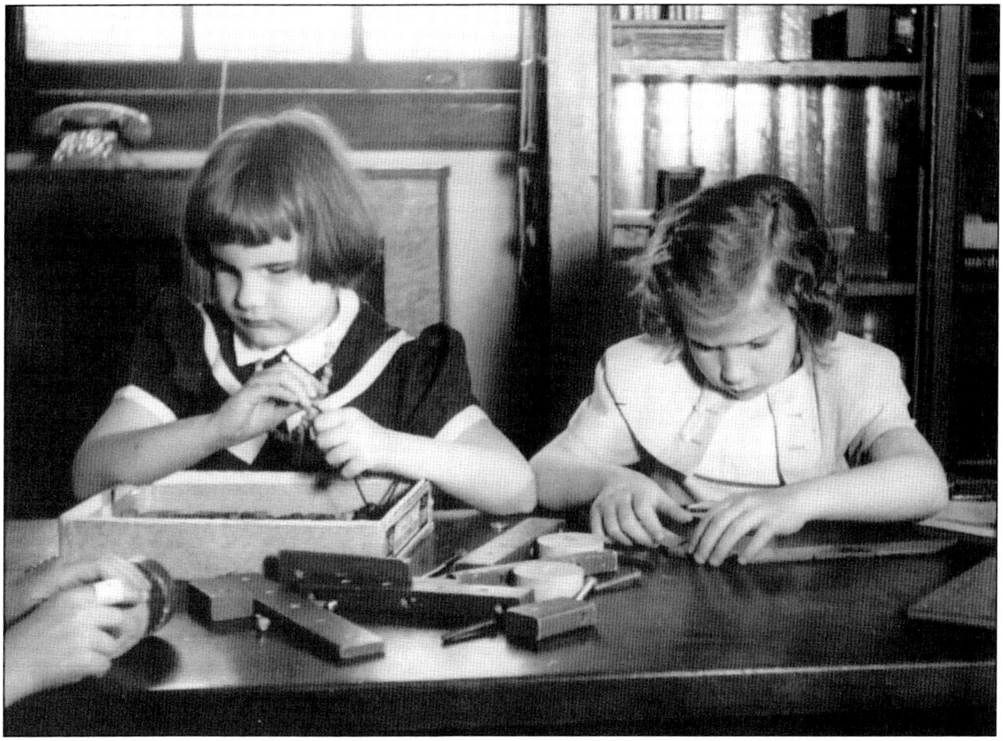

In the above view of the Maryland School for the Blind, kindergarten students, c. 1930, use building blocks. Below, little girls play house. (Courtesy of the Maryland School for the Blind.)

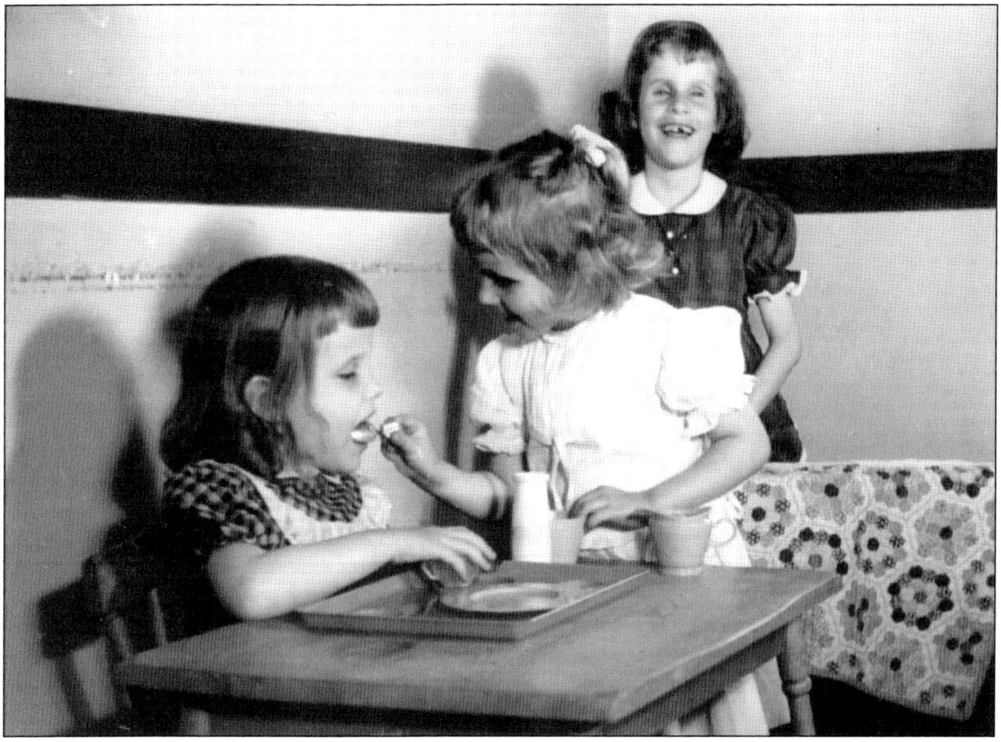

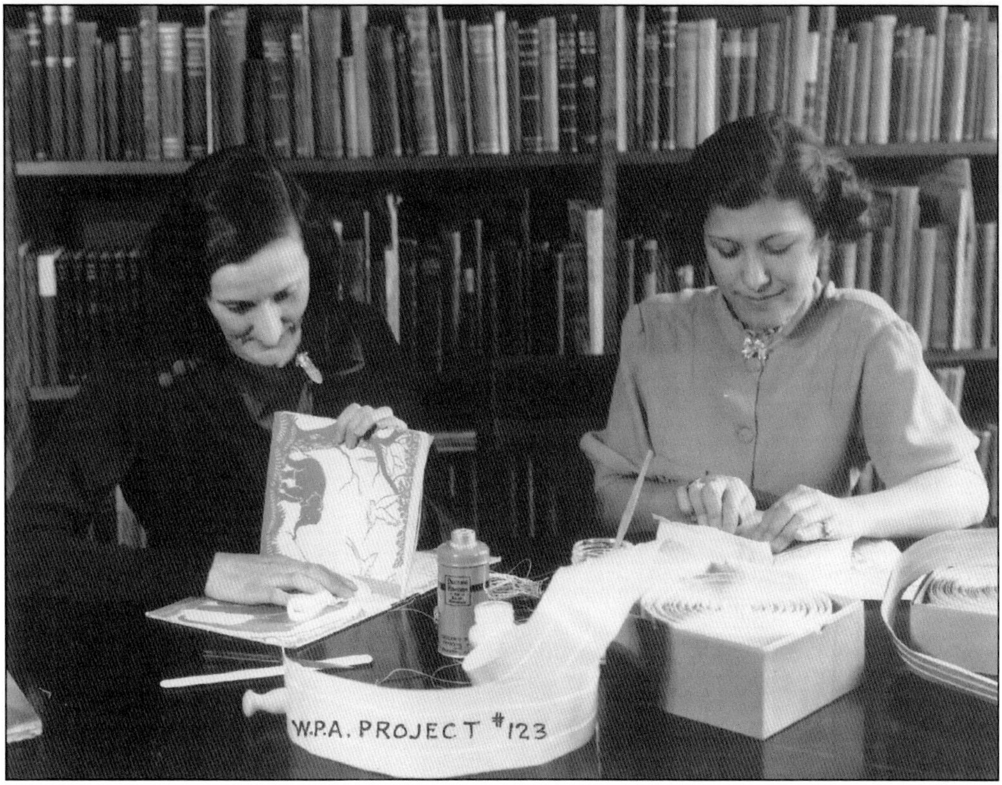

The Works Progress Administration (WPA), in addition to building roads and participating in other public service projects, also helped employ people to repair books and prepare food for schools, as seen in these *c.* 1934 images. (Courtesy of the Enoch Pratt Free Library.)

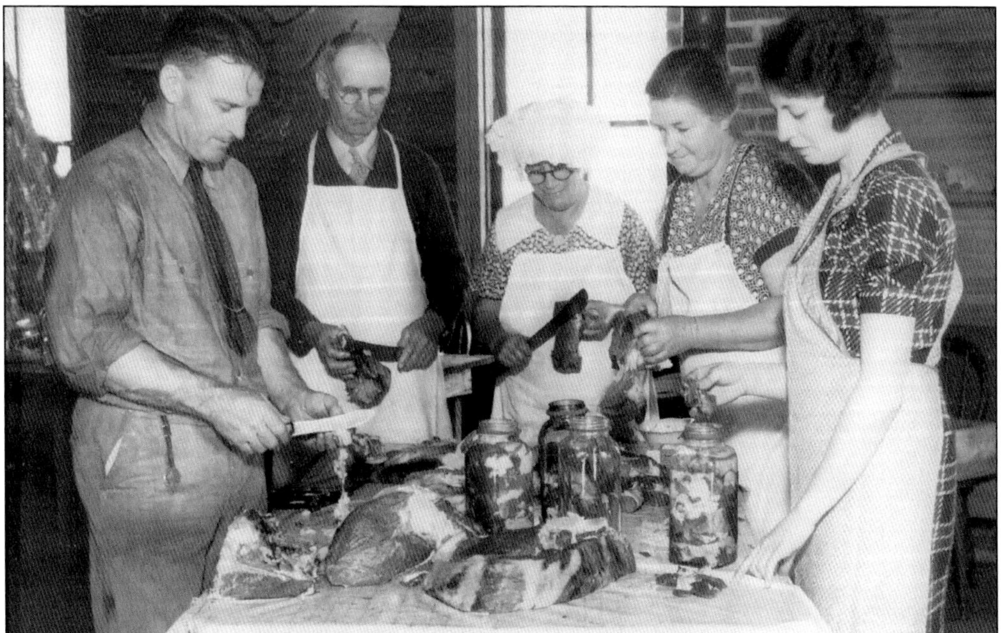

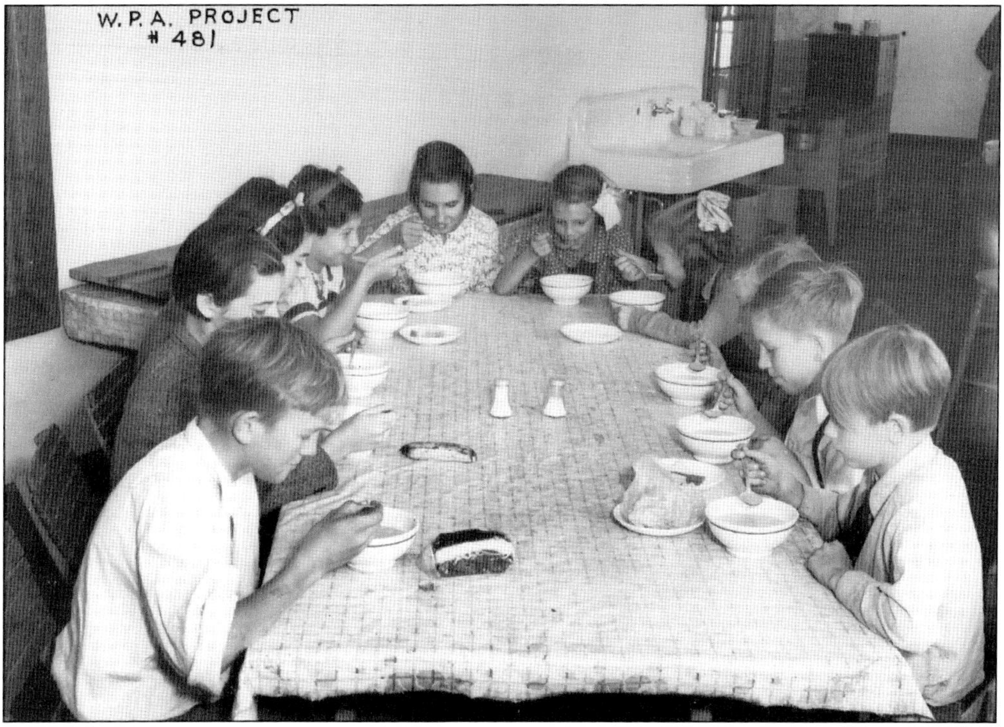

In the picture above, schoolchildren who could not afford food are fed through the WPA. Below, a WPA-run nursery school class is conducted. Both images were taken *c.* 1934. (Courtesy of the Enoch Pratt Free Library.)

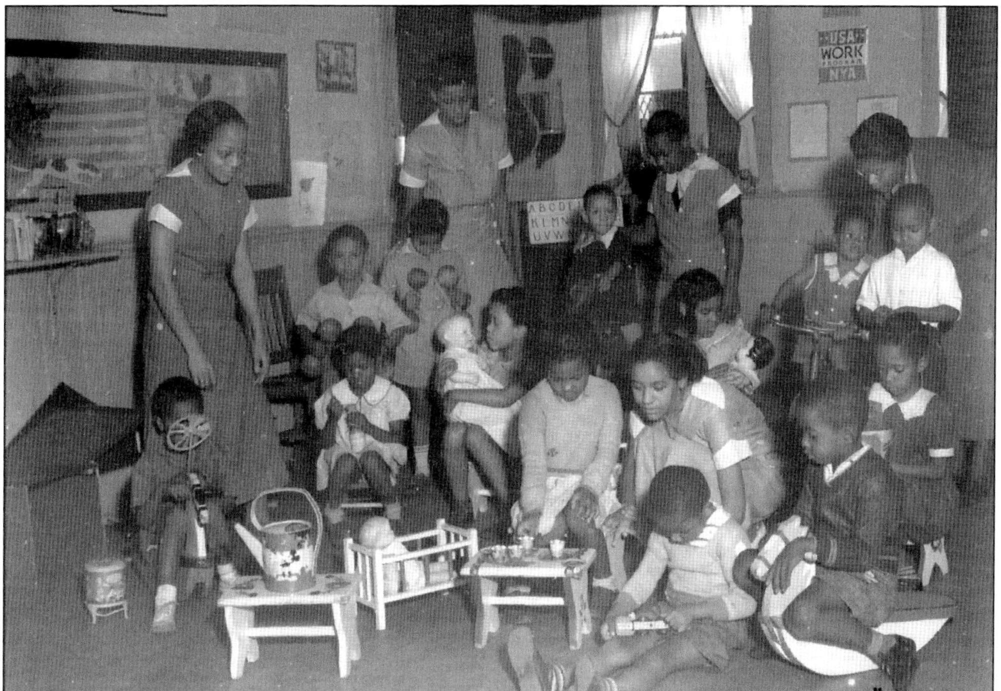

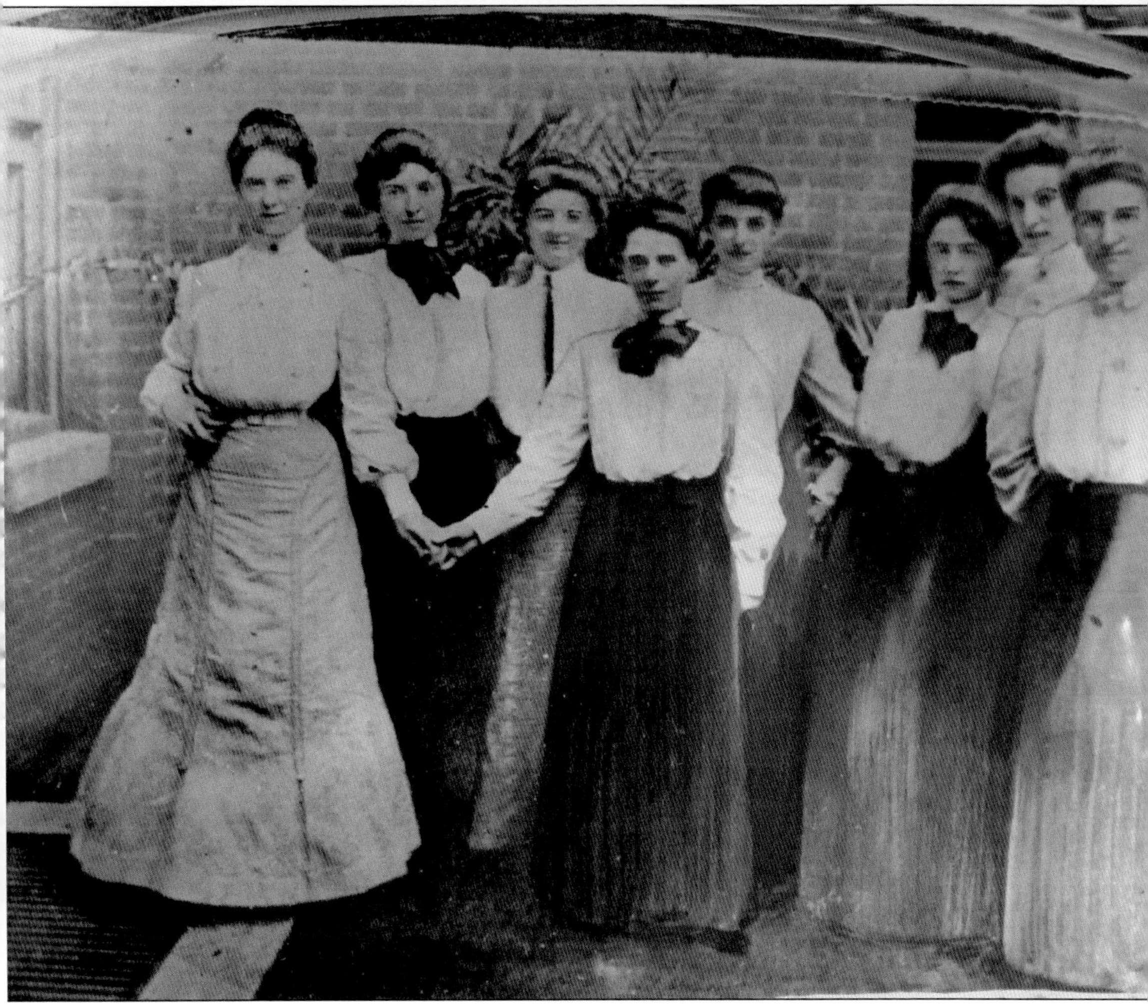

In 1881 Enoch Pratt broke ground on a project that would leave all the children of Baltimore a most precious gift. Pratt created a library system that would allow anyone and everyone holding a library card access to books. The library was never segregated (although attempts were made to do so after Pratt's death) and it was open to anyone who wanted to join. Pratt was known to sign for children who could not get a guardian to do so. The branch library system as we know it was almost nonexistent at the time Pratt put it into operation, establishing a trust that would continue supporting the library indefinitely. The effects of Pratt's incredible gift are still felt, although there are always threats of branch closures and lack of funds. The small branches that have survived are still loved and used by neighborhood children throughout Baltimore, and the beautiful Central Branch has resources plentiful enough for any bibliophile. Pictured above is the Enoch Pratt Free Library staff in the 1880s. Pratt thought women were better workers for several reasons, including the fact that he felt they had better handwriting. (Courtesy of the Enoch Pratt Free Library.)

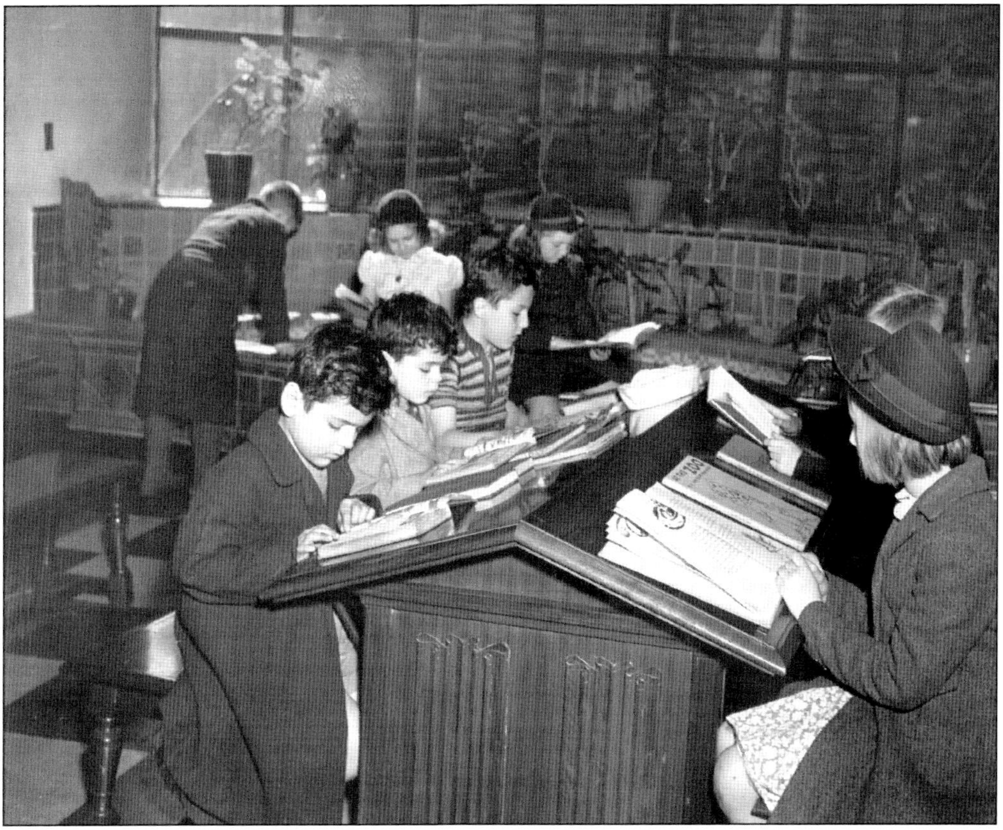

Above, schoolchildren enjoy the tranquil atmosphere of the children's room at the Enoch Pratt Free Library's Central Branch. Below, schoolchildren of the 1930s use the Enoch Pratt Free Library Branch #12. (Courtesy of the Enoch Pratt Free Library.)

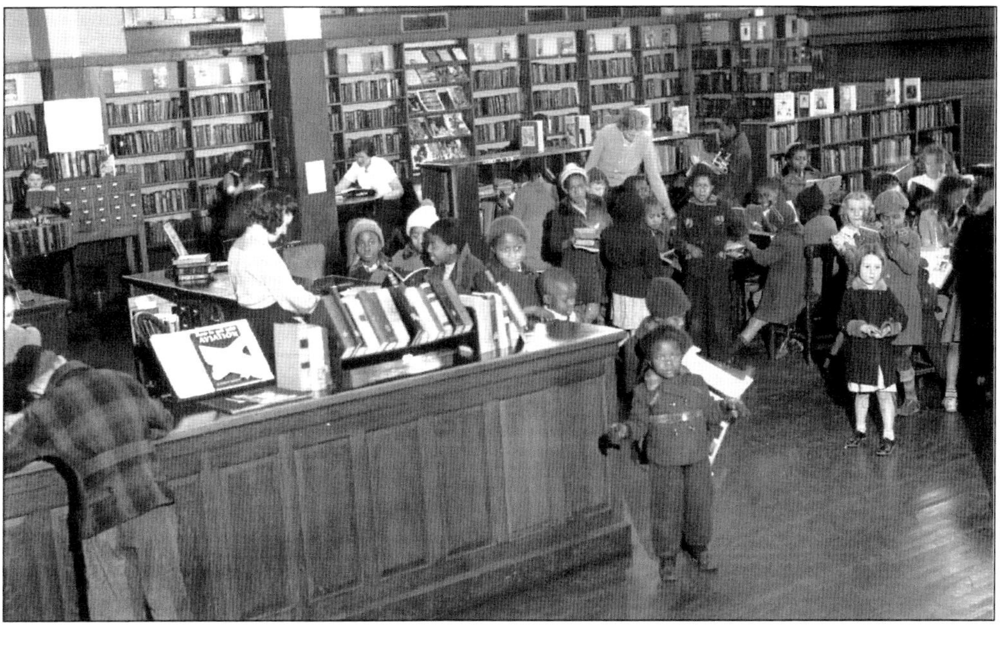

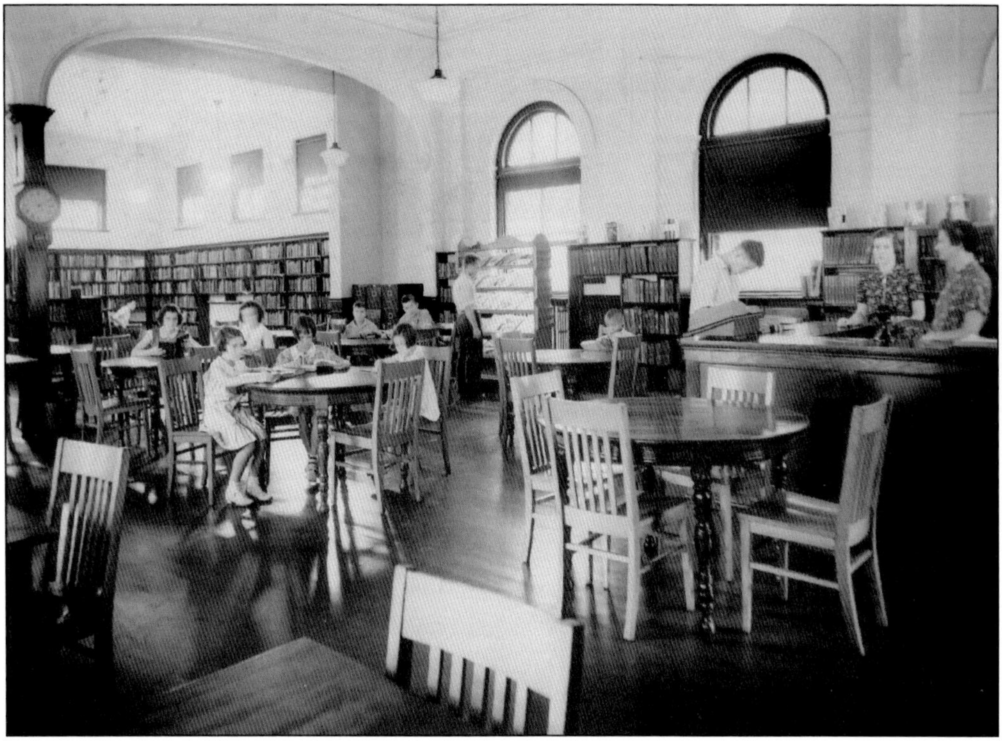

Enoch Pratt Free Library Branch #7 in Hampden, pictured above, is still one of the most popular neighborhood branches in the system. Below, schoolchildren are pictured outside of Enoch Pratt Free Library Branch #13. (Courtesy of the Enoch Pratt Free Library.)

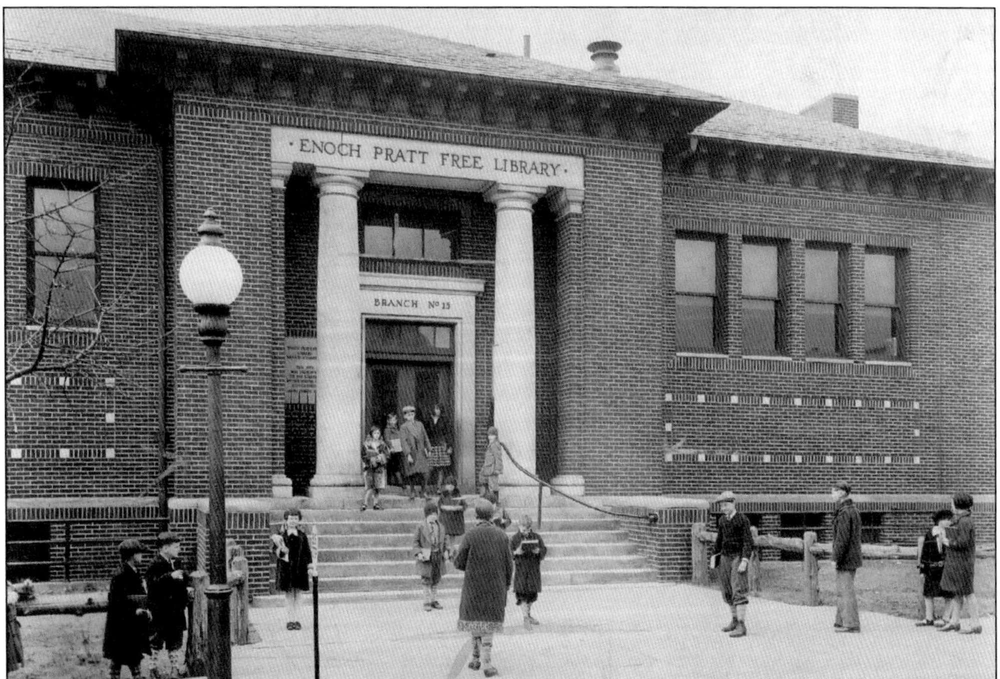

Three

CHILDREN AT WORK

In 1909 Lewis Hine set out to change the way Americans saw child labor. In fact, before Hine, few people ever knew what was going on behind the scenes at canneries, mills, mines, and factories around the nation. Consumers would buy their canned beans without knowing whose tattered little fingers worked for 10 hours each day stringing them. But "children at work" does not only imply suffering. Many kids had after-school jobs or helped with the family's income without being exploited and without being forced to give up school for work. Work could often be a source of pride and independence for kids. Unfortunately, the sense of pride derived from a job was often exploited by employers looking for cheap labor. Even those kids most at risk, given terrible jobs for almost no money, wanted to work just like the older kids in their families. This was all they knew. "Work even for the little hands" seems to have been the slogan of many factory managers. Far from trying to hide the desire for cheap child labor from parents, cannery, mill, and factory managers encouraged parents to bring their wee children to work. With promises to find jobs for even the youngest toddlers, parents were often thrilled to bring home a few extra pennies. Laws that kept children under the age of 14 from working required only a signature from parents stating the fact that they were of age. In several inquests, after the death of children in work-related accidents, it was uncovered that children as young as nine were "signed off" by their parents. The mines or factories claimed no responsibility. It is heartbreaking to read the accounts of children who died in mines or mills, tiny children who were given the "okay" to work by their desperate, often illiterate parents. You can see in the faces of these kids, as Lewis Hine did, that there was little hope for anything else.

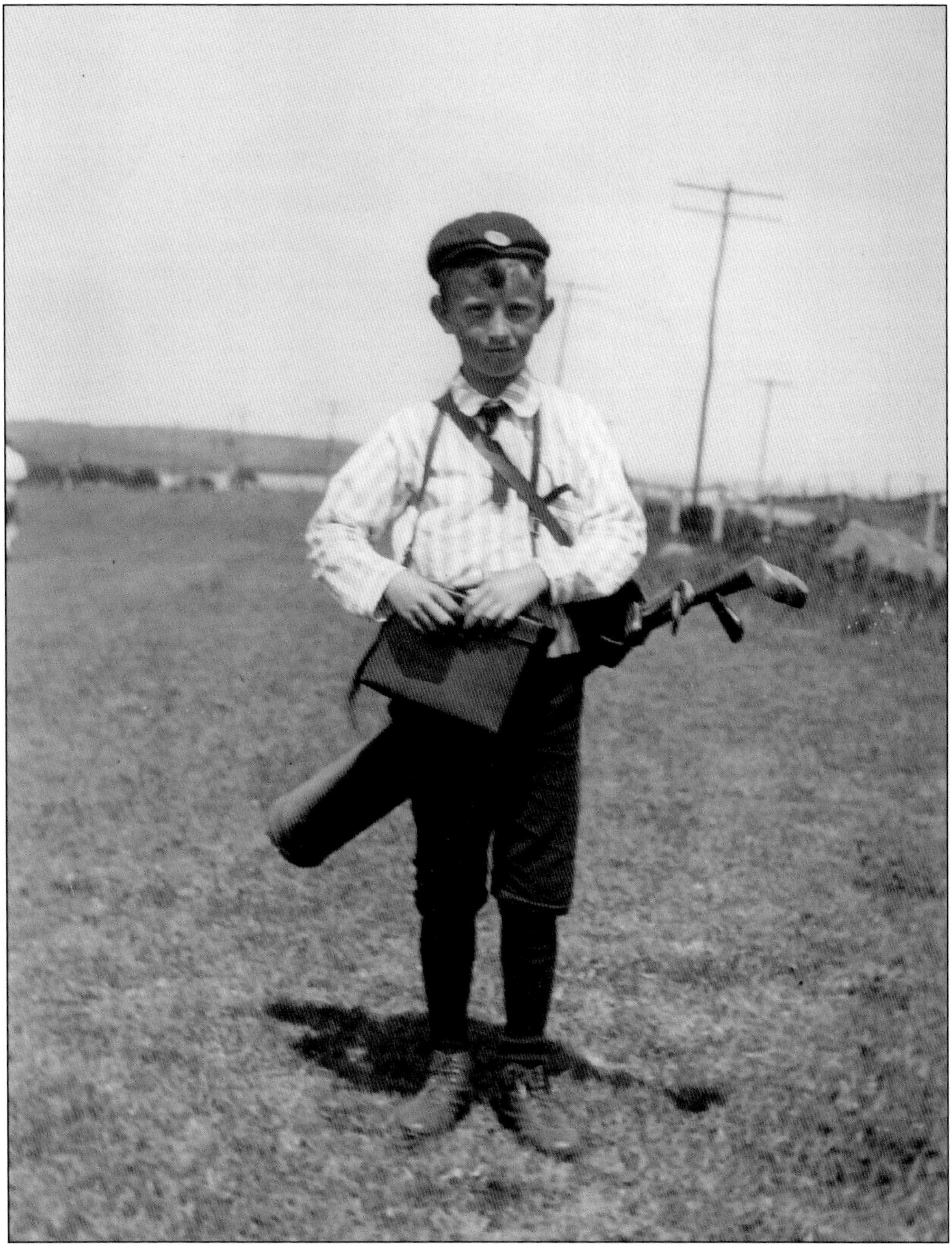

Although the legacy of child labor is a tragic one, children at work are not always suffering. Here a little boy works as a caddy on a public golf course in Baltimore city. He may be working to help his family, but he may also be enjoying the freedom of earning and spending money he made himself. One can suppose his hours are not excessive and his working conditions are not detrimental to his health and well-being. There is a clear difference between having an after-school job and being a victim of forced labor. (Courtesy of the Enoch Pratt Free library.)

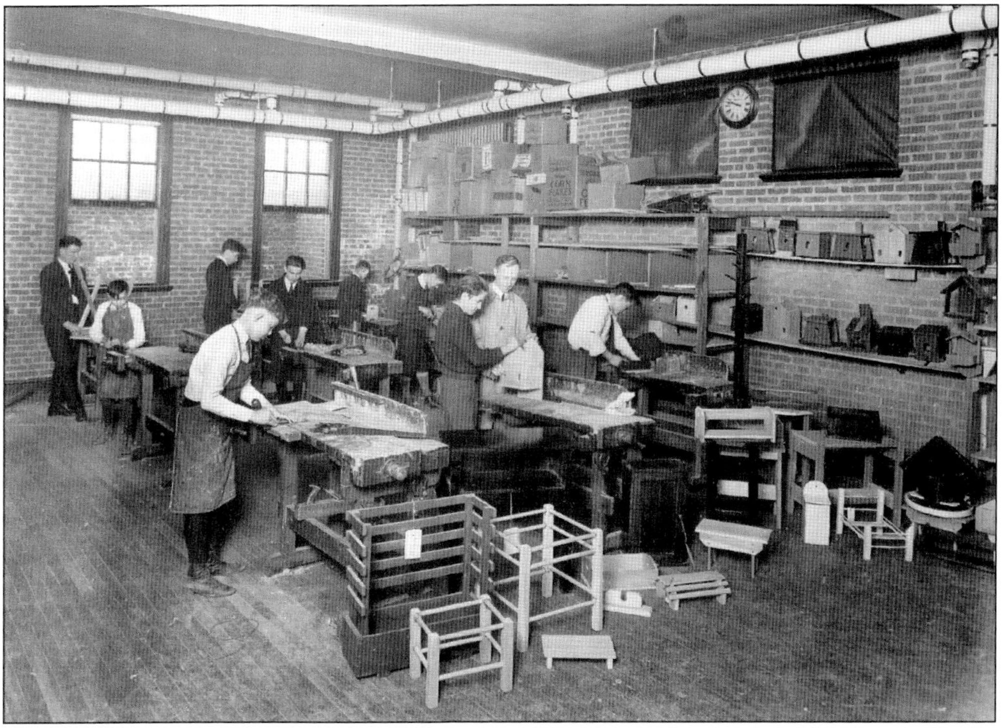

The Maryland Workshop for the Blind, run through the Maryland School for the Blind, was established in 1874, but the project did not have very positive results. Attempting to instruct and put to work both adults and children together was difficult for those in charge. After a final attempt in 1878, the workshop was abandoned. In 1908 a workshop for blind adults was created and formally opened in 1909. These photos, taken c. 1878, show both youngsters and adults learning to make brooms and construct other items in a workshop. The items made in these workshops were sold to the public. (Courtesy of the Maryland School for the Blind.)

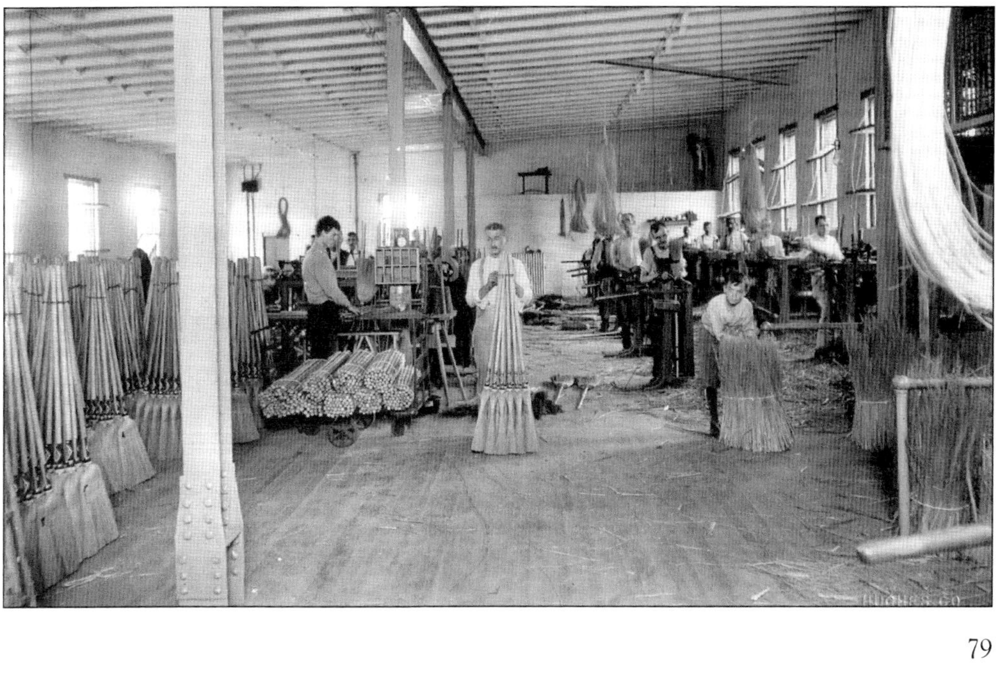

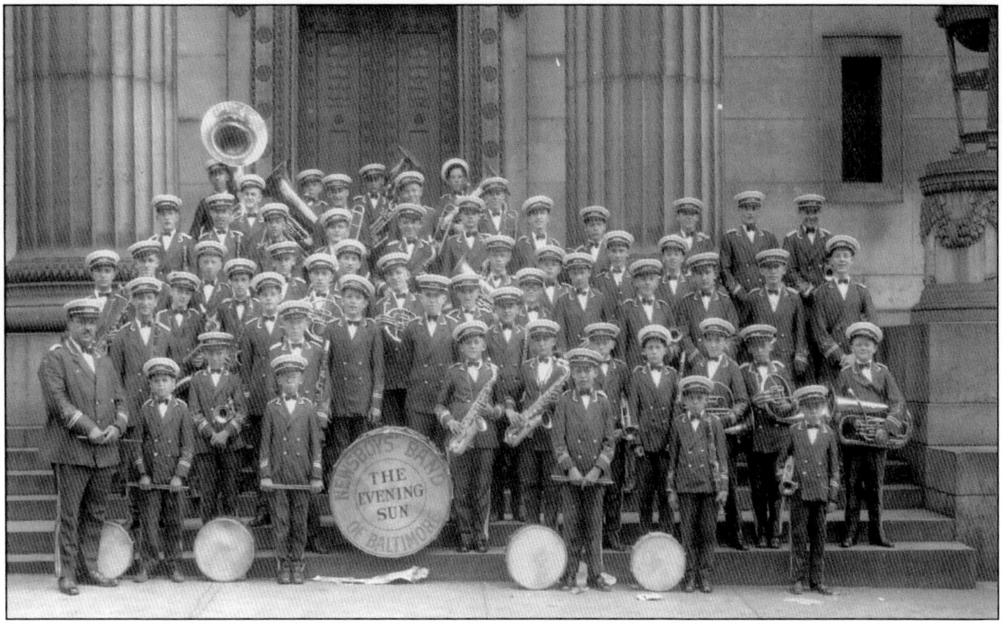

The Baltimore *Evening Sun* band, above, was formed in 1922 as a promotion gimmick for the newspaper. The boys played in parades and at other events and became very popular. John Philip Sousa led one concert and Babe Ruth once performed with them. On July 4, 1924, the 59-member band was returning from a performance in Crisfield when their ship, *Three Rivers*, caught fire. The newsboys were cited as heroes—many helping to save lives—but 10 people died, 5 of whom were newsboys. The tragedy overwhelmed the public and a monument was erected by the *Sun* in memory of the boys who died. Below, the *Sun* newsboys are pictured, c. 1910. (Courtesy of the Enoch Pratt Free Library.)

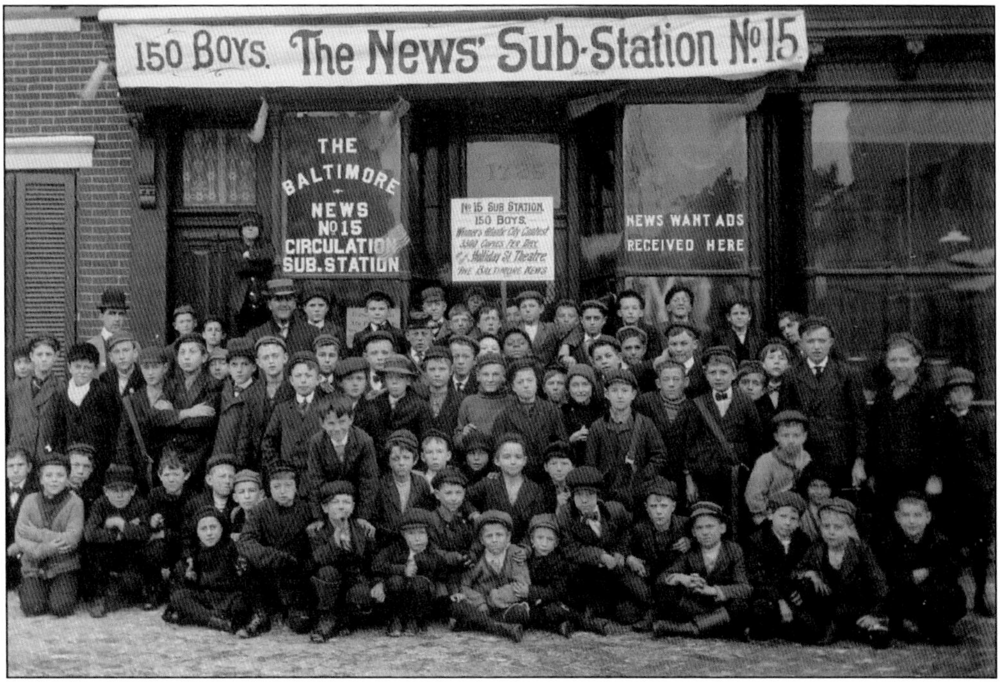

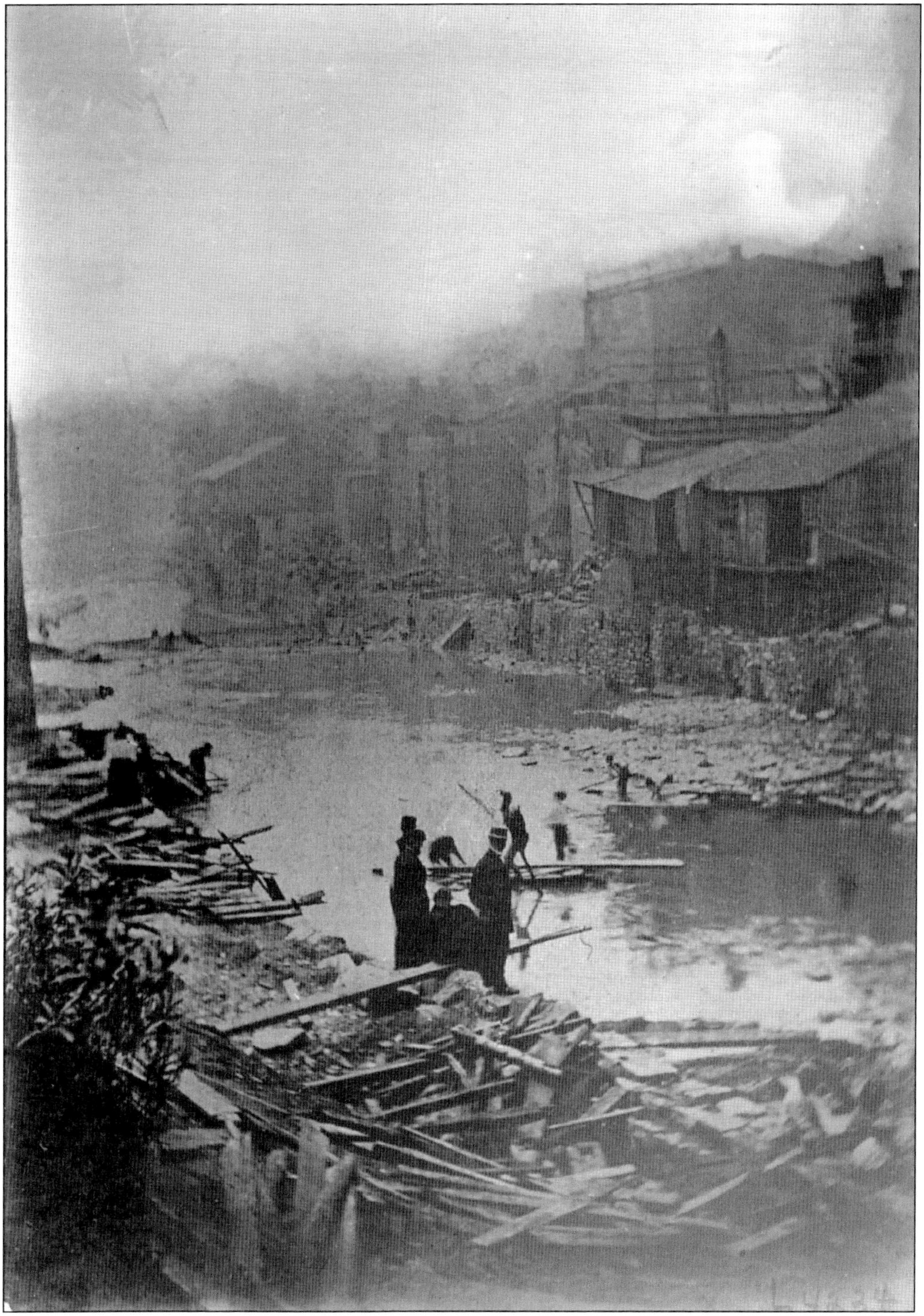

Children and adults scavenge Jones Falls after the devastating flood on July 28, 1868. Mills were destroyed throughout the Patapsco valley and over 1,000 lives were lost. B'nai B'rith, North America's oldest international service group, organized the first disaster relief campaign to come to the aid of Baltimore's flood victims. (Courtesy of the Enoch Pratt Free Library.)

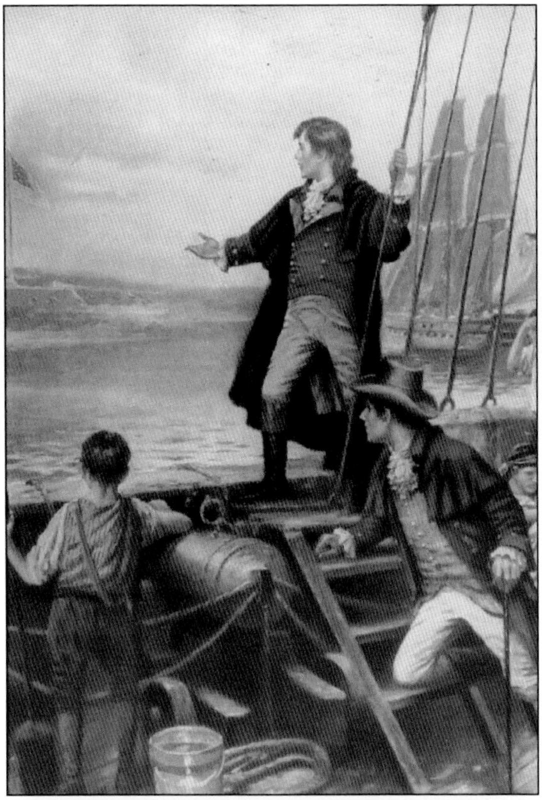

Francis Scott Key was born in Frederick County (a section that later became Carroll County) in 1779. At the time of the War of 1812 he was practicing law in Georgetown. He was securing the release of a prisoner aboard a ship in the harbor during the bombardment of Fort McHenry and, inspired by what he saw there, wrote the "The Star-Spangled Banner." In this 1915 painting by Edward Percy Moran (1862–1935), *The Dawn's Early Light*, we see Key being inspired while a young "powder monkey" is working on deck. A "powder monkey," or "powder boy," was the name given to boys who worked on ship caring for cannons. Their job was to clean, swab, and maintain the cannons and bring and load the gunpowder. Whether there was actually a "powder monkey" standing next to Key, or whether there was even a cannon aboard that ship, is unknown. Using artistic license, Moran gives us a glimpse at what it was to be a child working on a ship at that time. (Courtesy of the Enoch Pratt Free Library.)

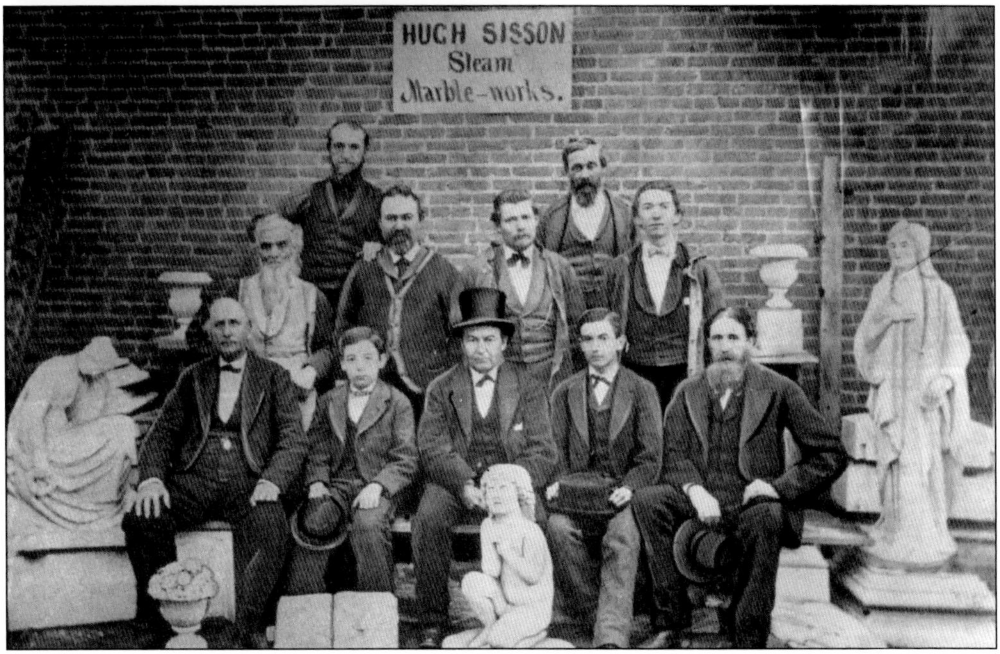

In a family business like Sisson Marble Works, the boys most likely worked as apprentices. If they stood to inherit the company, they would need to learn the ropes. (Courtesy of the Enoch Pratt Free Library.)

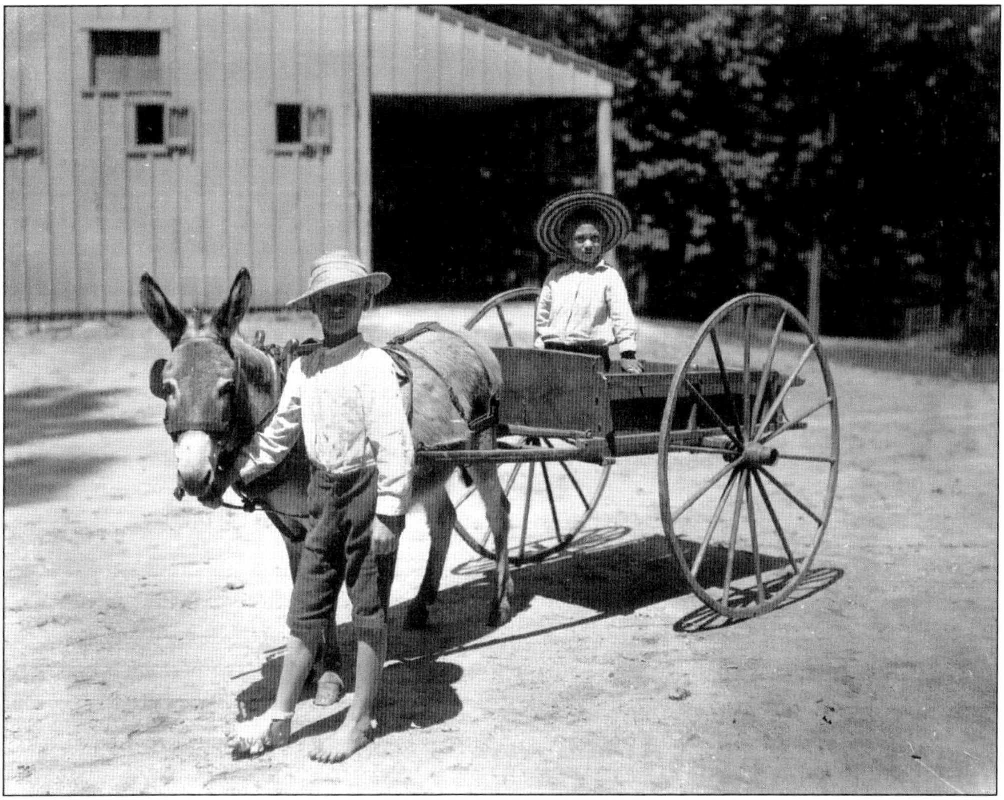

Taking tourists for sightseeing excursions at nearby farms was a common occupation for youngsters of Baltimore's environs. Country outings were and still are popular among city dwellers. This boy worked in Green Spring. (Courtesy of the Enoch Pratt Free Library.)

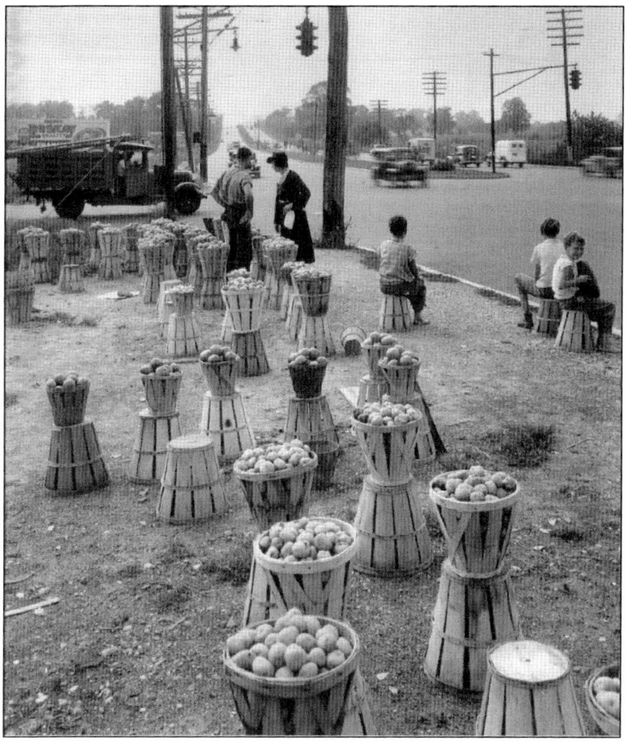

Farming families from the Baltimore area would often come with their harvest and set up shop on street corners like this. Children, having helped in the fields, would vend as well. This scene from 1936 is just as familiar to the modern eye. (Courtesy of the Enoch Pratt Free Library.)

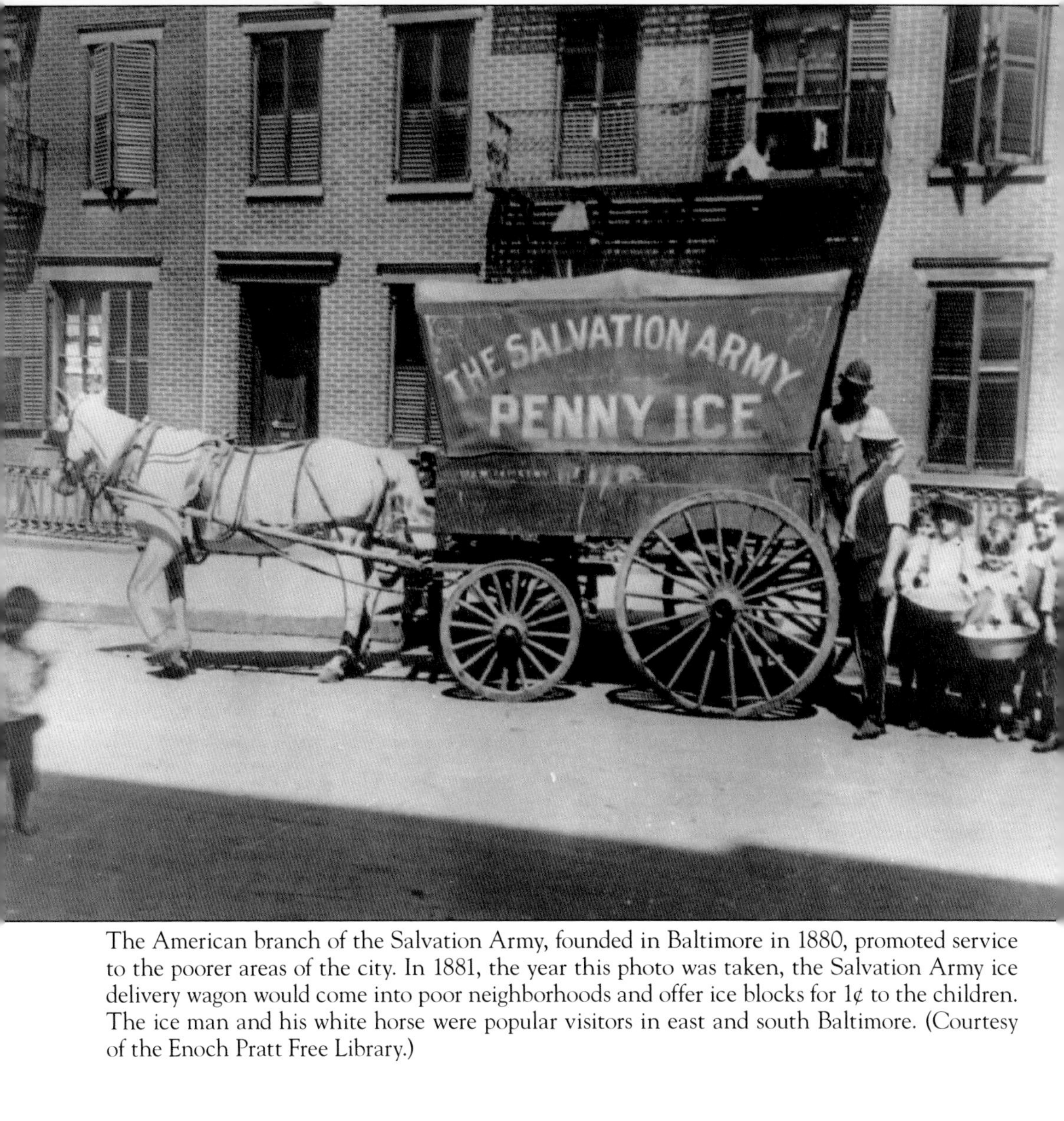

The American branch of the Salvation Army, founded in Baltimore in 1880, promoted service to the poorer areas of the city. In 1881, the year this photo was taken, the Salvation Army ice delivery wagon would come into poor neighborhoods and offer ice blocks for 1¢ to the children. The ice man and his white horse were popular visitors in east and south Baltimore. (Courtesy of the Enoch Pratt Free Library.)

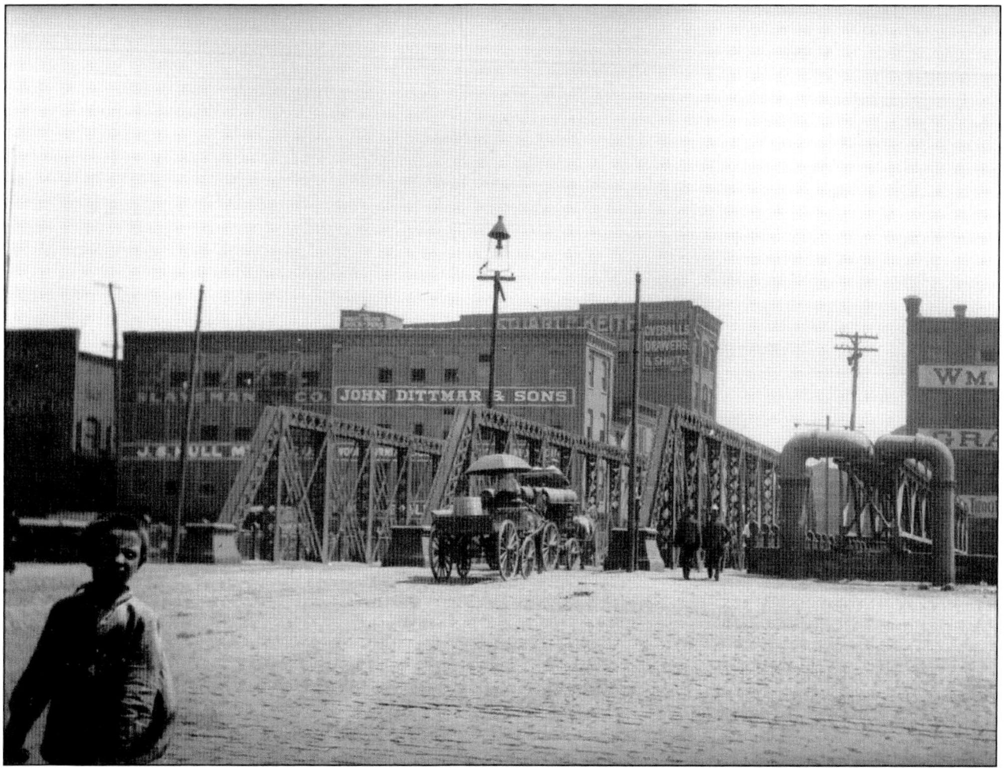

The scene at right was not an uncommon sight at the harbor and brings to mind ships traveling in third-world countries as tourists throw coins in the water for children to fetch. The Depression was devastating, and this scene, taken in 1930, shows some of the results. Impoverished children of the city often had to be quite resourceful. Above, a little boy wanders Pratt Street in 1910 hoping for handouts. (Courtesy of the Enoch Pratt Free Library.)

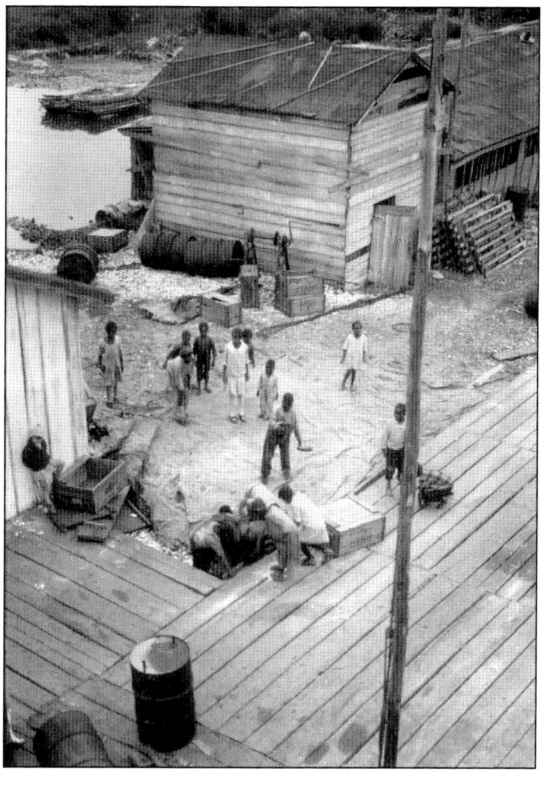

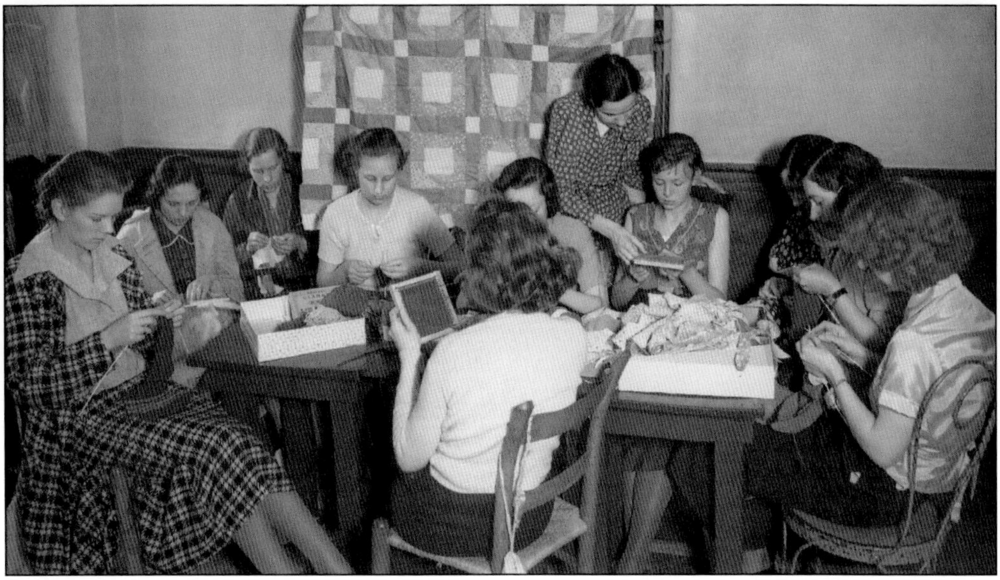

The National Youth Administration (NYA) was formed in 1935 as a relief program for young people suffering financially from the Depression. In 1936 the NYA offered instruction in various crafts to a select number of teens under the direction of Elizabeth Winn, a Virginian then living in Baltimore. The teens were taught folk arts at locations such as the Roosevelt Recreational Center in Hampden and the YMCA. The Defense Department also had kids in machine shop and other useful instructional programs. By 1941, the NYA came under much scrutiny and the program was determined not cost effective. What was taught at a significant expense could be taught in the public schools, and the program was abandoned. (Courtesy of the Enoch Pratt Free Library.)

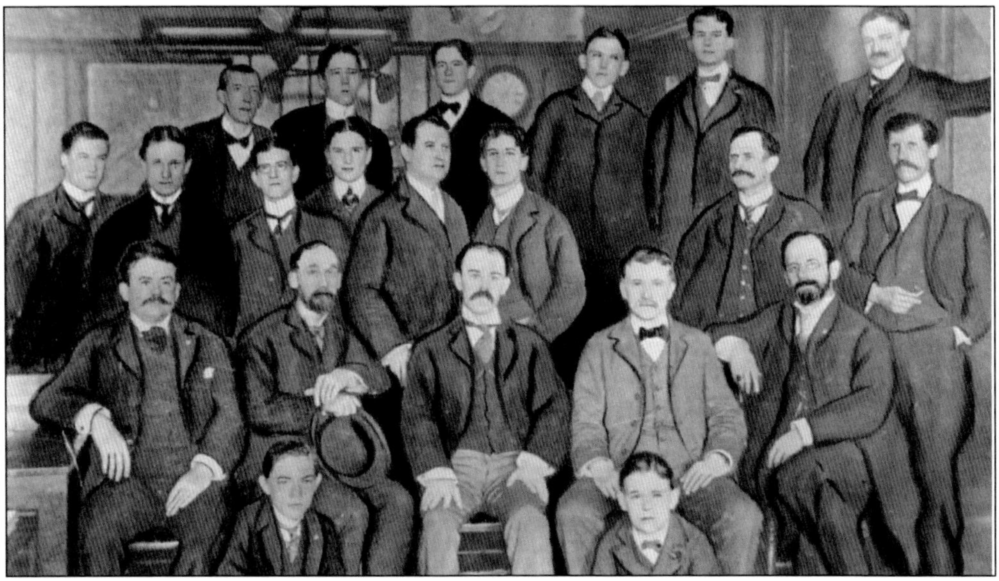

These Hibernian Society men made up the staff of the *Baltimore Herald*, c. 1900. H.L. Mencken is the second man from the right in the back row. The two boys in the front were copy boys, and the boy on the left went on to work for the *Evening Sun*. (Courtesy of the Enoch Pratt Free Library.)

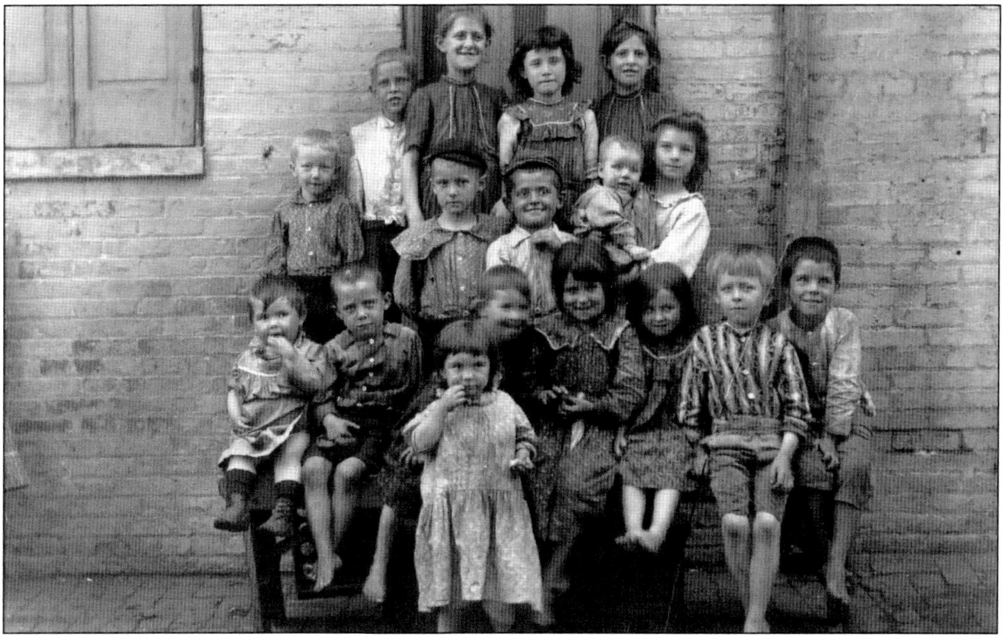

This c. 1910 photo by Jim Lewis shows the children of industrial Baltimore. The kids were responsible for themselves for the most part. They may have worked or cared for younger siblings and maintained their homes while their parents and older siblings worked. (Courtesy of the Enoch Pratt Free Library.)

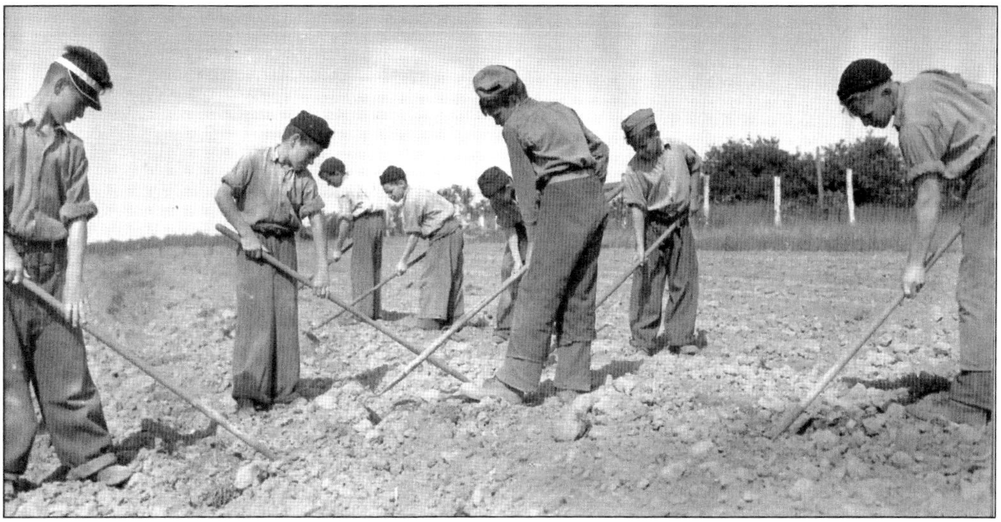

Maryland Training School for Boys was called the House of Refuge from 1831 to 1910. The name was changed to Maryland School for Boys (1910–1918) and then to Maryland Training School for Boys. Serving as an all-white, segregated reform school for boys, it was considered to be one of the biggest and strictest in the area. Uniforms were imposed as well as a militaristic regime. In 1940 three health delegates came to check the conditions of several of the reform schools, and Maryland Training School for Boys was considered unacceptable. It was overcrowded, had poor facilities, and the food was inedible, leaving many boys malnourished and underfed. In addition to racial segregation, the school maintained a policy of refusing entrance to boys who had low IQs. This photo was taken in 1936. (Courtesy of the Enoch Pratt Free Library.)

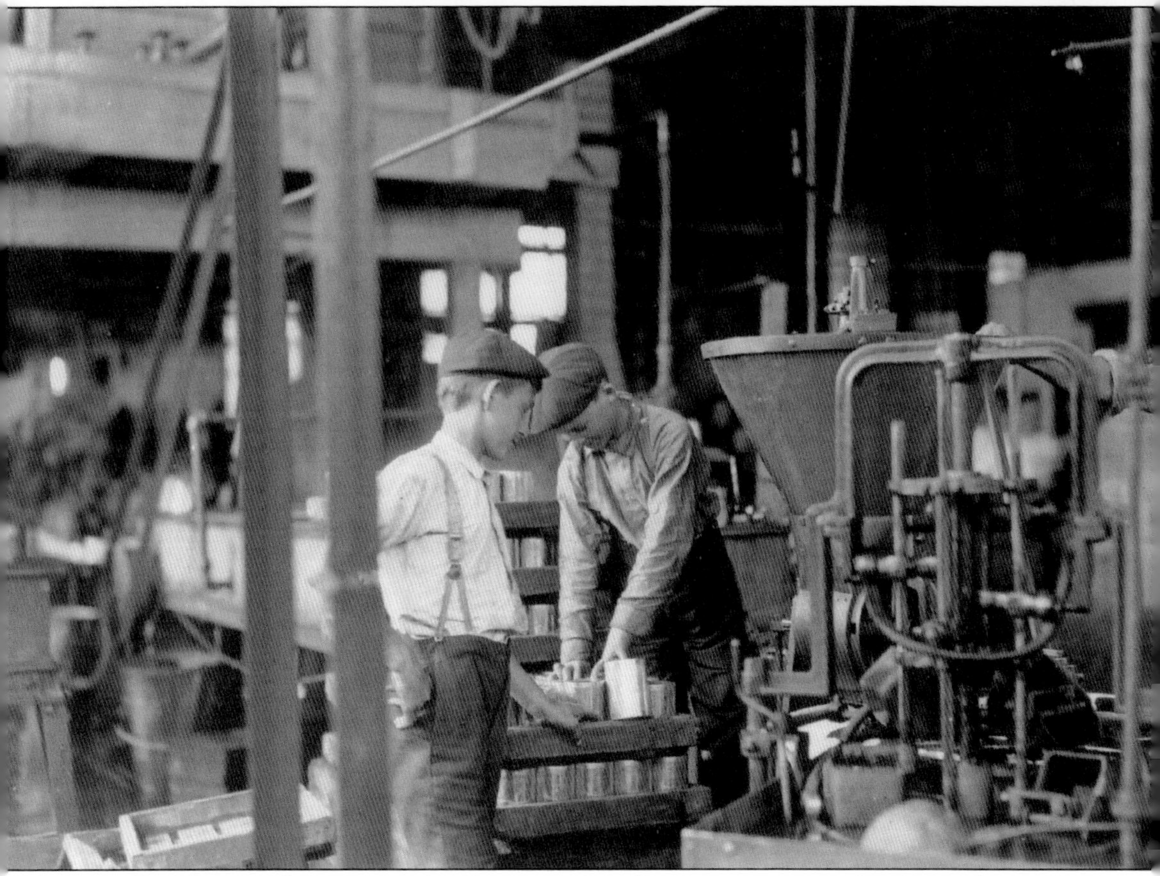

The following photos were taken by Lewis Hine during his tenure at the National Committee for Child Labor. Hine, a former teacher and amateur photographer turned activist, became involved in the plight of working children. He joined forces with the anti-child labor movement and went around the country photographing children. These photos were meant to inspire public outcry and action against the forced labor of children. Although there were laws put into place as early as 1894, no action was really taken to protect these children. Laws against underage children—those younger than 14—working were easily circumvented if parents signed a paper stating that their child was of proper age. One case in which a little boy was crushed to death while working in a mine, the manager of the plant admitted that the boy looked small for 14 but that most of these undernourished kids were small. Since the boy's parents, most likely desperately poor and in dire need of the pittance that their small son could earn, signed for him. The boy, as it was discovered, was just 9 years old. Often risking his own life, Lewis Hine managed to get into mills and factories by claiming he was taking photographs for the fire department or offering other fabricated reasons. His dedicated and persistent work is often considered to have been the most poignant and effective measure leading to child labor reform. This photo was taken at J.S. Farrand Packing Company in Baltimore city on July 7, 1909. The canning machines were very dangerous and little, if any, precautions were taken to guard the boys' safety. (Courtesy of Photography Collections, University of Maryland, Baltimore County.)

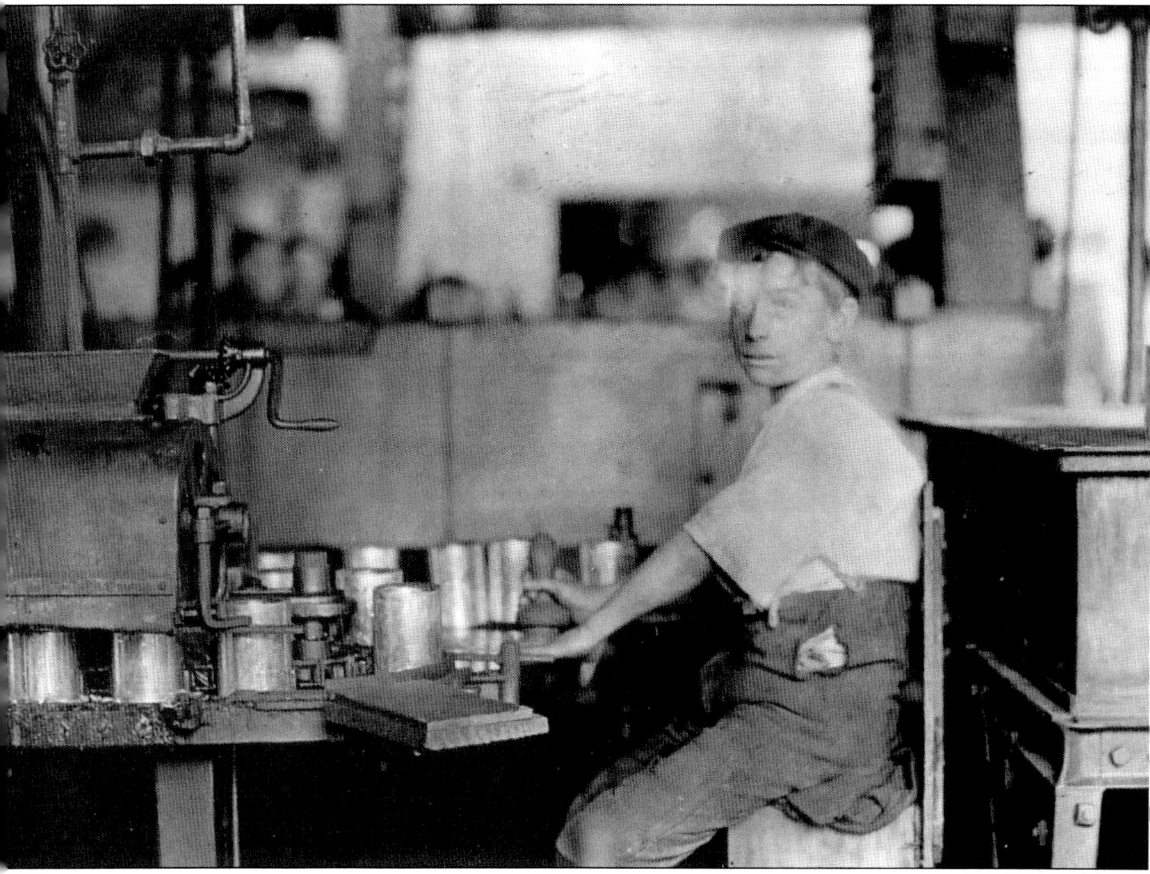

This photo, also taken at J.S. Farrand Packing Company in Baltimore city, was given the title "Dangerous Business" by Hine. He also noted that many such boys worked at "canning machines with open grating." They were in grave danger of losing fingers and getting metal slivers. There was no support for an injured child. There would be no help, only hardship for parents who were most likely unable to stay home and care for him. Many families were loaded into wagons and taken to the berry fields outside of Baltimore. Several families would live together in makeshift huts, sleeping on hay with little or no protection from inclement weather. They cooked on open fires and had few comforts, if any. (Courtesy of Photography Collections, University of Maryland, Baltimore County.)

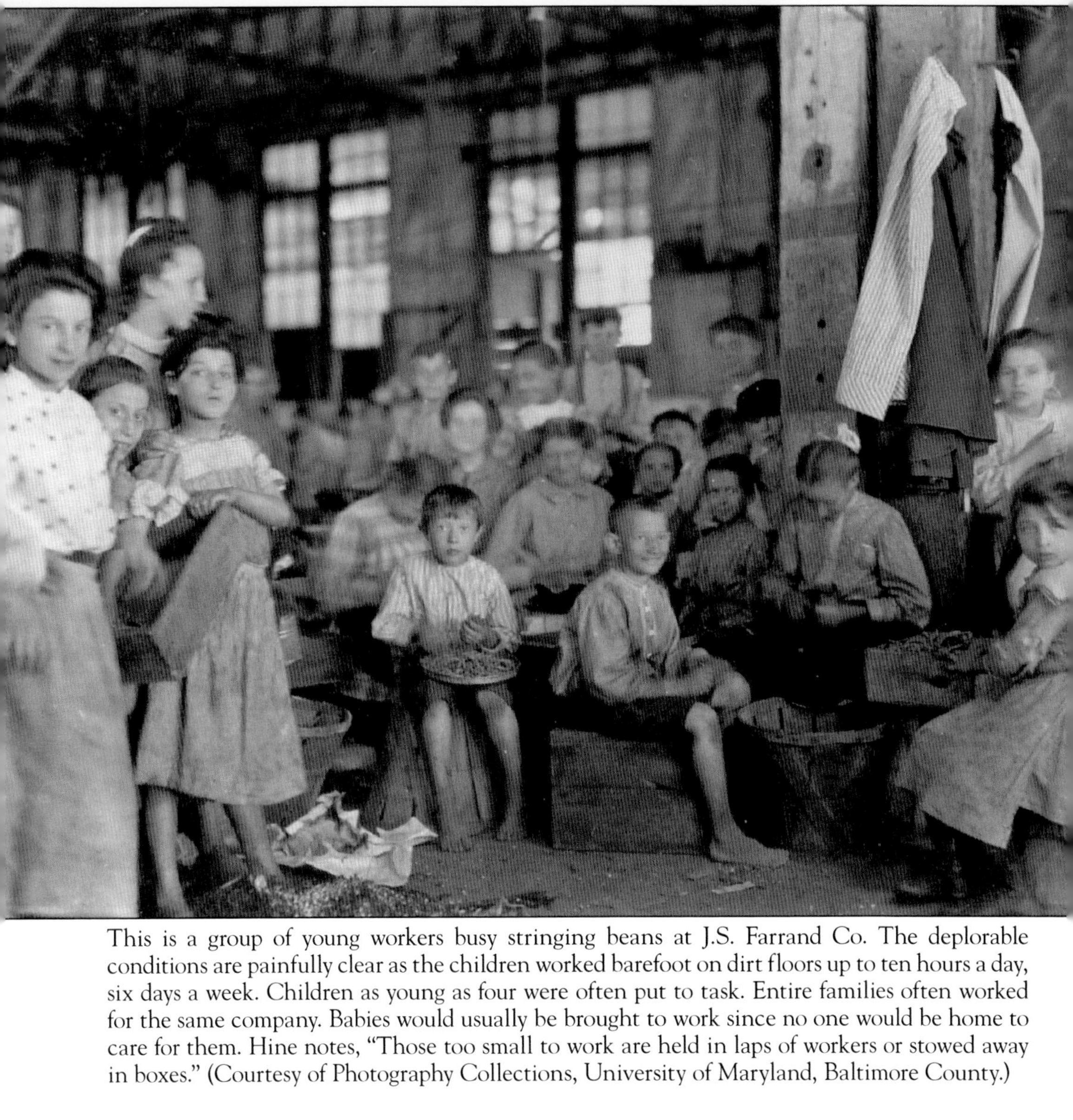

This is a group of young workers busy stringing beans at J.S. Farrand Co. The deplorable conditions are painfully clear as the children worked barefoot on dirt floors up to ten hours a day, six days a week. Children as young as four were often put to task. Entire families often worked for the same company. Babies would usually be brought to work since no one would be home to care for them. Hine notes, "Those too small to work are held in laps of workers or stowed away in boxes." (Courtesy of Photography Collections, University of Maryland, Baltimore County.)

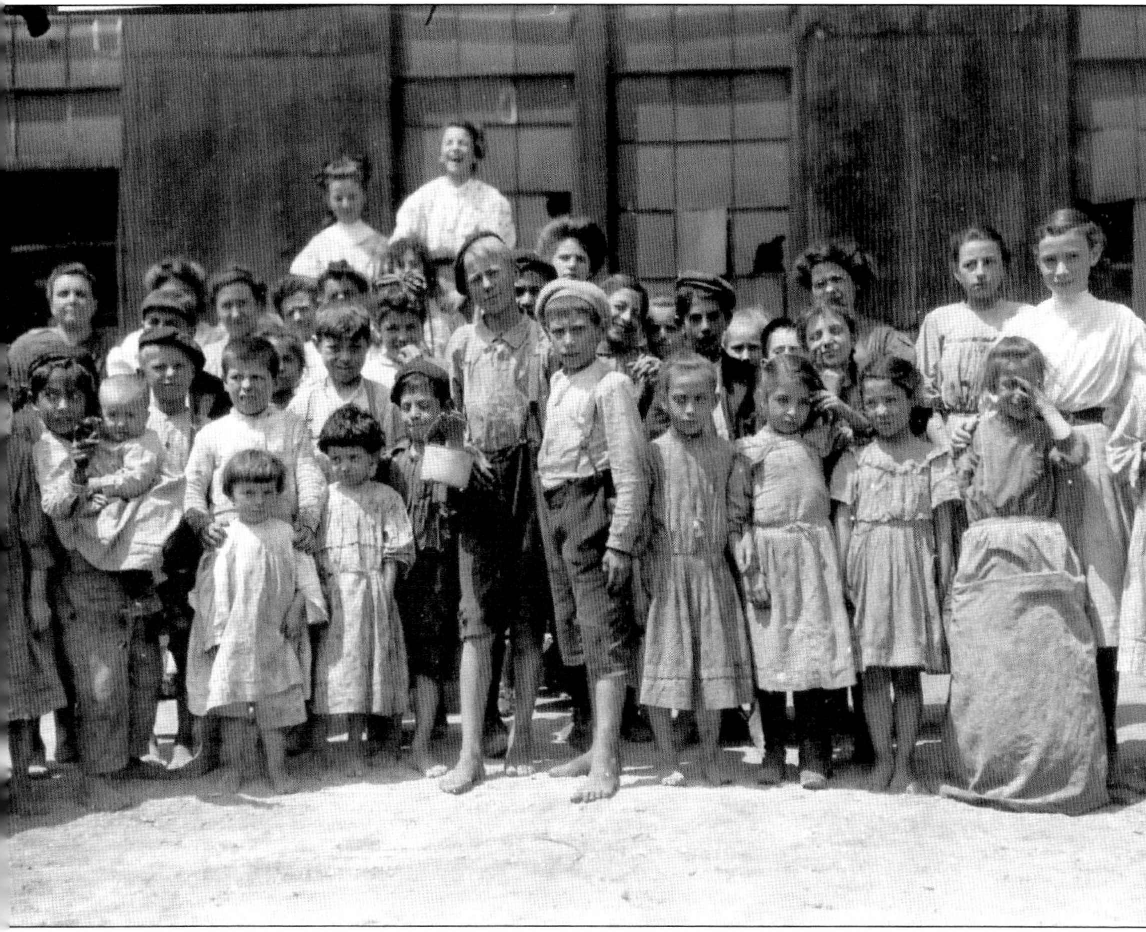

Some of the same faces can be spotted in this photo and the one previous. There seems to be a camaraderie among the young laborers, who must have grown to care for each other while working long hours together. Many children were from the same family with the younger sibling looking up to the elder and the elder looking out for the younger. Even a child as small as the little boy holding the baby to the left of the photograph took on a parental role. The very youngest were forced to spend days in these canneries and mills. (Courtesy of Photography Collections, University of Maryland, Baltimore County.)

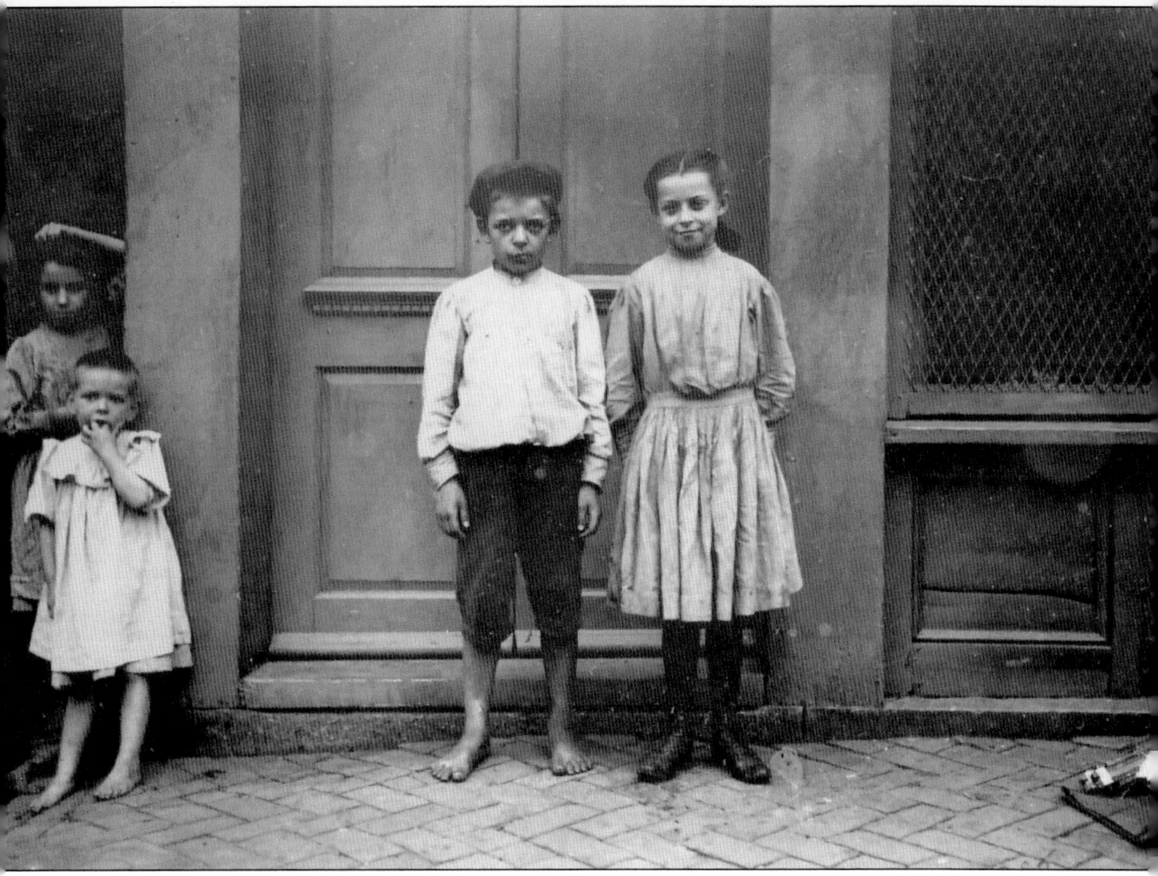

Siblings Albert and Marie Kawalski stand at 615 South Bond Street in Baltimore in this image. The plight of the Kawalski family was not unfamiliar. Immigrant families would have their fare paid on ships that would bring them to America to work. Sometimes, already here, they would be brought to Baltimore from other areas. Many families from the city would be taken by wagon to the outskirts of the city for whole summers to work in the berry fields. They would live, sometimes three families together, in tiny shacks. They would eat outside, cooking over fires, and sleep several to a straw mat. Hine notes on this photo, "Albert is 10 and Marie is 11 years old. They worked, with mother, last winter, shucking oysters for Vern & Beard Packing Co. Youngs Island, S.C. (near Charleston). Mrs. Kawalski did not have things represented to her correctly and she found that all the children that had fare paid were compelled to work for the company. Other smaller children worked some and went to school some." Marie and Albert, at their young age, had already been working "several summers in the berry, beans, and tomato fields" as well as in packing houses. (Courtesy of Photography Collections, University of Maryland, Baltimore County.)

Four

Children at Play

Kids will always be kids. Whether you give them a dirt lot or their own private baseball team, complete with uniforms, they will find a way to rejoice in play. Baltimore has a remarkable history when it comes to children and play. A pioneer city for child-friendly spaces, Baltimore was one of the first cities to have actual playgrounds. Parks have been a part of the cityscape since cities first came into existence, but the building of actual play areas for children is a relatively new idea that made its debut in the 1800s. In addition to playgrounds, Baltimore also has one of the country's oldest zoos, and the Maryland Science Center has existed, in one form or another, since 1797. Originally called the Maryland Academy of Science and Literature in 1826, the group reorganized after a fire destroyed most of their collection and became the Maryland Academy of Sciences in 1867, making it one of the oldest of such institutions in the country. During the Victorian era, Baltimore was home to several amusement parks and was a tourist destinations for many families, providing state-of-the-art entertainment for both kids and adults. The way people enjoyed themselves in the past reflects the enthusiasm we see today. And while the clothes and uniforms may look strange to us and the games played somewhat differently, the faces on the following pages look remarkably familiar. These are the faces of children at play.

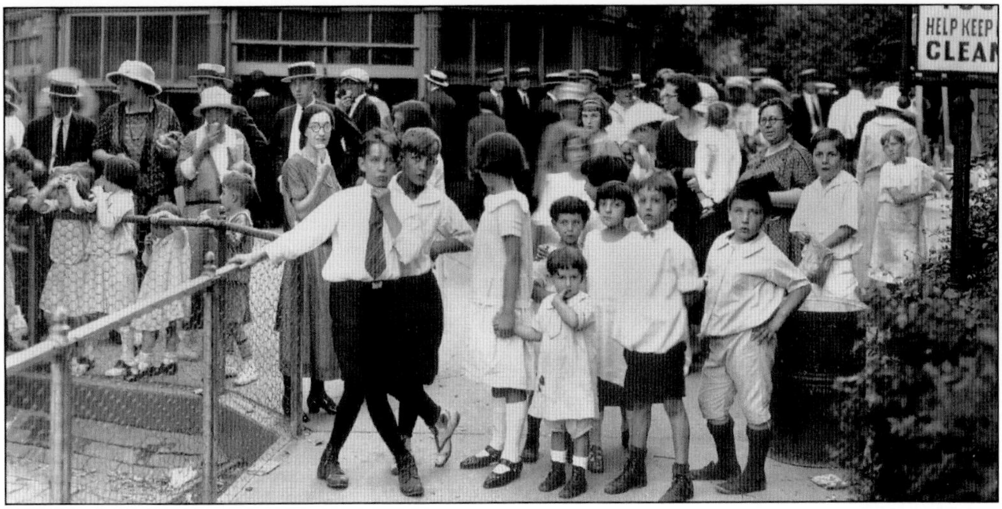

In 1688, the land on which the Baltimore Zoo is now located was a 2,000-acre estate known as "Hab Nab at a Venture." In 1741, after several plots were sold, a physician named George Buchanan purchased 578 1/2 acres and named it "Auchentorlie." The Buchanan home was destroyed by fire and a new house was built by Col. Nicholas Rogers after he inherited the land. He renamed the area "Druid Hill," as we know it today. The Rogers family mansion was also destroyed but rebuilt from plans of the other; it stands today as the administration building for the zoo. The city bought the land in 1860, and in 1867, Thomas Winans set 52 deer free to roam Druid Hill Park. Established April 7, 1876 by the Park Commission as a "Zoological Garden," the Baltimore Zoo is the third oldest zoo in the country. Eventually fences were put in place when athletic activities caused people and animals to get in each other's way. Structures were added, and by 1890, the zoo had camels, monkeys, birds, and one alligator. (Courtesy of the Enoch Pratt Free Library.)

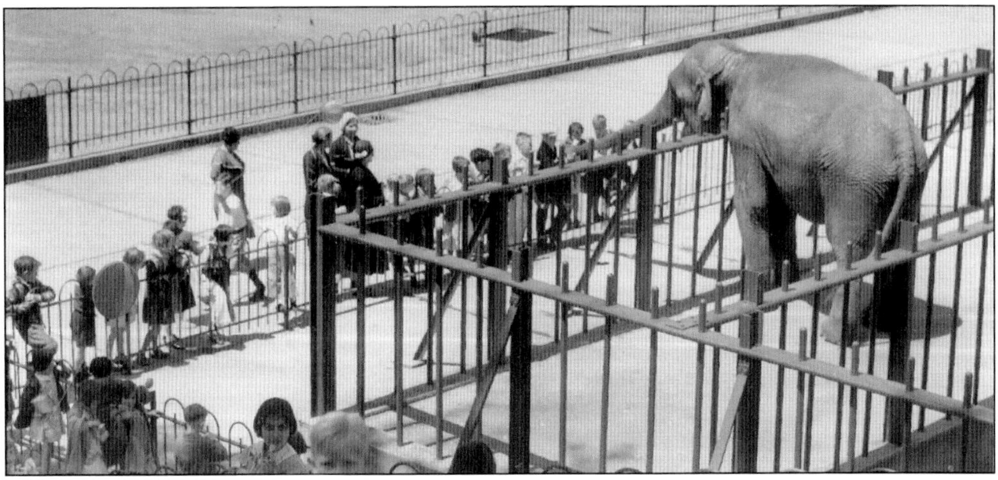

In 1925 the zoo's first elephant, Mary Anne, was purchased with pennies donated by the children of Baltimore. Mary Anne was part of some controversy in 1921 when Gwynn Oak Park (one of Baltimore's many amusement parks) decided that it wanted an elephant. "A Jungle Circle" was established—a "children's pro-elephant pressure group." Apparently, Howard Jackson, who was running for mayor, ran on a "pro-elephant ticket," promising Mary Anne a home in Druid Hill Park. He won and so did the children of Baltimore. Mary Anne was a part of the Baltimore zoo family until her death in 1941. (Courtesy of the Enoch Pratt Free Library.)

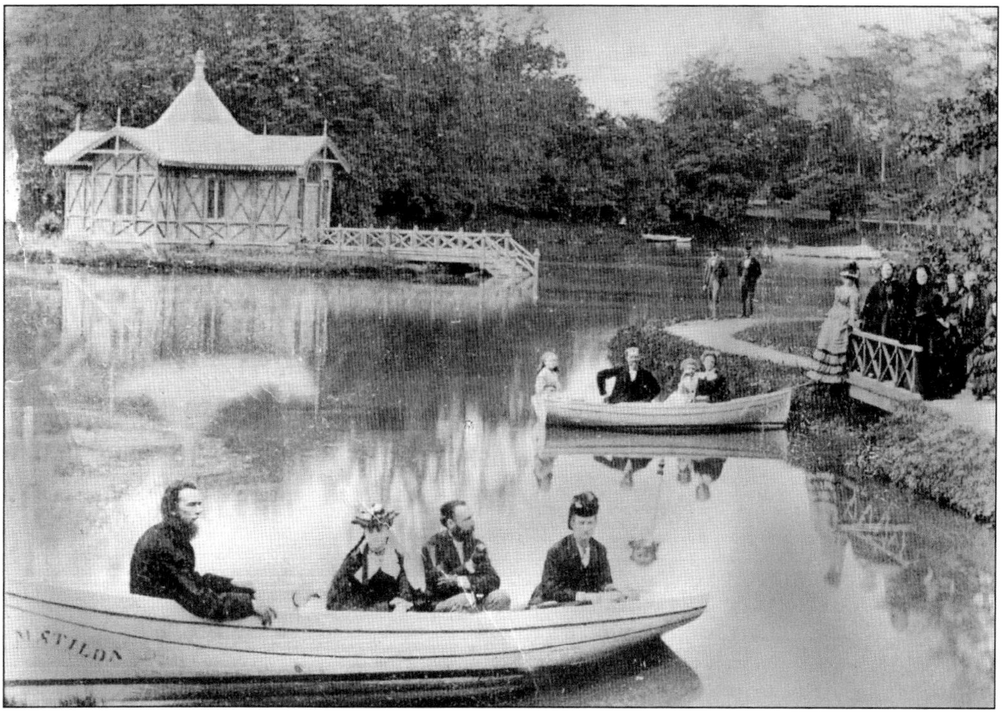

Pictured here is a lovely afternoon in Druid Hill Park in 1870. The boating area has been restored and is in the vicinity of the zoo. This pond was originally known as the "Upper Lake" and once a stream continued through it. A dam was built in 1865 to create a "skating lake." It was known as "Boat Lake" once a boat rental concession was added. (Courtesy of the Enoch Pratt Free Library.)

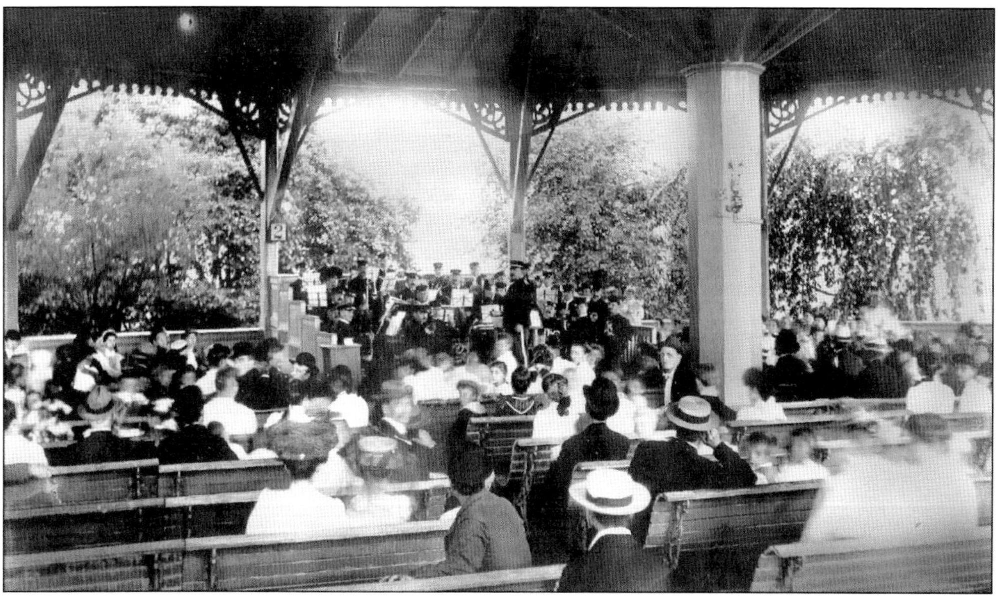

The Druid Hill Park band pavilion was a favorite spot for families on the weekends and for special events. The pavilion still stands as the entrance to the Baltimore Zoo. (Courtesy of the Enoch Pratt Free Library.)

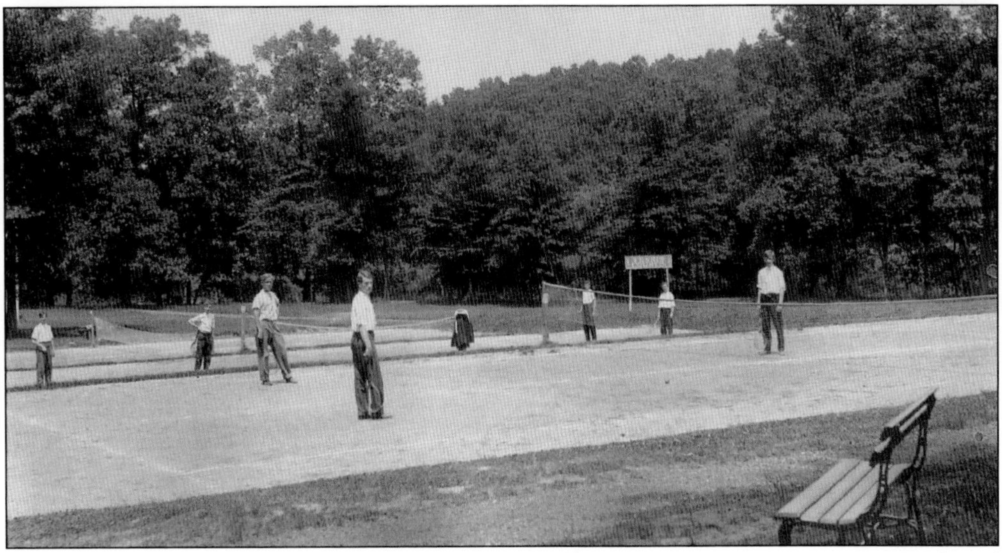

Gwynn Oak Park, established before the turn of the last century, was an amusement park and recreational area for families—white families, that is. Although many amusement parks were segregated, Gwynn Oak Park is notorious for its refusal to integrate after desegregation was enforced. The amusement park, which included a wooden roller coaster, a merry-go-round, pony rides, concessions, tennis courts, and swimming area, was inherited by the Price brothers in 1957. Their refusal to allow black families into the park—and the insistence that this was not bigotry, but business—made the Price brothers and the business the target of nationwide protests. In 1963 Sharon Langley, then 11 months old, was the first African-American child to ride the merry-go-round. The events at Gwynn Oak became national news. Baltimore County executive Spiro T. Agnew spoke out against the protesters while Sen. Hubert Humphrey condemned Gwynn Oak Park's trespassing law. Above, the Gwynn Oak Park tennis courts are pictured *c.* 1900. (Courtesy of the Enoch Pratt Free Library.)

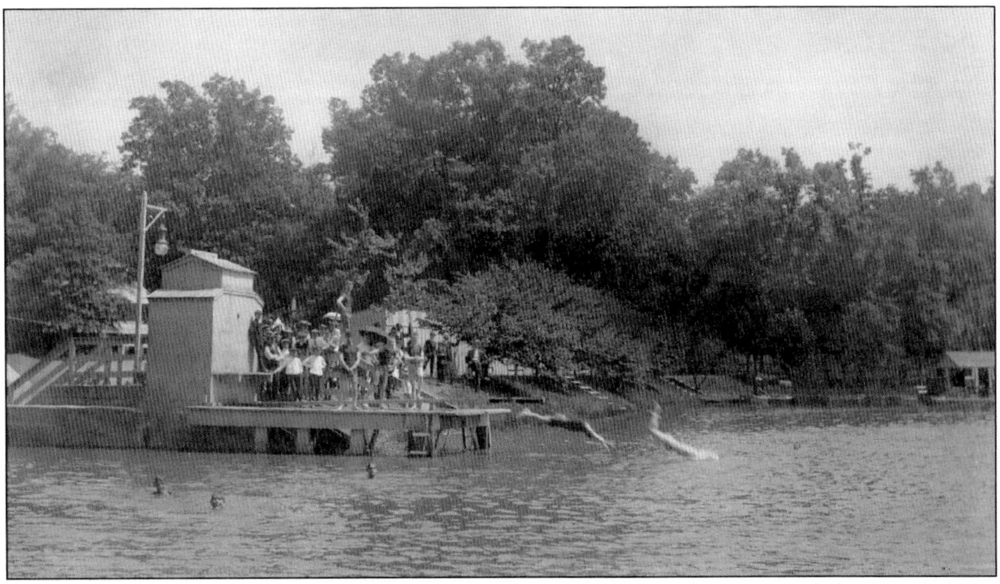

Pictured here is the Gwynn Oak Park swimming area, *c.* 1900. (Courtesy of the Enoch Pratt Free Library.)

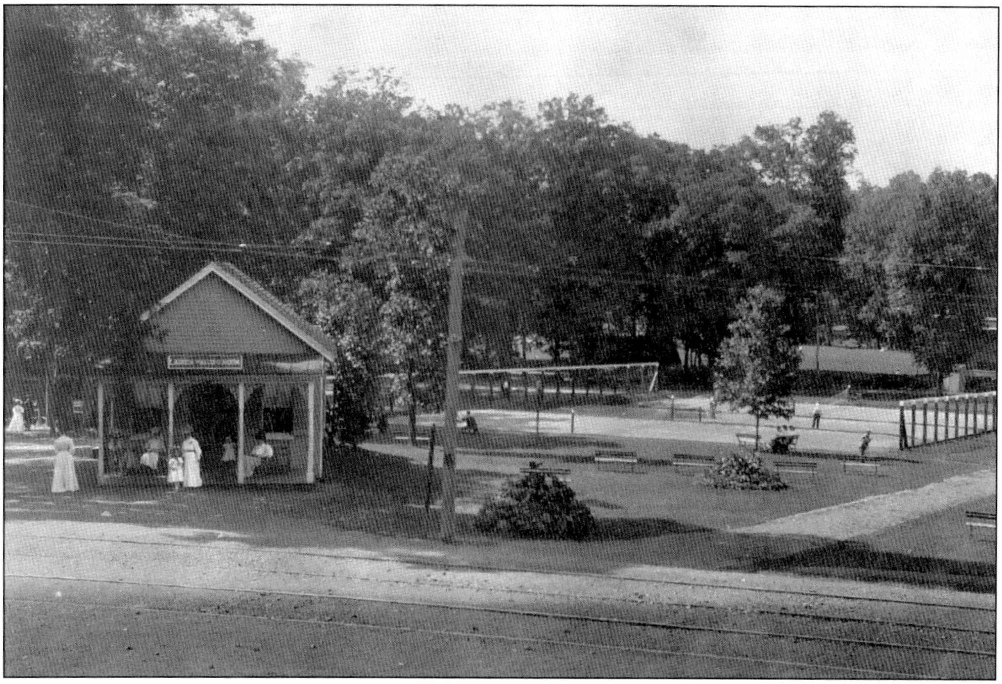

This photo, taken in 1900, shows the ladies' waiting room. This room gave women a private place to relax and get out of the sun. (Courtesy of the Enoch Pratt Free Library.)

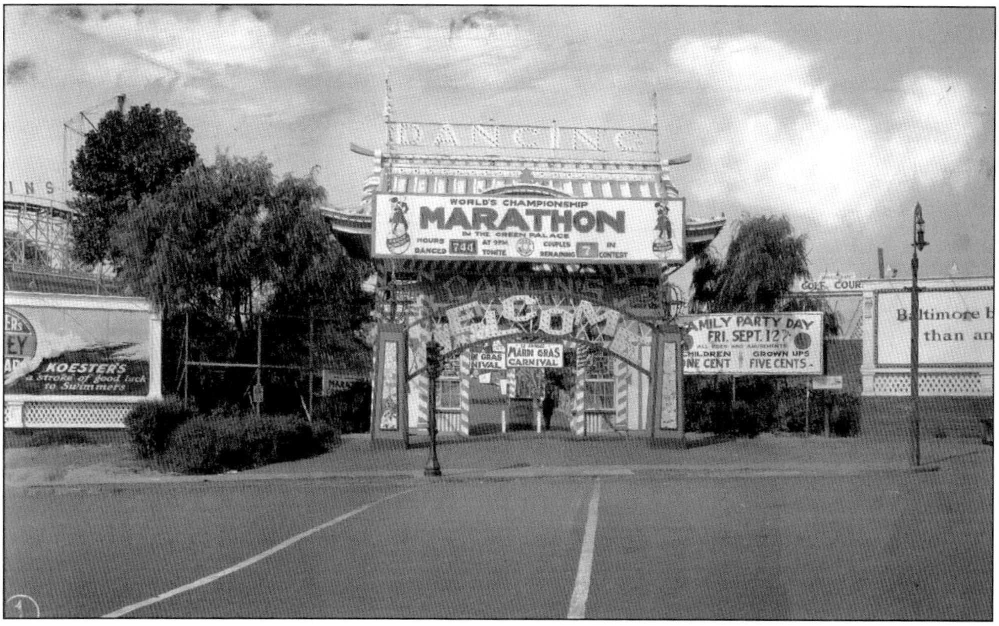

Carlin's Park, once called Liberty Heights Park, was built in 1919 and opened on June 6, 1920. Dancing was always a big part of the scene at this amusement park, and dance contests and dance marathons were regular events. In 1923 Rudolph Valentino judged a dance contest and was nearly smothered by his adoring fans. Fires were the downfall of this and many similar parks. The dancehall burned down in 1928 and two other fires in 1937 and 1956 marked the end of Carlin's reign. (Courtesy of the Enoch Pratt Free Library.)

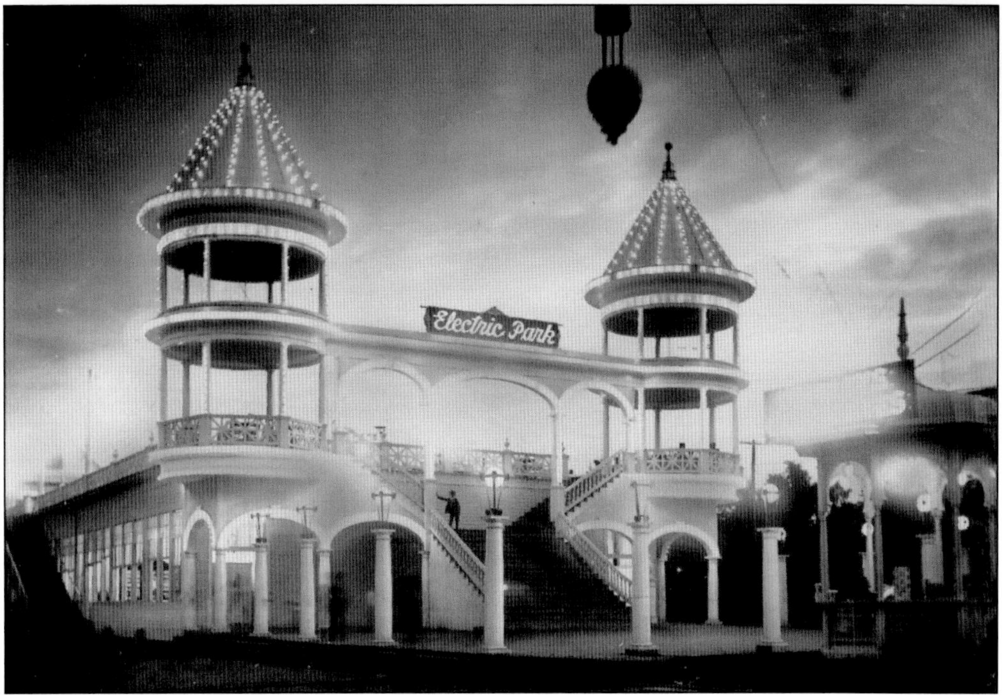

Electric Park, built in the 1890s and located at Belvedere Avenue and Reisterstown Road, contained rides, a casino, a bowling alley, and a swimming pool. The casino auditorium featured magic acts and comedy as well as circus sideshow acts. The park was closed and torn down in 1916. Above, Electric Park is seen in its full electric splendor in 1905. Below is the Electric Park swimming pool, *c.* 1900. (Courtesy of the Enoch Pratt Free Library.)

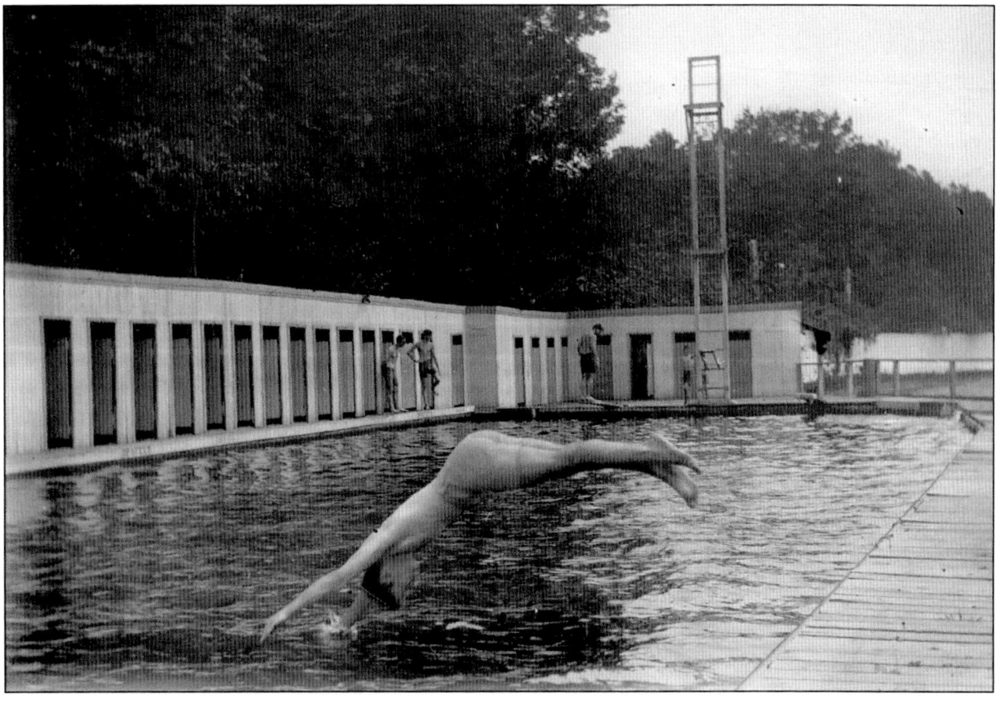

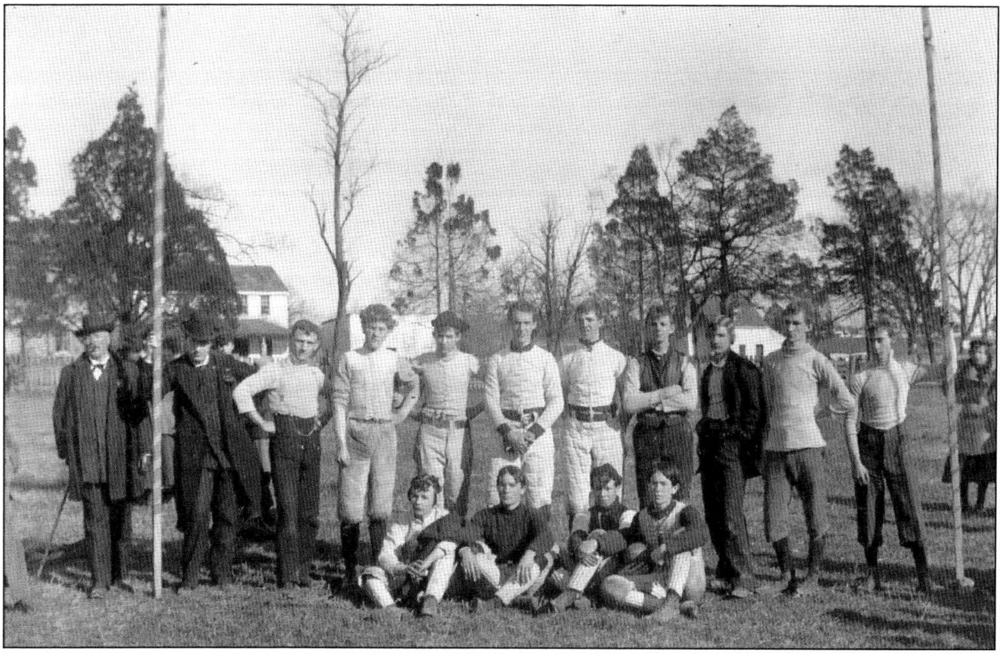

These photos depict the Madison Athletic Club, later called the Druid Outing Club. Both the athletes and the rooters are seen aboard the double-decker bus in 1889. (Courtesy of the Enoch Pratt Free Library.)

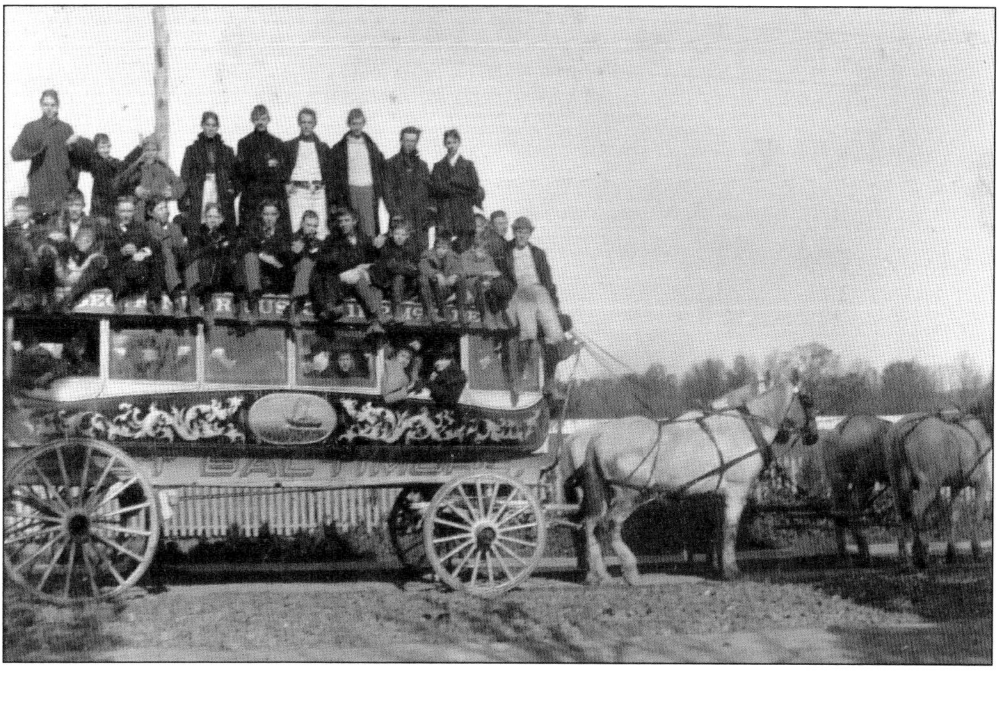

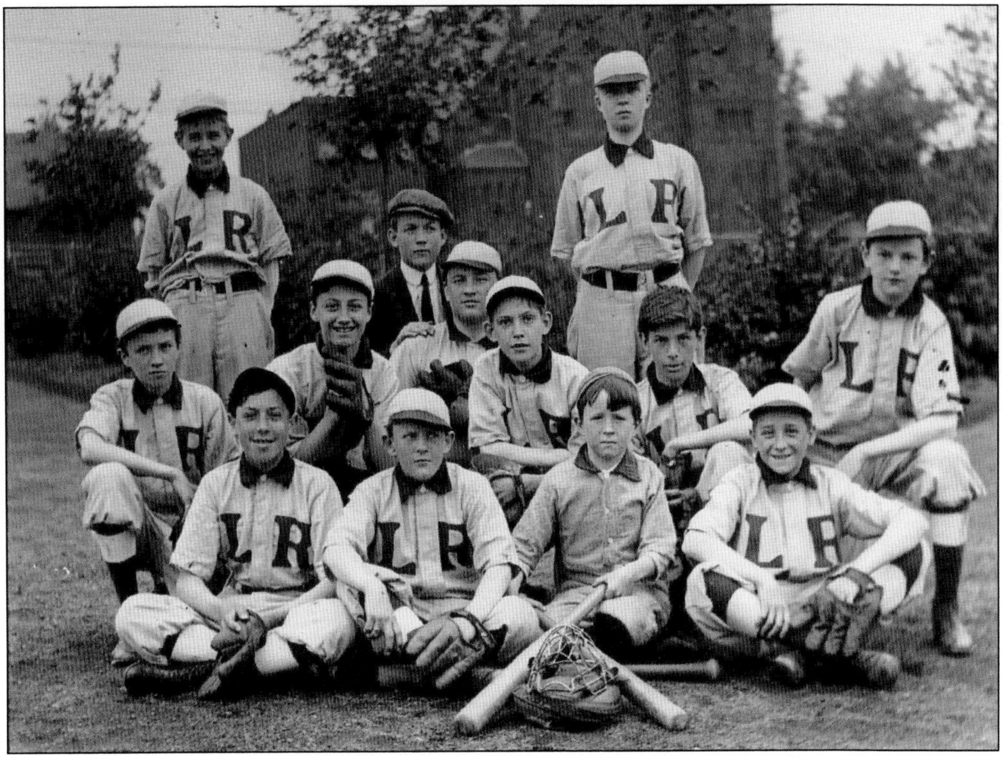

These young men, called the Lafayette Reserves, played baseball at Latrobe Park around the turn of the century. This photo was taken by the Baltimore Camera Club on May 16, 1908. (Courtesy of the Enoch Pratt Free Library.)

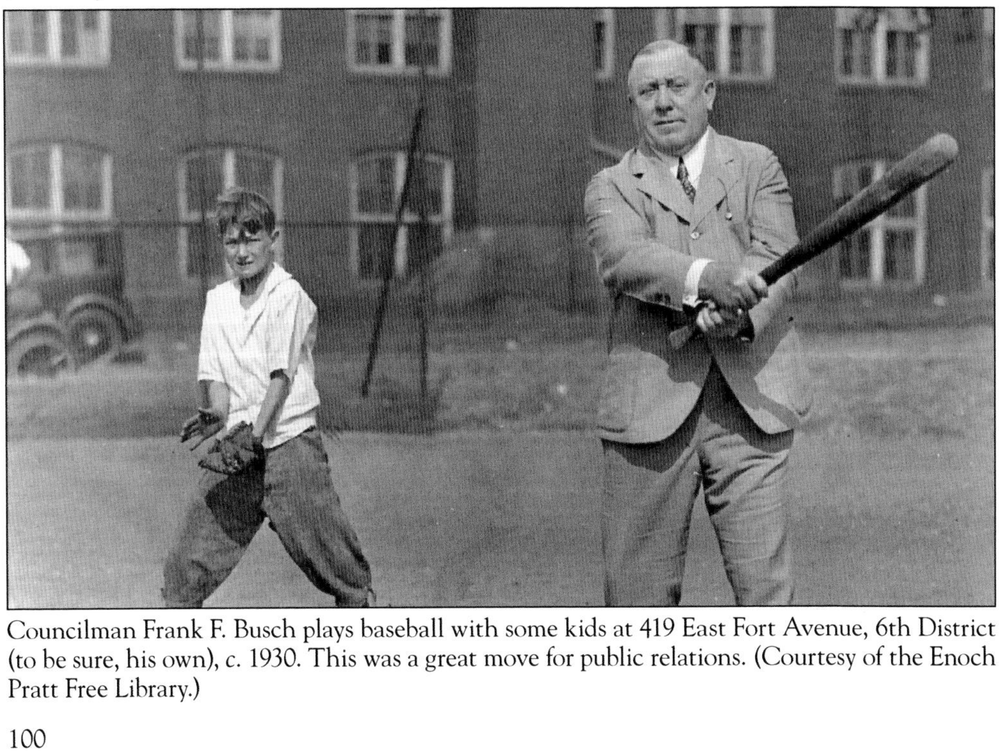

Councilman Frank F. Busch plays baseball with some kids at 419 East Fort Avenue, 6th District (to be sure, his own), c. 1930. This was a great move for public relations. (Courtesy of the Enoch Pratt Free Library.)

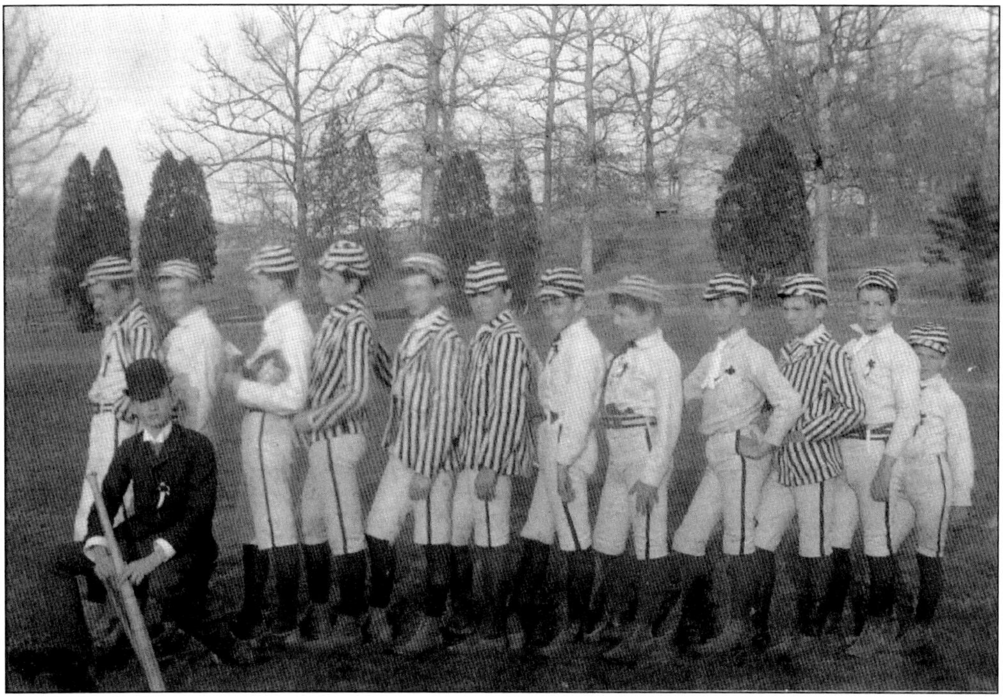

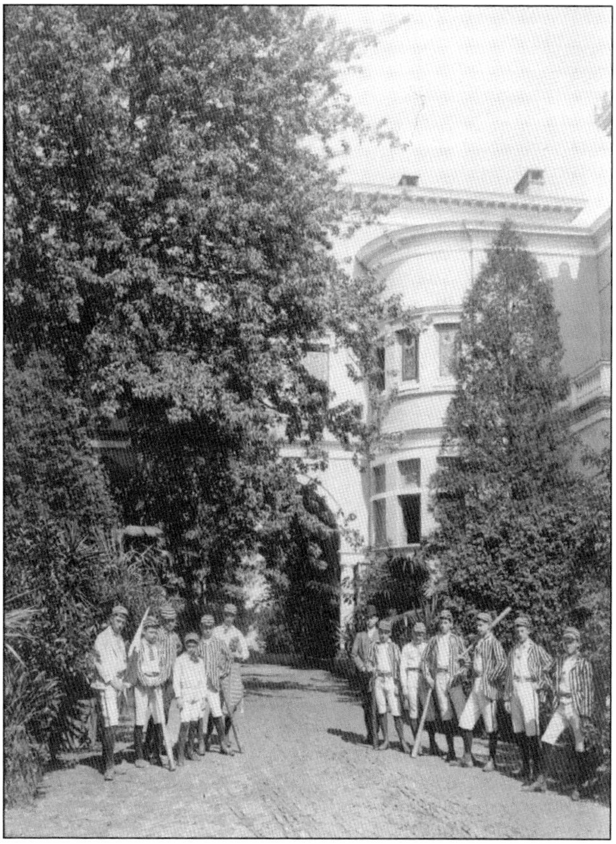

Children of the elite also engaged in fun and games, although not barefoot on dirt lots. Their uniforms were perhaps a bit brighter and their equipment newer than those of the city kids playing in public parks, but the games were the same. Above, the Garrett boys and their friends pose for a photograph of their own private baseball team, the Evergreen Baseball Club. From left to right, they are Graeme Turnbull, John Garrett, John Frick, E.G. Gibson, S.H. Browne, Horatio Turnbull, Horatio Garrett, Harry Turnbull, Edward Frick, Robert Garrett II, Henry B Spencer, Douglas Turnbull, and Vivian Spencer. At right, the boys stand in front of the mansion. The photo was taken by a "Miss Banman of Townsontown on April 2, 1888." (Courtesy of the Evergreen House Foundation, The Johns Hopkins University.)

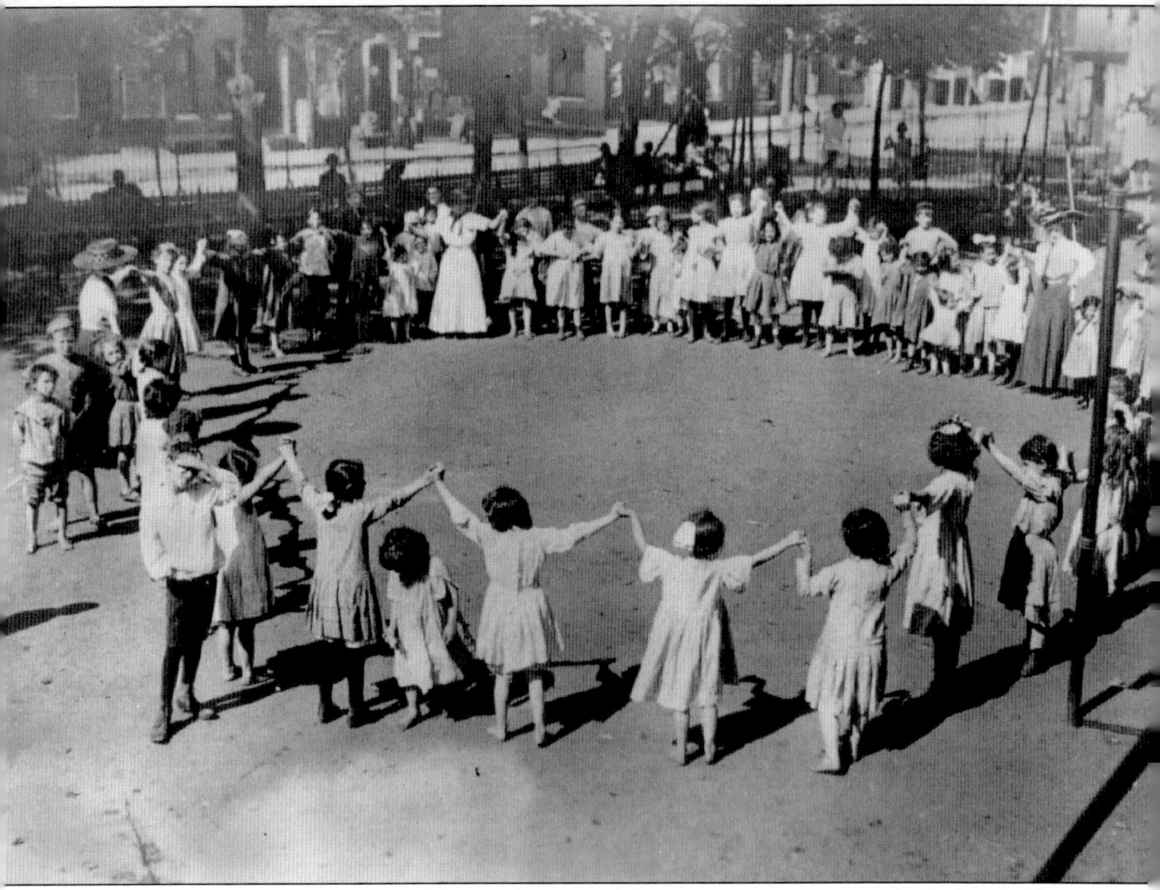

In this c. 1905 photo the Children's Playground Association's supervisors lead the children in games. In 1897 the first true playground was created in Baltimore. Eliza Ridgely and Eleanor Freeland applied for space at Druid Hill Park to create a playground where Baltimore's children could get exercise. They created the Children Playground Association (CPA) and, by 1902, were operating playgrounds in parks throughout the city. The CPA provided leaders and supervisors to play with the children and teach crafts. Leaders received some training and were almost exclusively women. They operated on private funds but were given a meager subsidy by 1907. Public Athletic League, founded by former Olympic star Robert Garrett, served boys from the age of seven. In 1922 Garrett announced that the two programs would operate as one under the name—Playground Athletic League (PAL). Robert Garrett, although he gave much to the city's parks, was a fierce segregationist. He made it difficult for the Parks Board to move towards desegregation. By 1949 he was forced to resign because of his position. (Courtesy of the Enoch Pratt Free Library.)

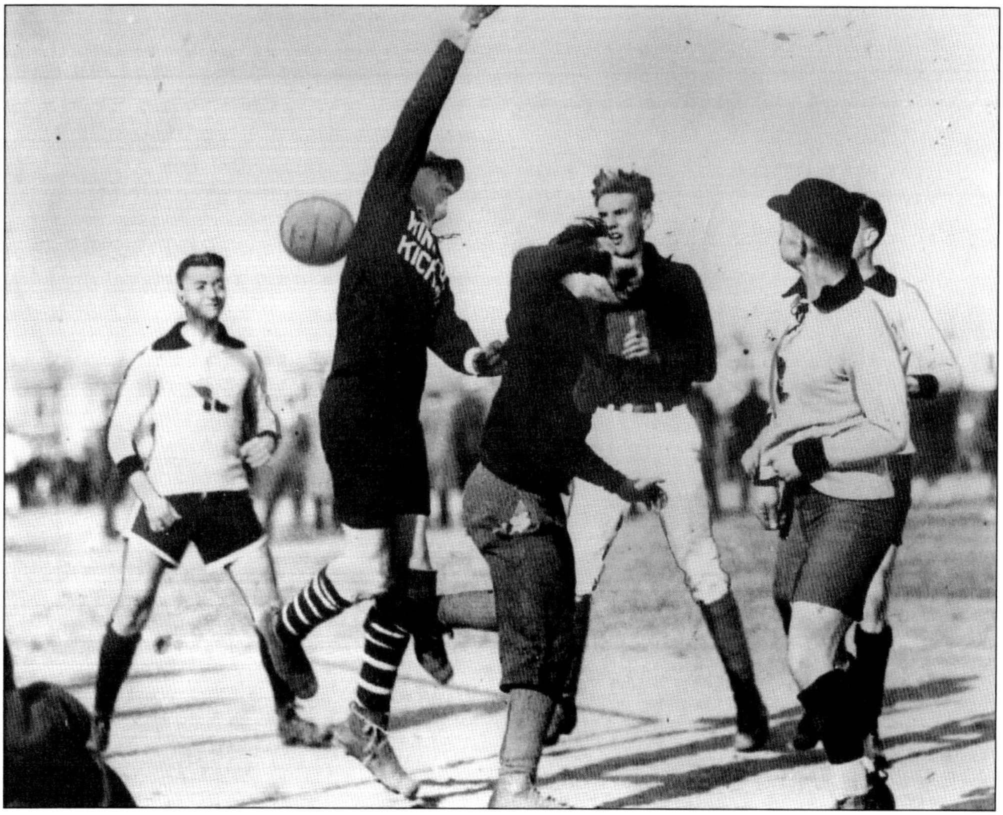

A boys' soccer competition run by PAL is pictured above in the 1920s. (Courtesy of the Enoch Pratt Free Library.)

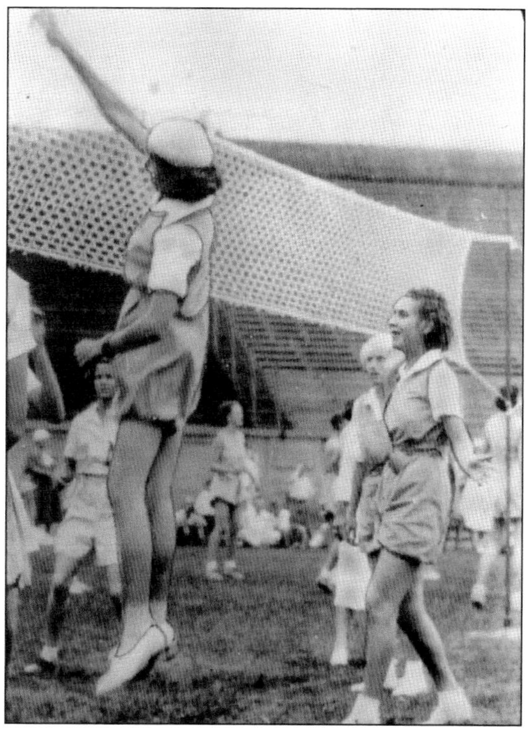

Pictured here is a PAL girls' volleyball contest in the 1920s. (Courtesy of the Enoch Pratt Free Library.)

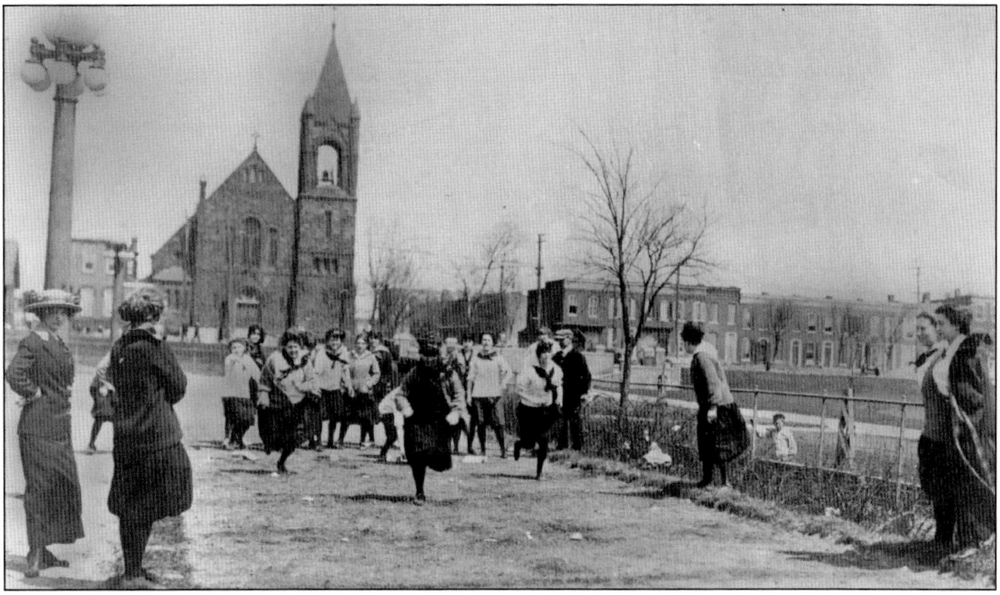

The Children's Playground Association (later PAL) leads a girls' footrace in Latrobe Park in 1913. (Courtesy of the Enoch Pratt Free Library.)

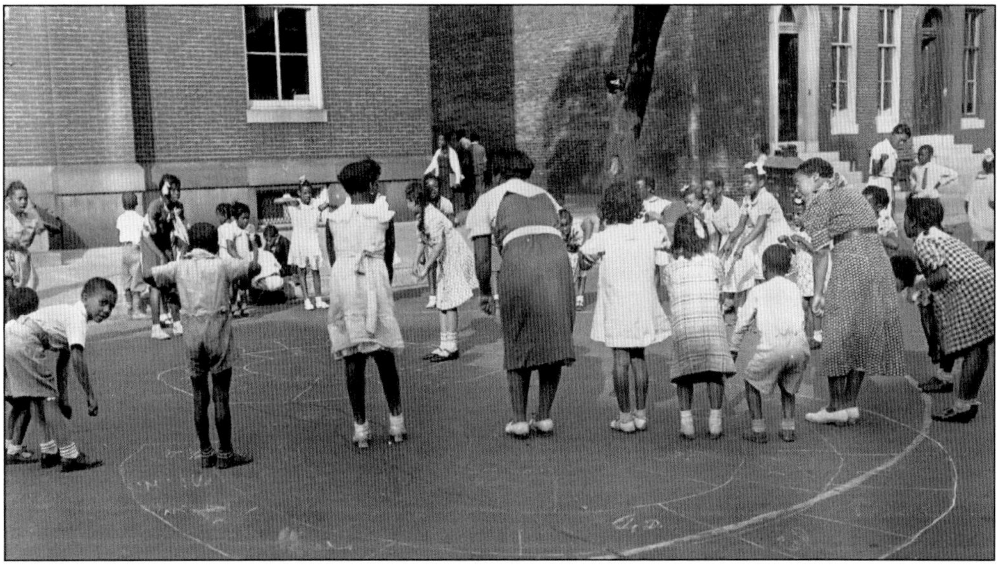

In the post–New Deal years, Maryland benefited greatly from various work programs created by the government. The Public Works Administration (PWA) and Civil Works Administration (CWA) were federally sponsored work relief programs that hired tens of thousands of Maryland residents. PWA was created to complete large-scale projects and hired more skilled than unskilled workers. CWA, created in 1933, hired over half of its workers from the relief rolls. In 1935, the CWA was replaced by the more permanent Works Progress Administration (WPA). WPA spent $58 million on Maryland projects before it was dismantled in 1943. Here we see various activities under project #7012 between 1934 and 1935. According to all of the photos from this era, project #7012 seems to have been exclusively for African-American children and adults. Here children are being supervised in play by members of the WPA team. (Courtesy of the Enoch Pratt Free Library.)

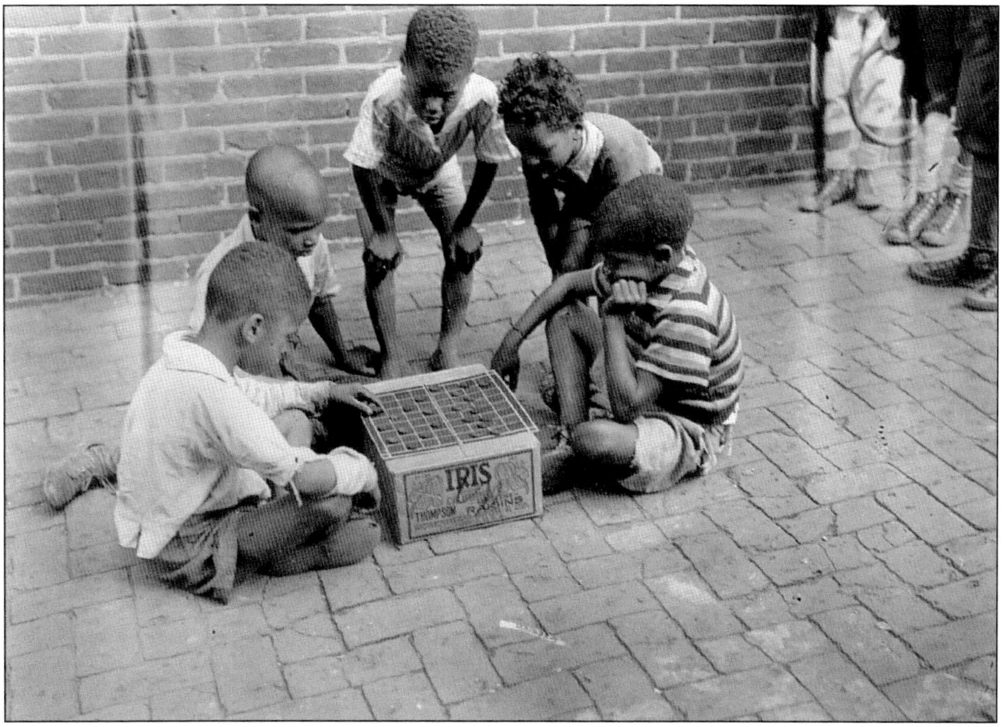

Here little boys play a WPA-supervised checker game in a schoolyard. (Courtesy of the Enoch Pratt Free Library.)

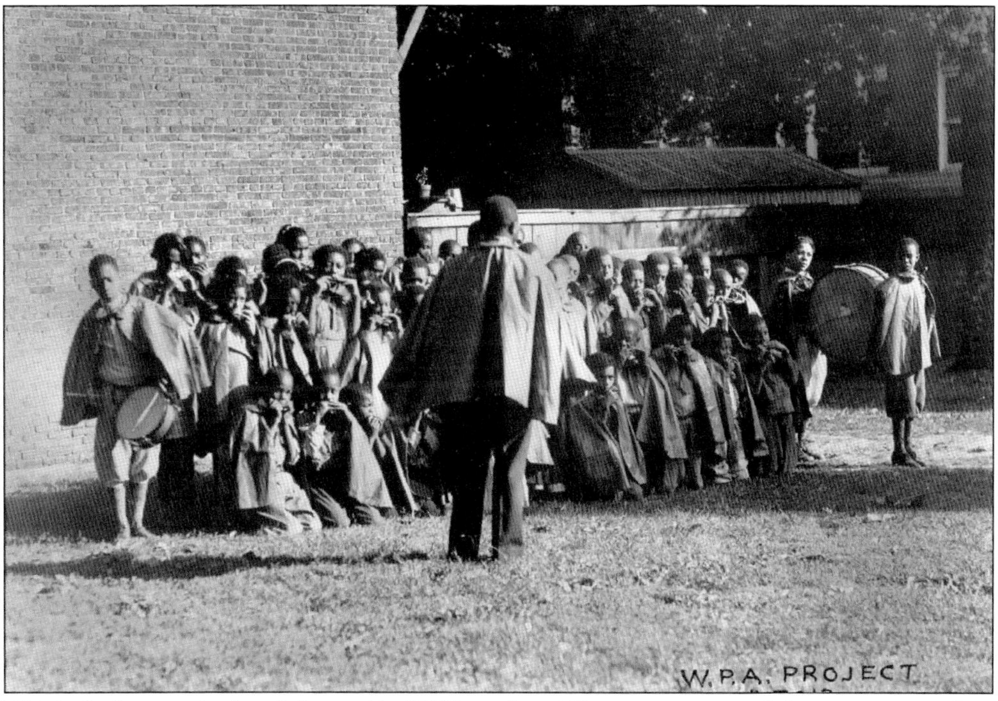

This is the harmonica band directed by WPA workers. The capes were made by women attending recreation centers. (Courtesy of the Enoch Pratt Free Library.)

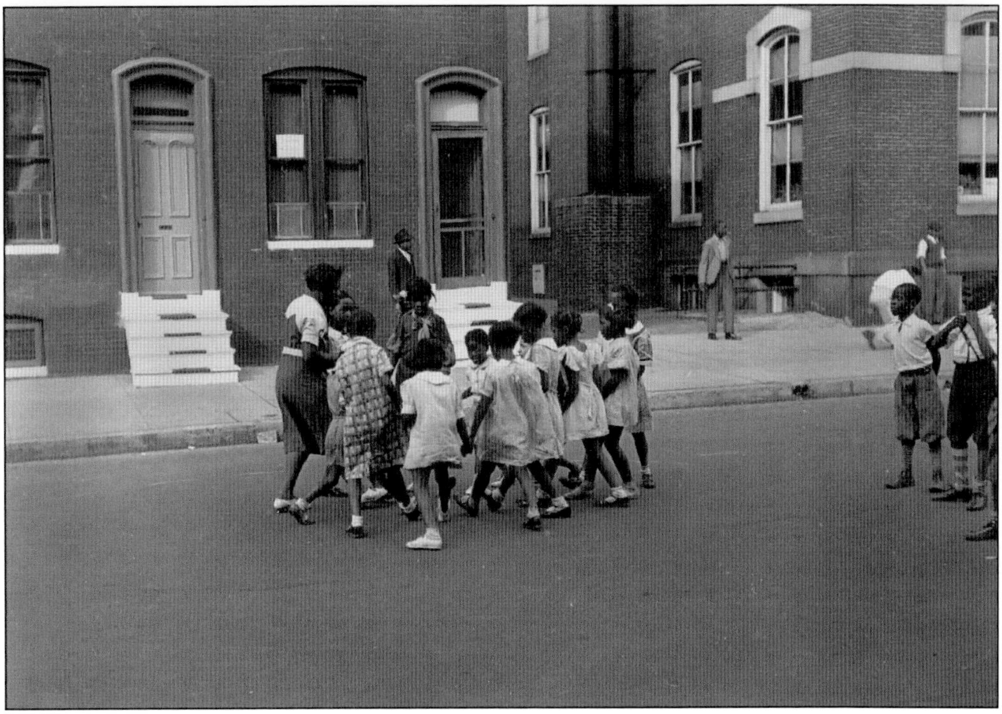

City officials roped off this street for play with WPA supervisors. (Courtesy of the Enoch Pratt Free Library.)

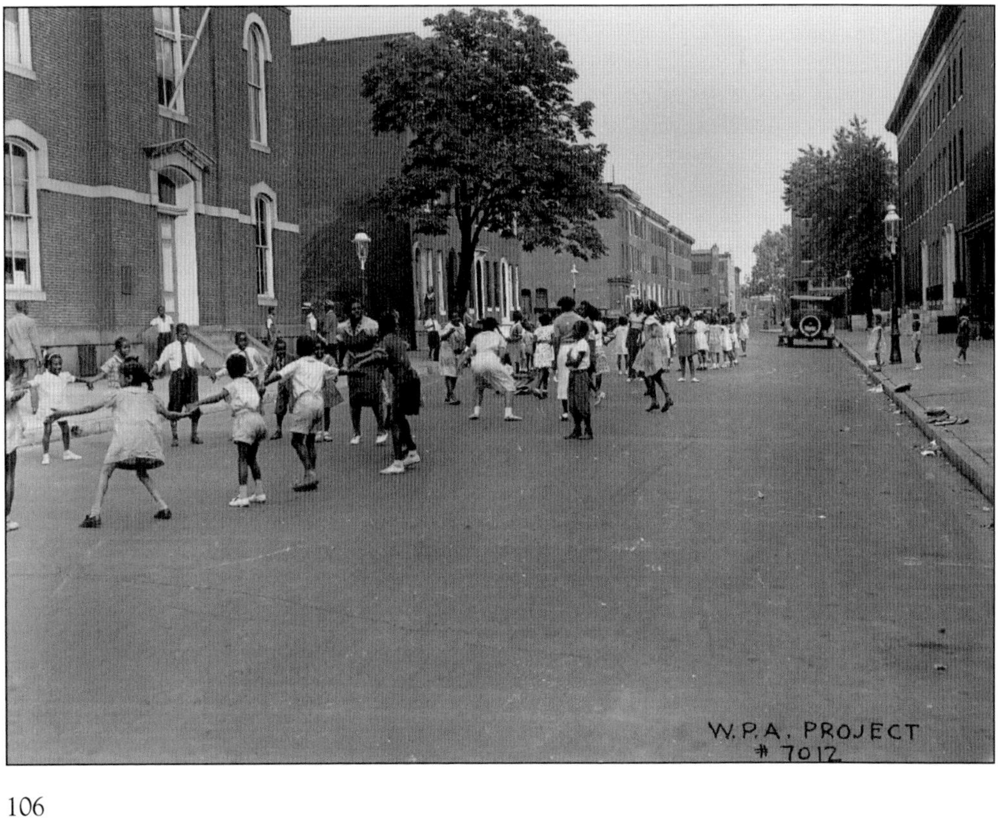

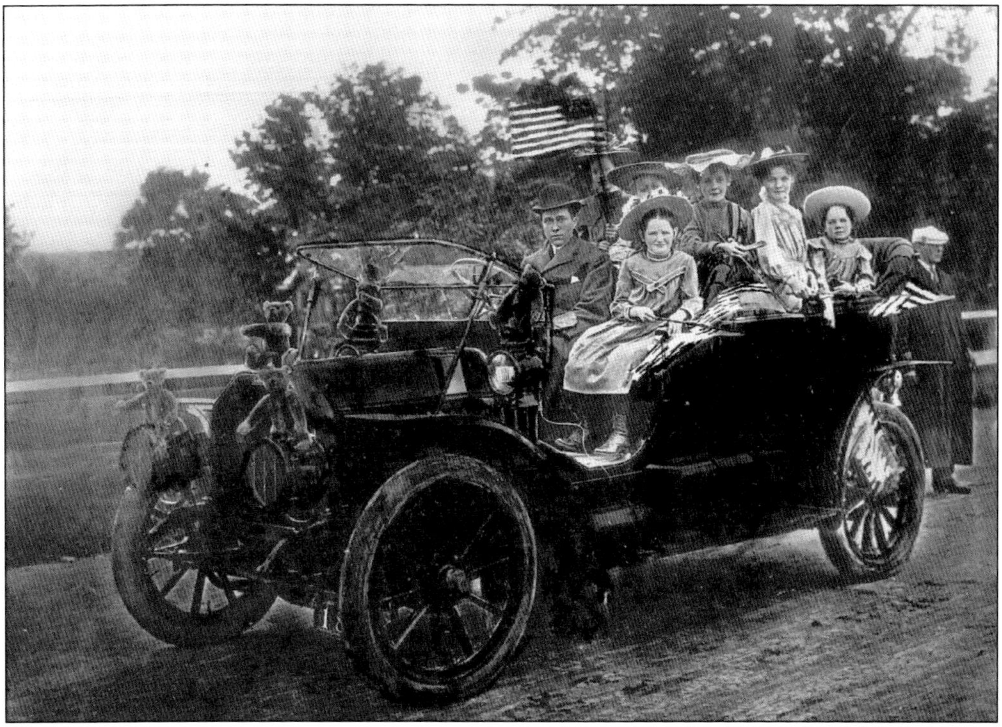

This is a photo of the Kernan Benefit for Crippled Children, c. 1910. Kernan Hospital, at that time, was an orthopedic hospital for children. (Courtesy of the Enoch Pratt Free Library.)

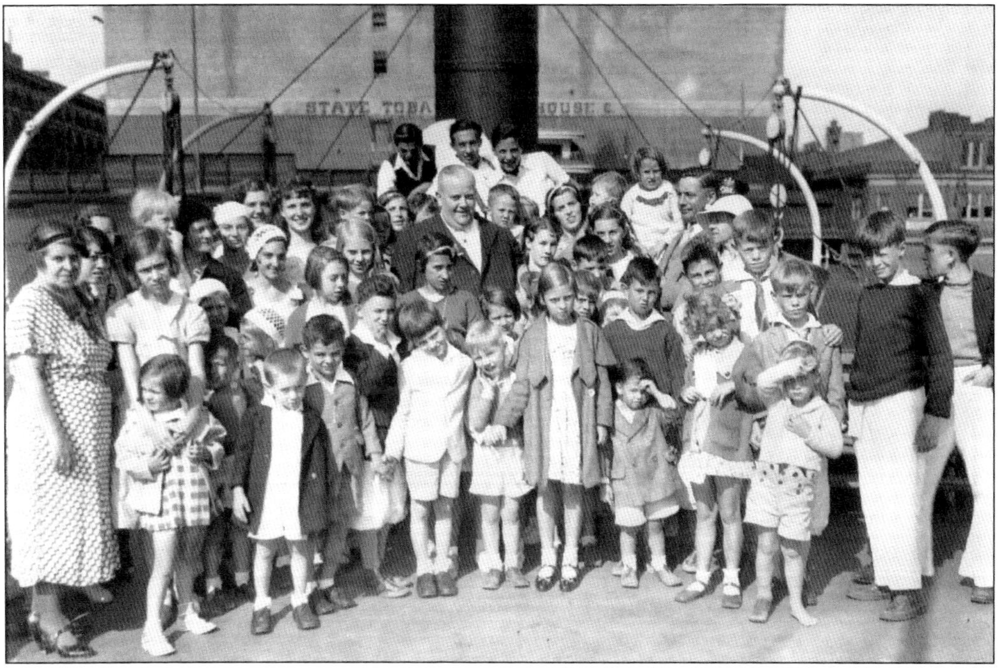

With his public relations team hard at work, Lester Mueller, then president of the city council, is seen here taking poor kids to Fairview for a day's outing in 1934. (Courtesy of the Enoch Pratt Free Library.)

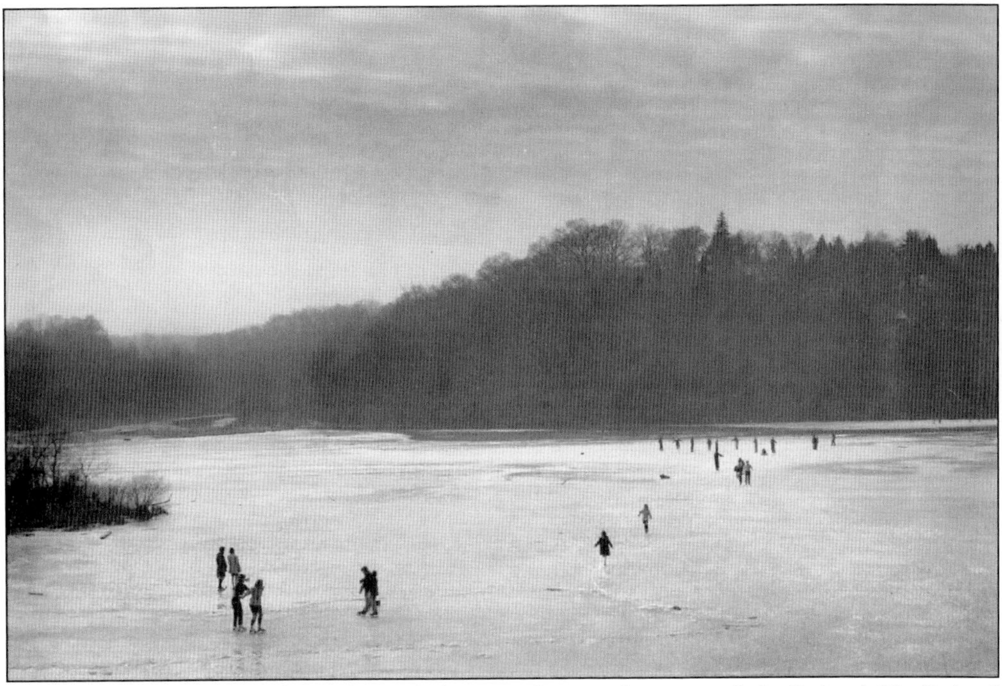

A timeless place that has always drawn kids to ice skate in the winter, Lake Roland, like Roland Park, gets its name from Roland Thornberry. The man-made lake was created *c.* 1853. (Courtesy of the Enoch Pratt Free Library.)

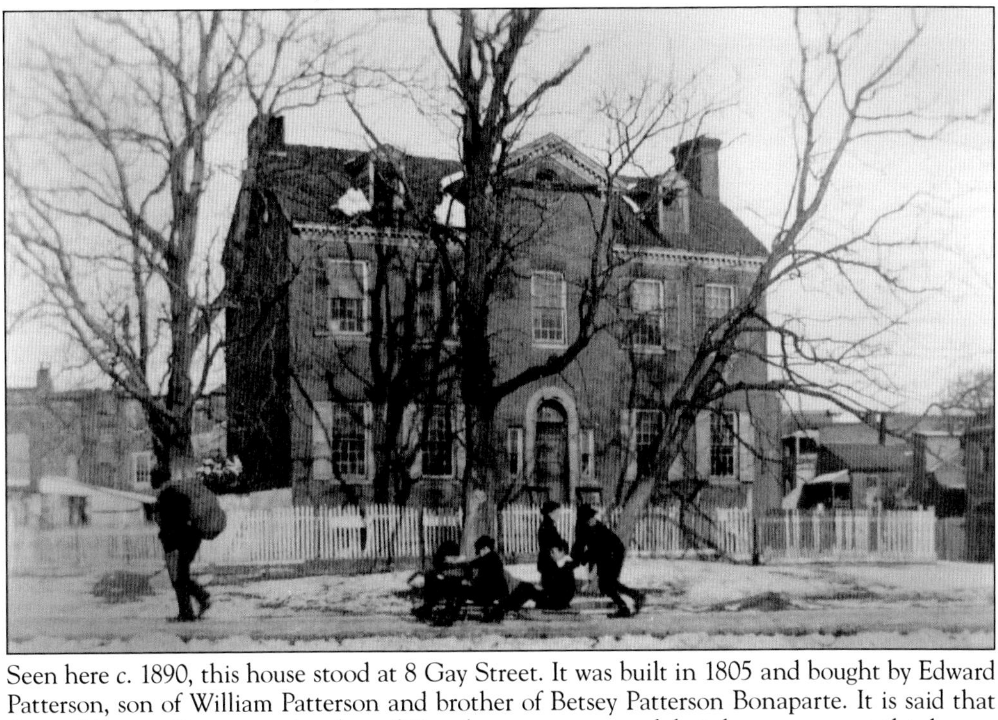

Seen here *c.* 1890, this house stood at 8 Gay Street. It was built in 1805 and bought by Edward Patterson, son of William Patterson and brother of Betsey Patterson Bonaparte. It is said that she and Jerome Bonaparte, brother of Napolean, spent part of their honeymoon at this house. (Courtesy of the Enoch Pratt Free Library.)

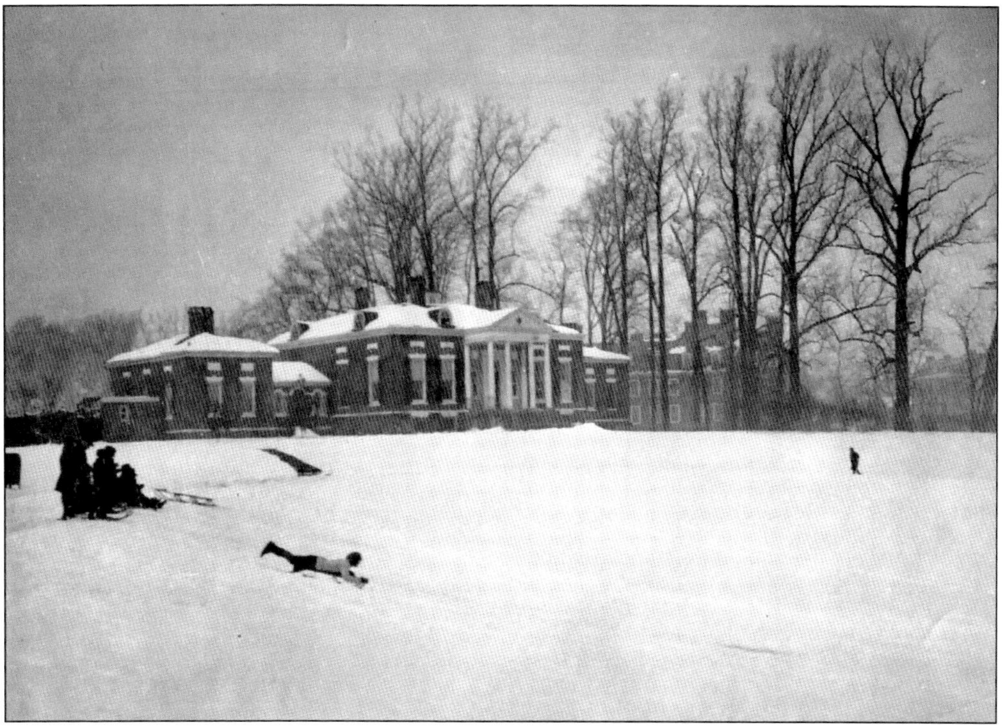

Sledding at Homewood is seen in this photograph. The house in the background was built by Charles Caroll Jr., the son of the signer of the Declaration of Independence, and sold in 1840 to Samuel Wyman. It was used by the Gilman School (then called the Country School) until October 1910 and is now a part of Johns Hopkins University. (Courtesy of the Enoch Pratt Free Library.)

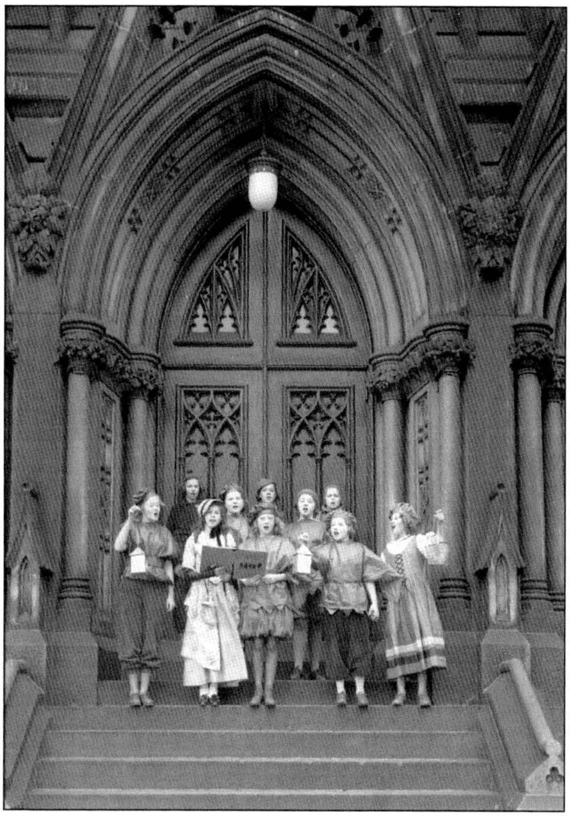

Kids carol at the Mount Vernon Place Church, which still stands in all its splendor. This photo was taken at Christmas in 1935. (Courtesy of the Enoch Pratt Free Library.)

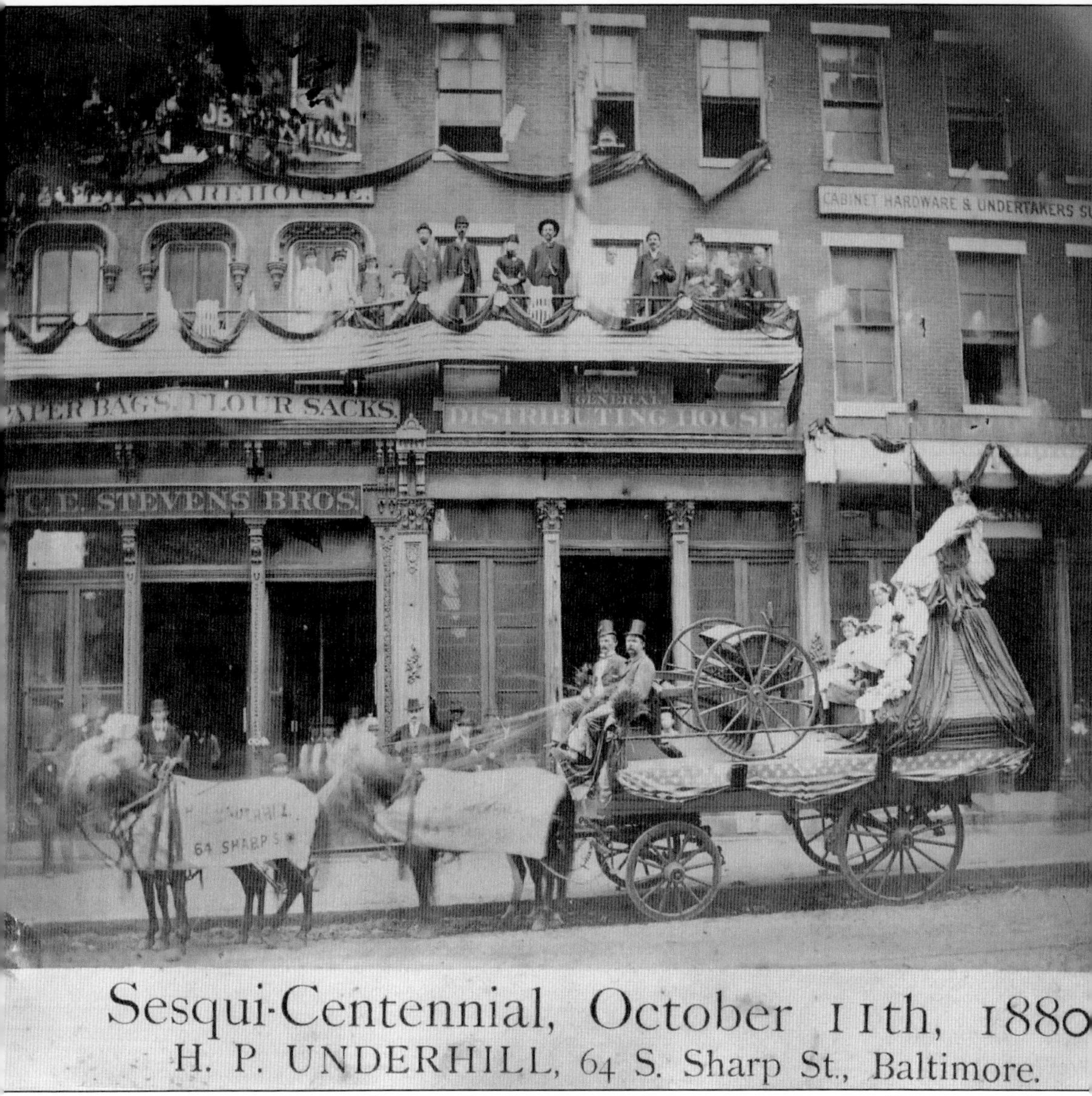

This scene shows the celebration of Baltimore's 150th anniversary in 1880. (Courtesy of the Enoch Pratt Free Library.)

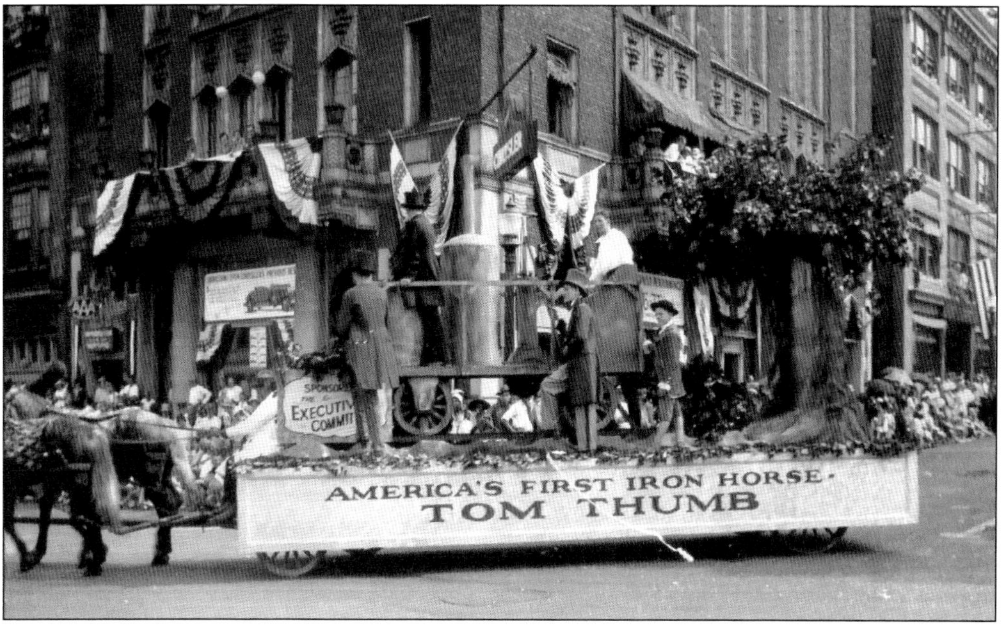

Fifty years later, in 1930, Baltimore's 200th anniversary was also the occasion of a parade. (Courtesy of the Enoch Pratt Free Library.)

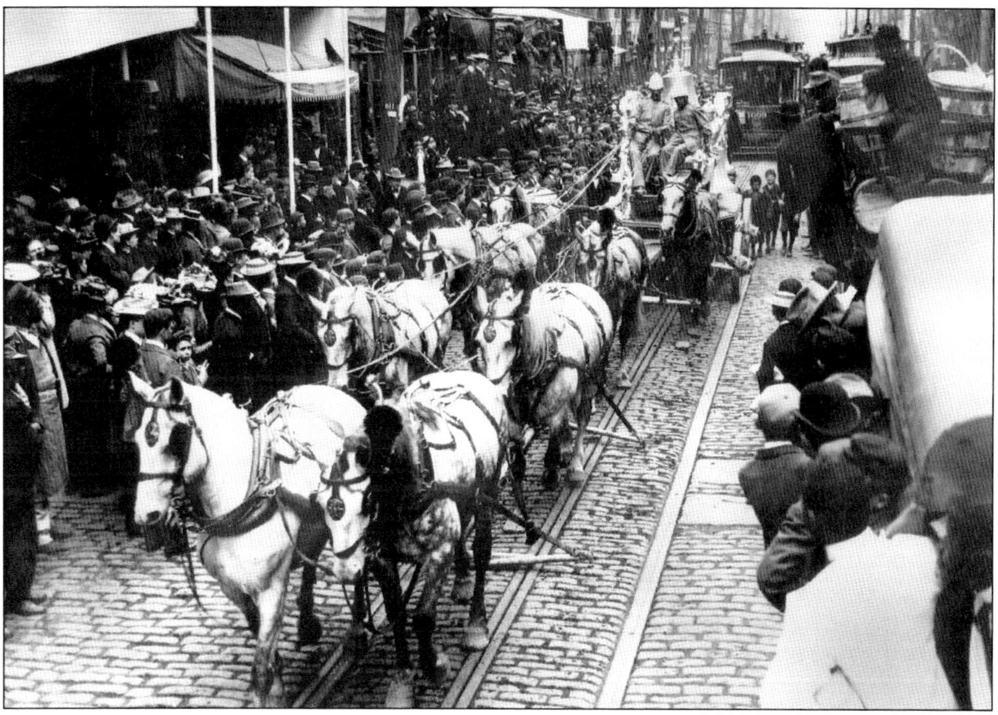

This parade photo was taken on East Baltimore Street looking east from Charles Street. Although the photo is titled "Bell Parade," there has been some dispute over whether this is the Liberty Bell on loan to the city or the huge bell created by Regester Bell Company. The Regester Bell was carried through the streets before every parade. (Courtesy of the Enoch Pratt Free Library.)

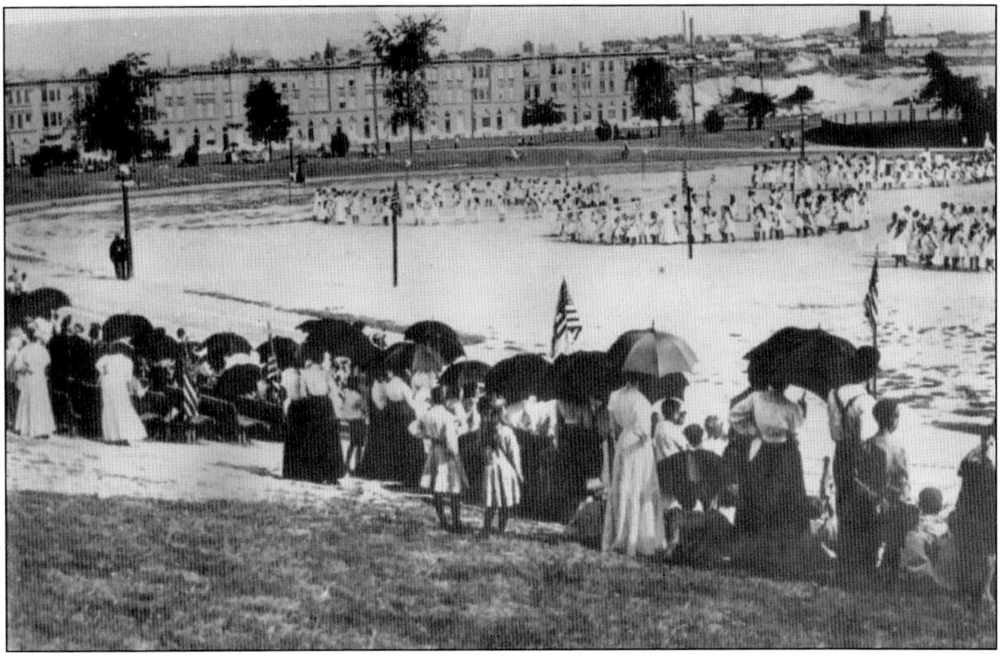

This is a late 19th-century event, most likely a May Day celebration, at Patterson Park. (Courtesy of the Enoch Pratt Free Library.)

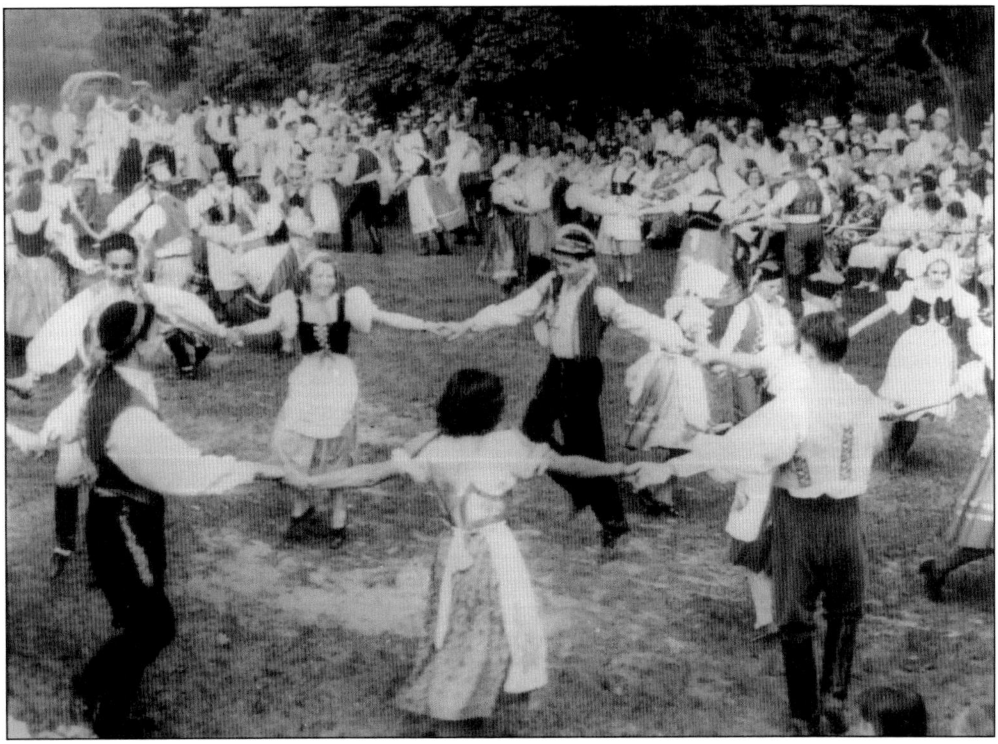

Baltimore is a city of great diversity, and the many ethnic residents celebrate their differences in a variety of ways. Here, the United Czechoslovakian Society of Baltimore celebrates at a camp picnic at Sokol Camp Tyr on June 26, 1938. (Courtesy of the Enoch Pratt Free Library.)

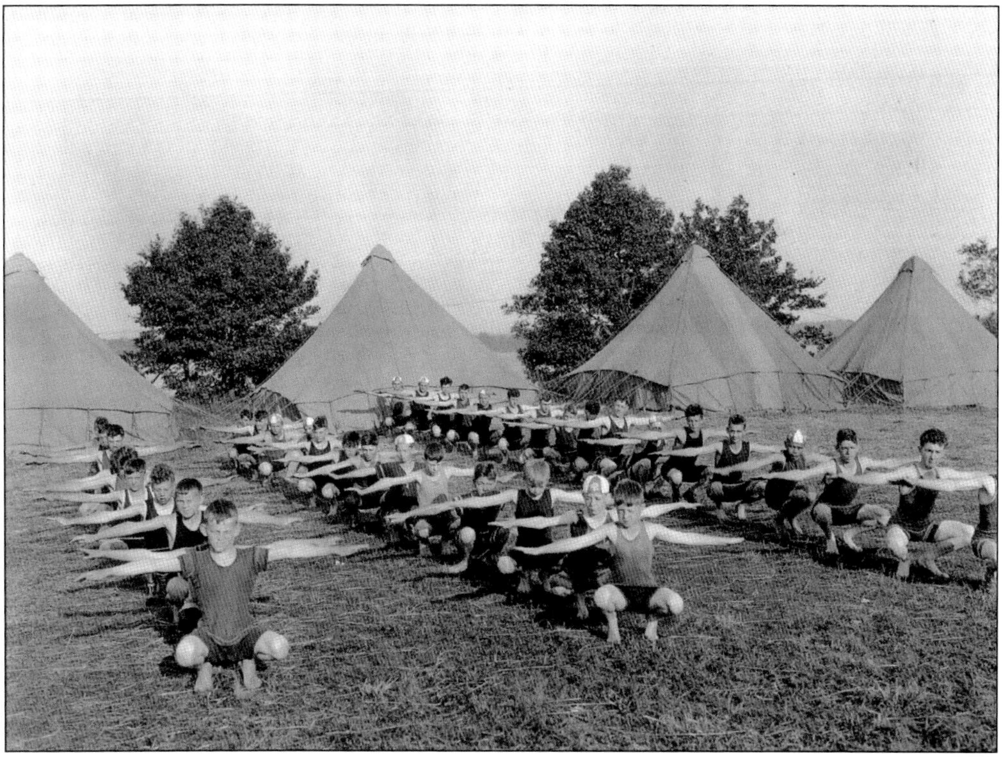

In this 1936 image, young campers are doing their morning exercises. (Courtesy of the Enoch Pratt Free Library.)

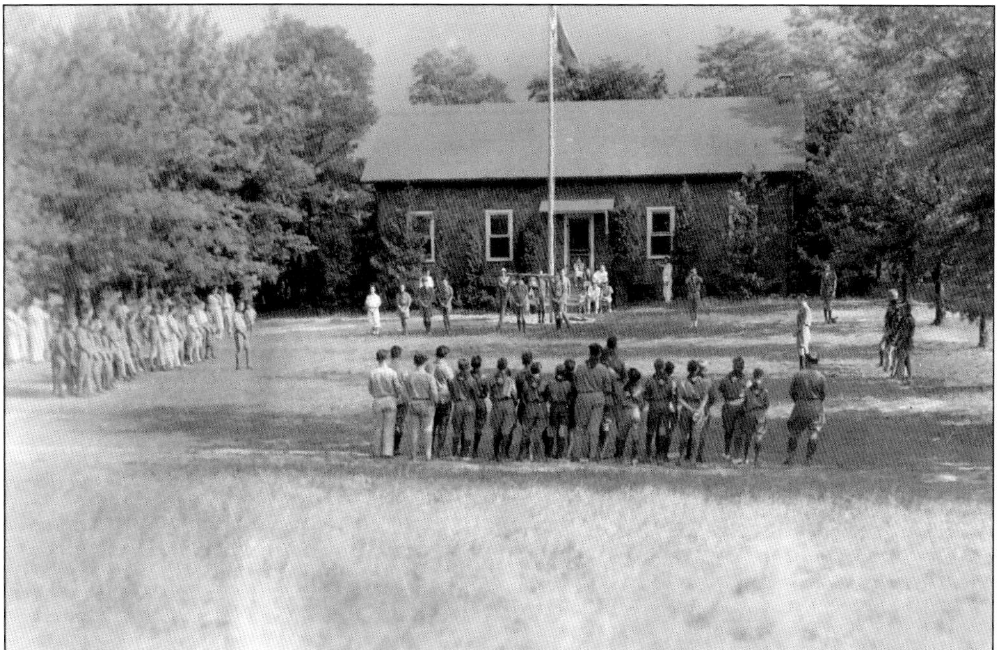

These boys are at Camp Linstead, a Boy Scout camp in Baltimore, in 1936. (Courtesy of the Enoch Pratt Free Library.)

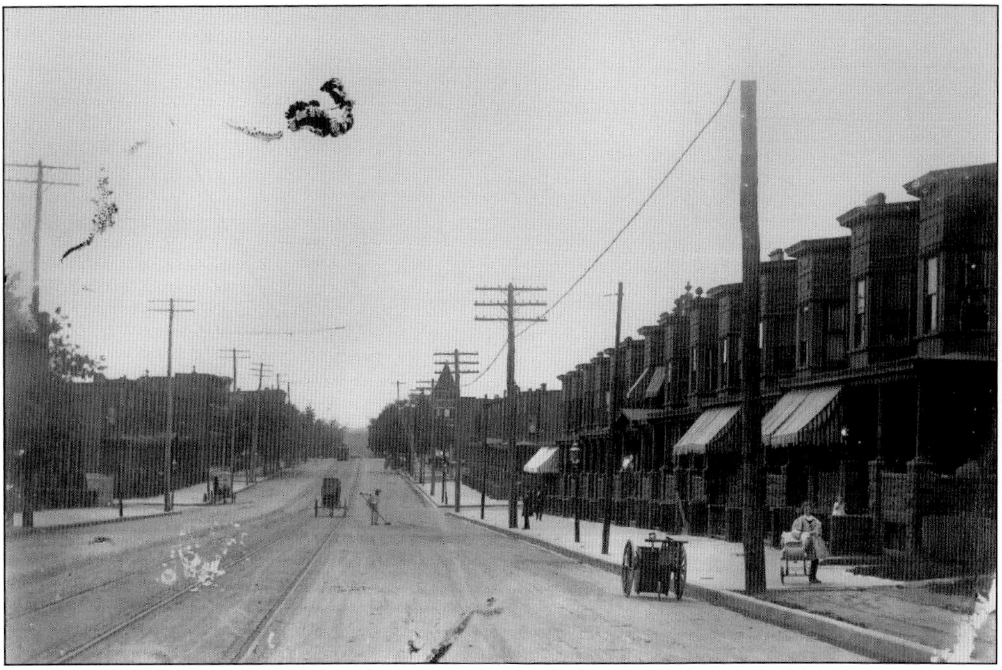

The little girl on the right of the photo takes her doll for a walk down Guilford Street, *c.* 1890. (Courtesy of the Enoch Pratt Free Library.)

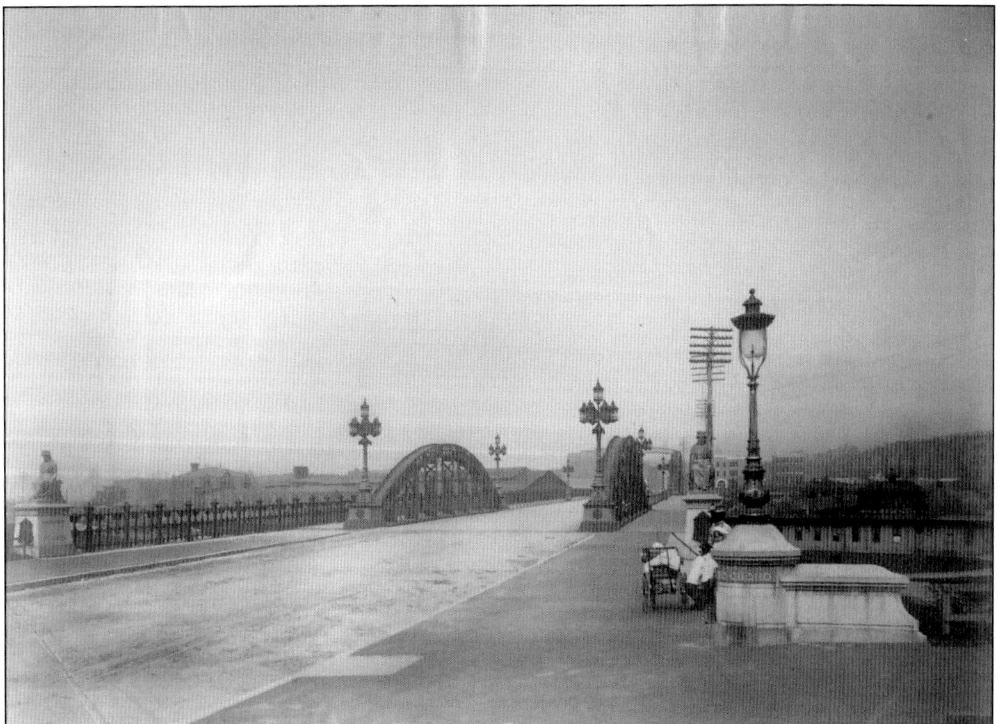

An African-American nanny takes her white charge for a stroll. Here, they rest on the St. Paul Street Bridge near Union Depot, *c.* 1880. (Courtesy of the Enoch Pratt Free Library.)

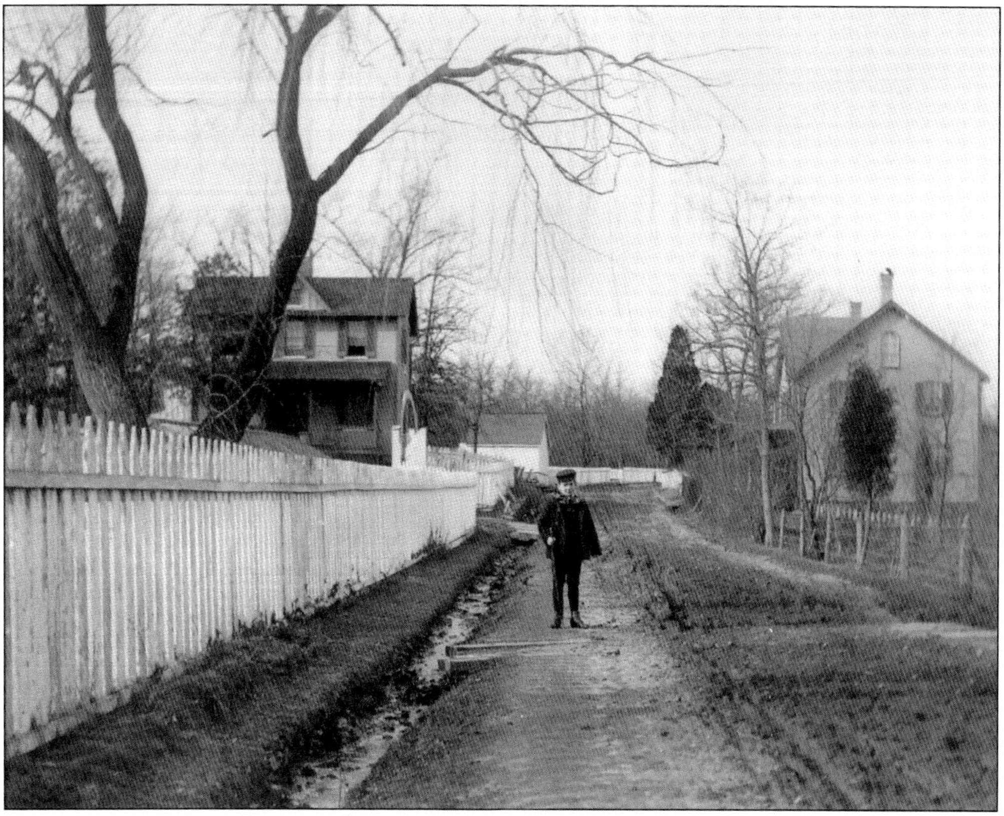

Above, a young boy takes a walk on a cool afternoon in 1899. (Courtesy of the Enoch Pratt Free Library.)

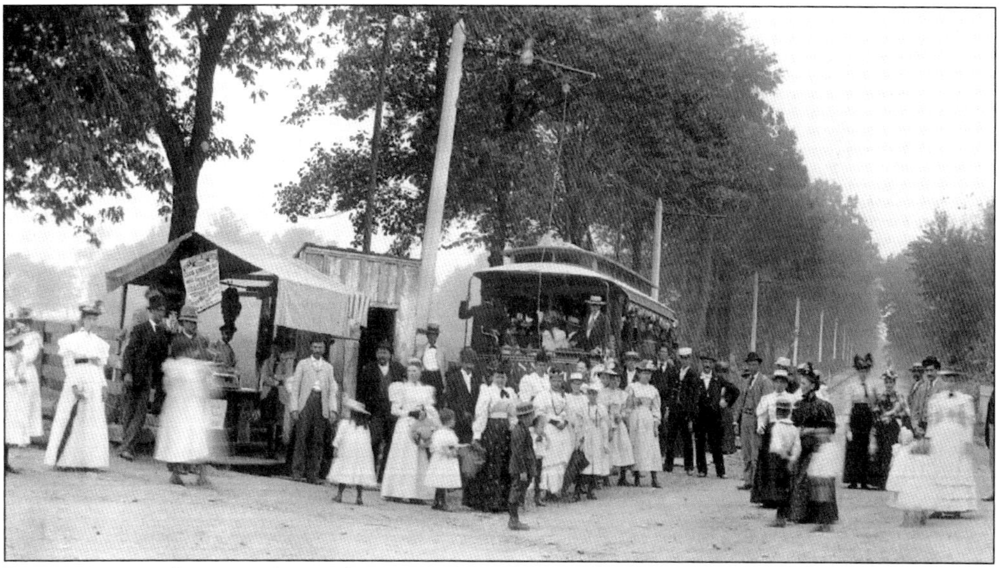

Picnics were a frequent form of entertainment in Victorian Baltimore. Pictured here is an organized social event in 1900, complete with refreshment stands. (Courtesy of the Enoch Pratt Free Library.)

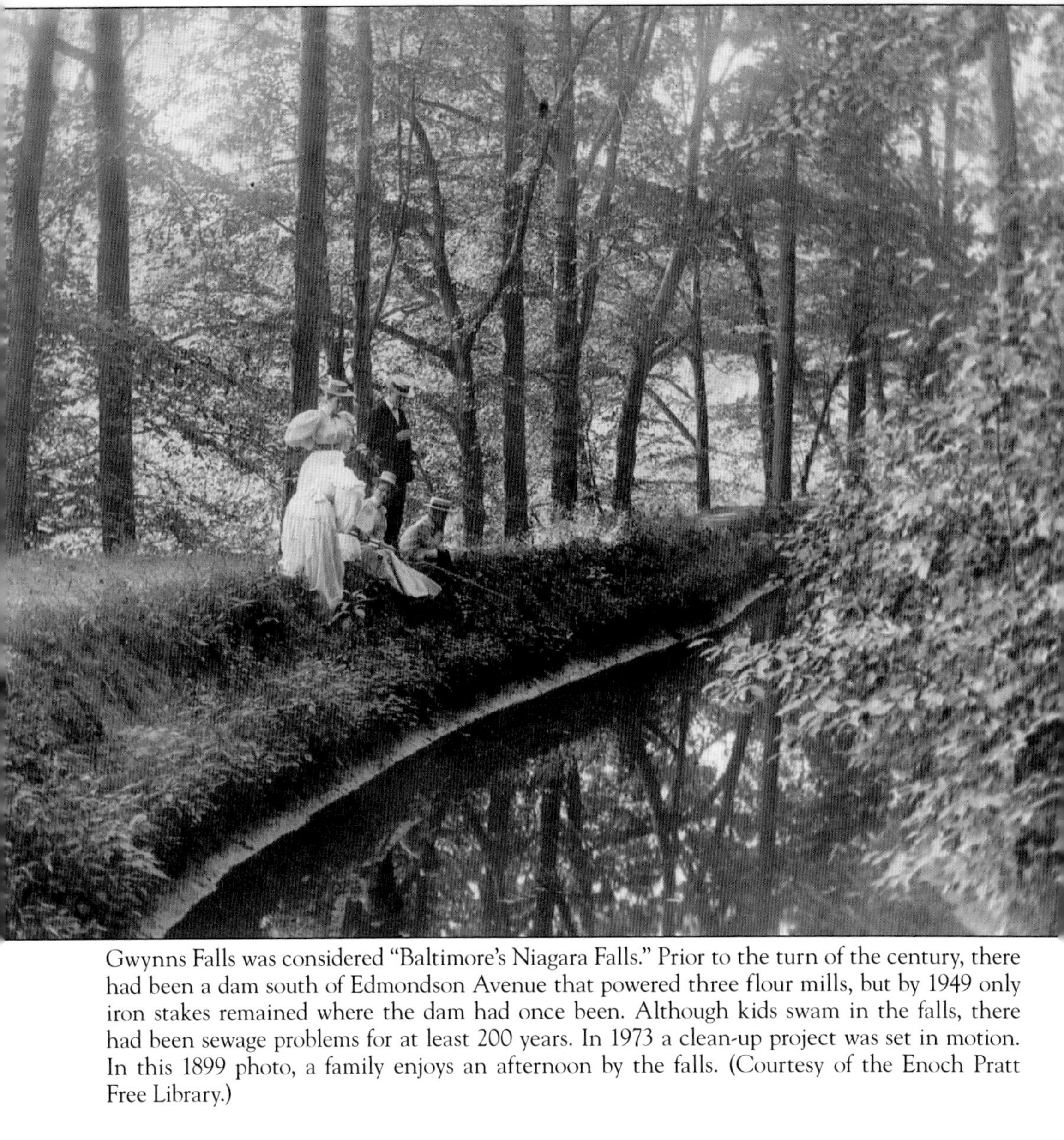

Gwynns Falls was considered "Baltimore's Niagara Falls." Prior to the turn of the century, there had been a dam south of Edmondson Avenue that powered three flour mills, but by 1949 only iron stakes remained where the dam had once been. Although kids swam in the falls, there had been sewage problems for at least 200 years. In 1973 a clean-up project was set in motion. In this 1899 photo, a family enjoys an afternoon by the falls. (Courtesy of the Enoch Pratt Free Library.)

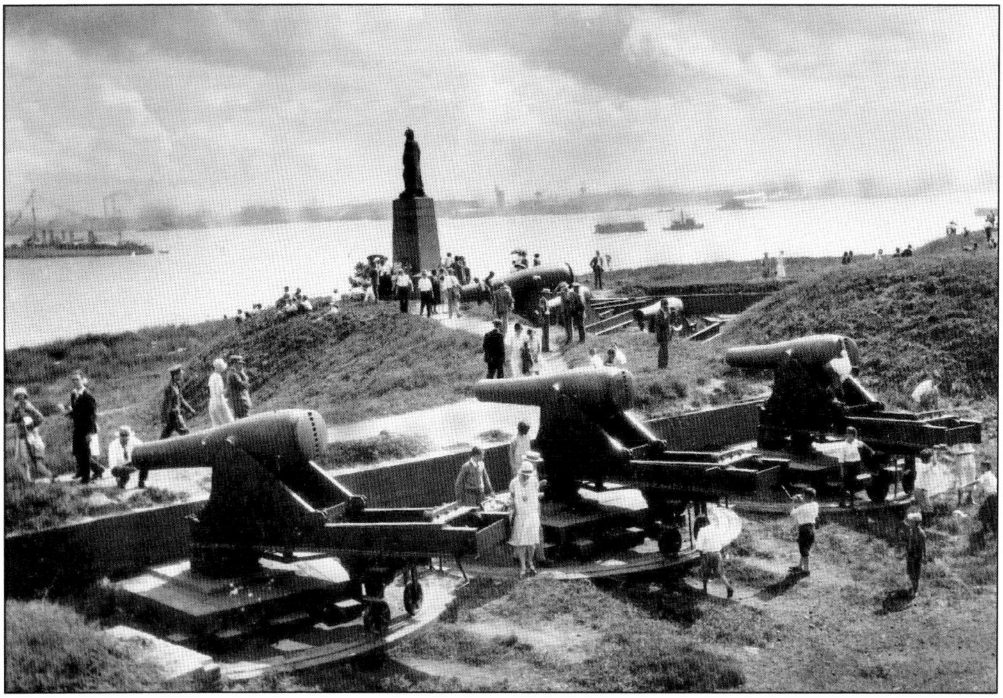

The famous site of the battle that inspired Francis Scott Key to write his immortal poem "The Star-Spangled Banner," Fort McHenry is still a tourist venue. Here, tourists investigate on a sunny afternoon in 1920. (Courtesy of the Enoch Pratt Free Library.)

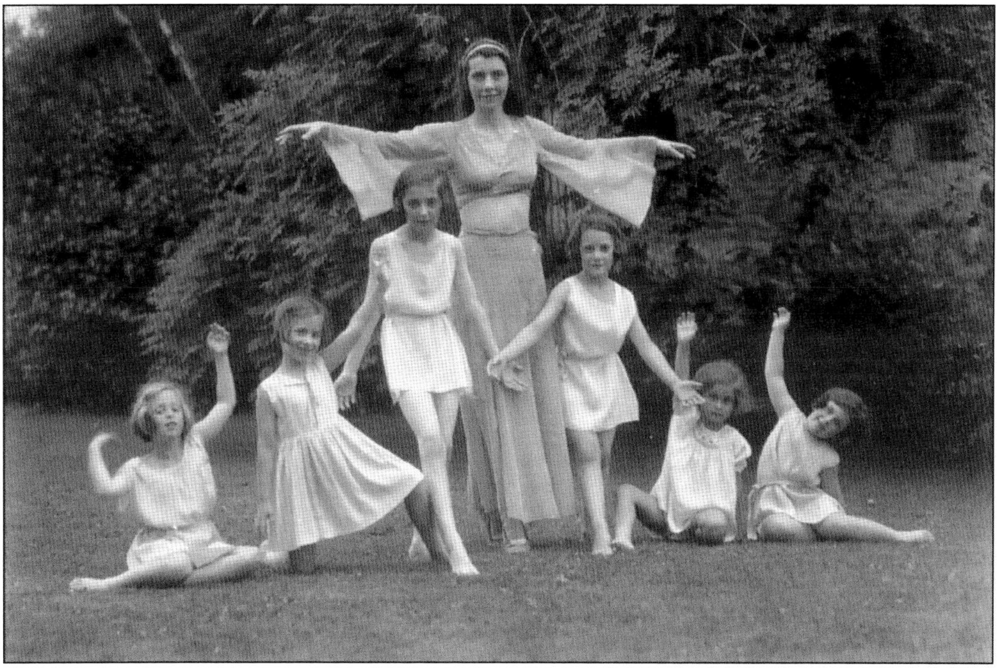

The Weiler family house on Slade between Park Heights and Reisterstown Road was an expansive house with a beautiful lawn. Many afternoons were spent playing here. This photo was taken *c.* 1935. (Courtesy of Liz Moser.)

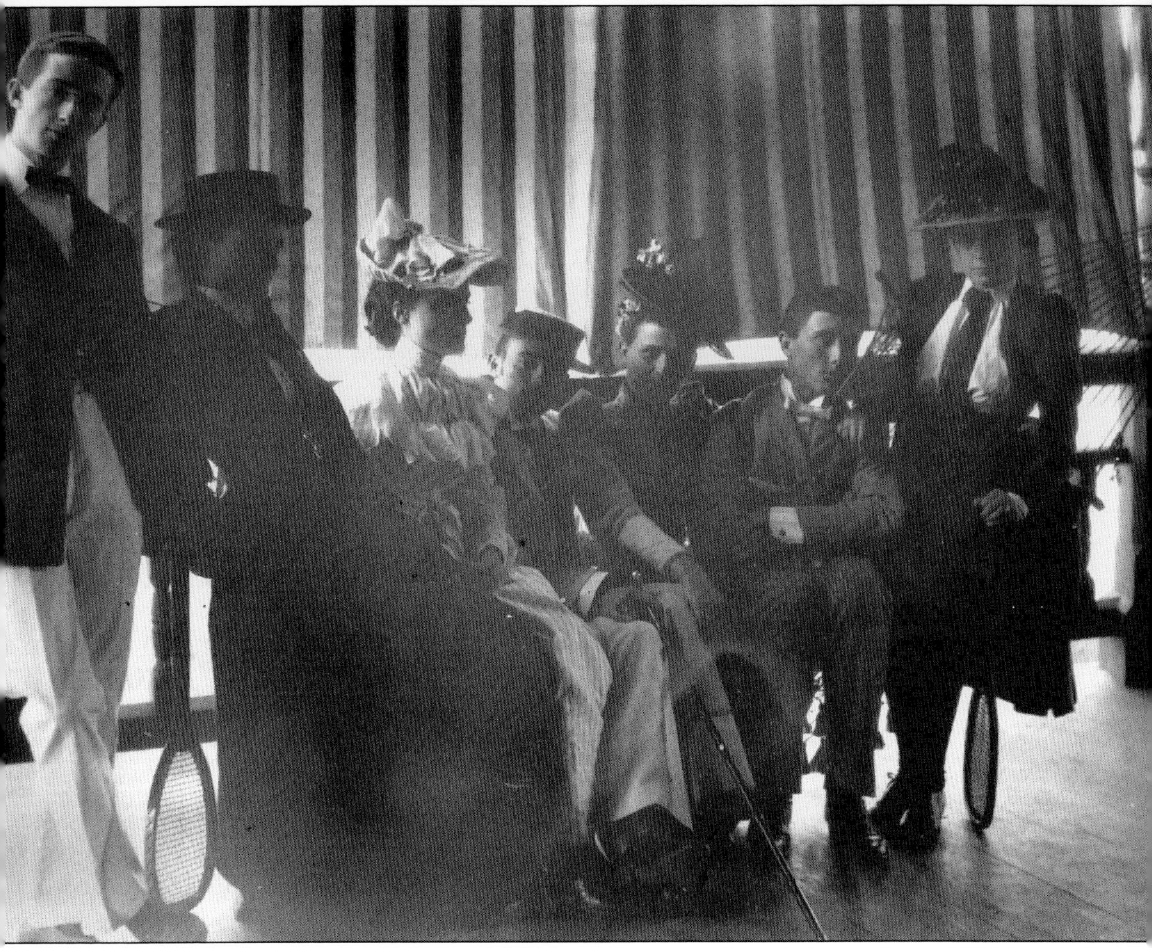

These are the Turnbull and Garrett children as teenagers. From left to right are H.W. Turnbull, Lisa Turnbull, Anne Turnbull, John W. Garrett, unidentified, Robert Garrett, and Lillie Turnbull. They seem to be taking a break from playing tennis. (Courtesy of the Evergreen House Foundation, The Johns Hopkins University.)

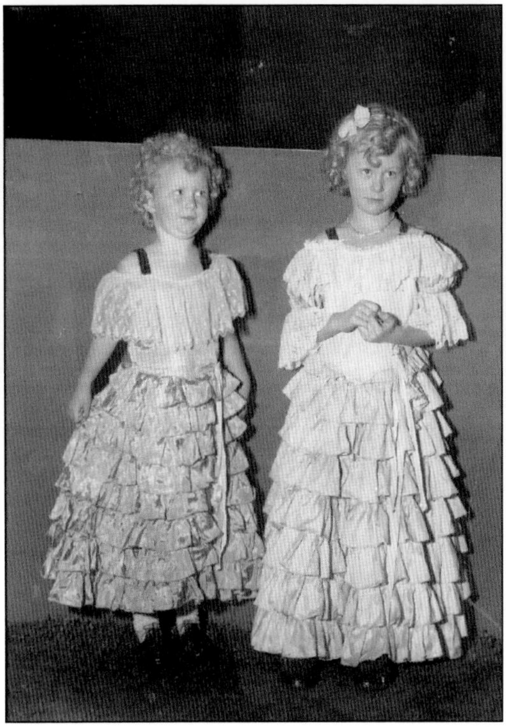

Two little girls participate in the Tercentenary Pageant at Municipal Stadium, the site of Memorial Stadium, in October 1934. Memorial Stadium, which itself was torn down in 2001, was built on top of the old stadium. (Courtesy of the Enoch Pratt Free Library.)

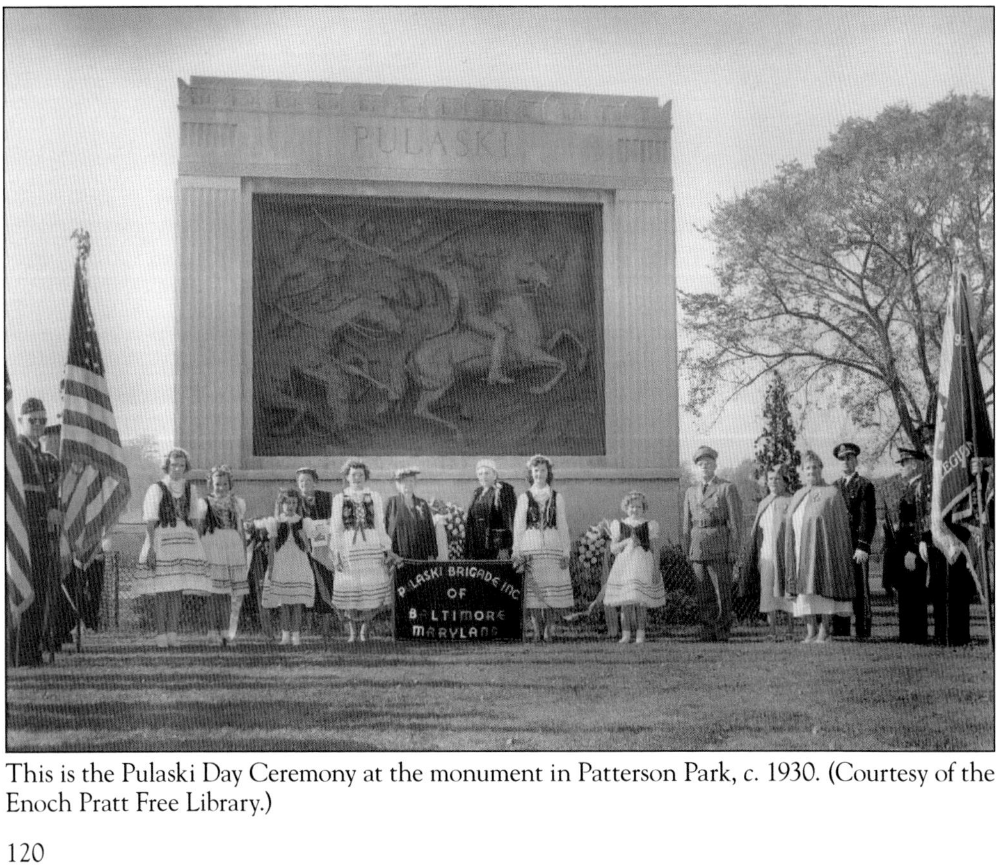

This is the Pulaski Day Ceremony at the monument in Patterson Park, c. 1930. (Courtesy of the Enoch Pratt Free Library.)

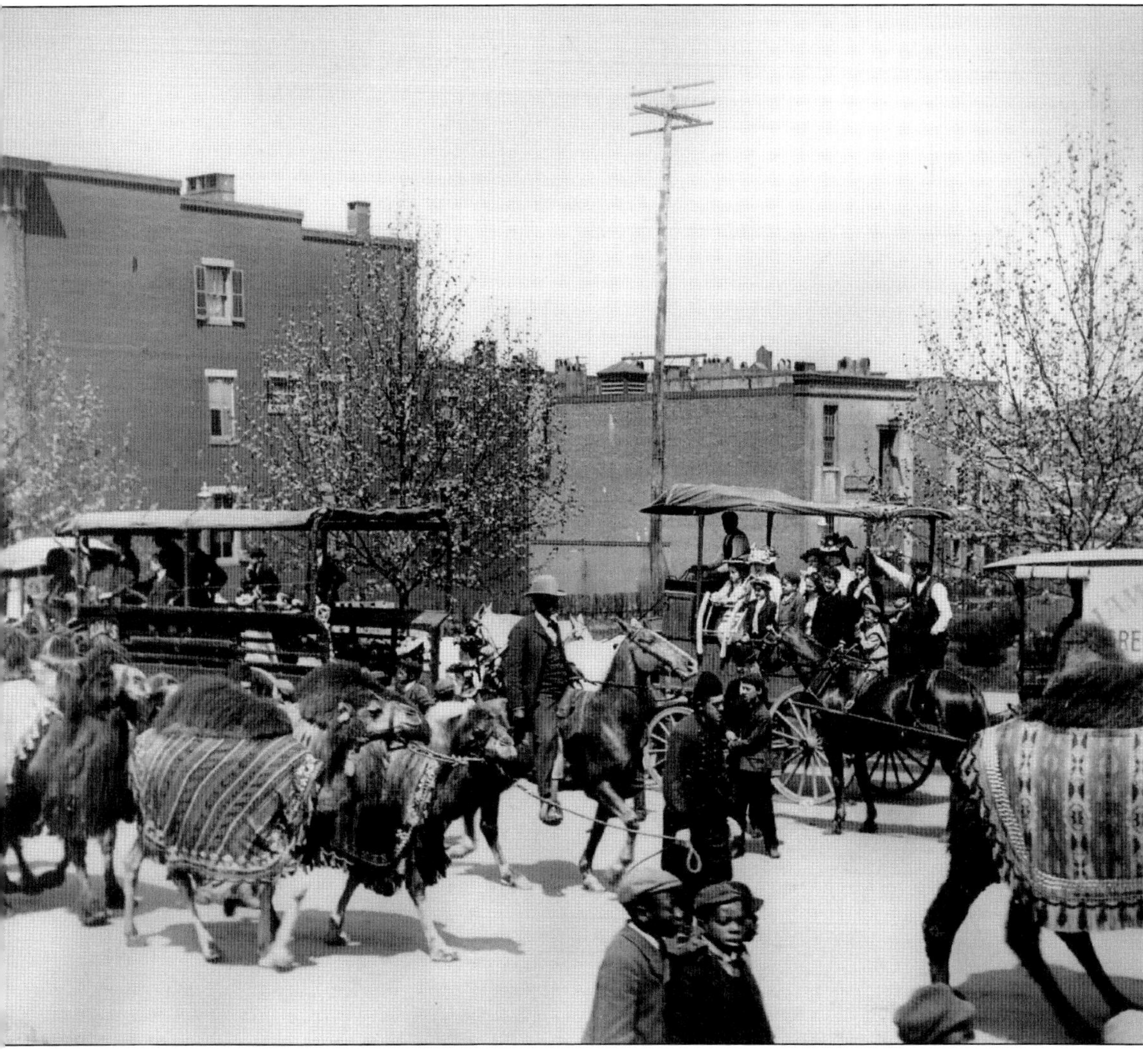

The circus was in town on this day in Victorian Baltimore, and visiting fairs and circuses were a fun part of life in the city and were a frequent sight and welcomed source of entertainment. Circus parades were anticipated with great excitement by children and adults of all ages and backgrounds. (Courtesy of the Enoch Pratt Free Library.)

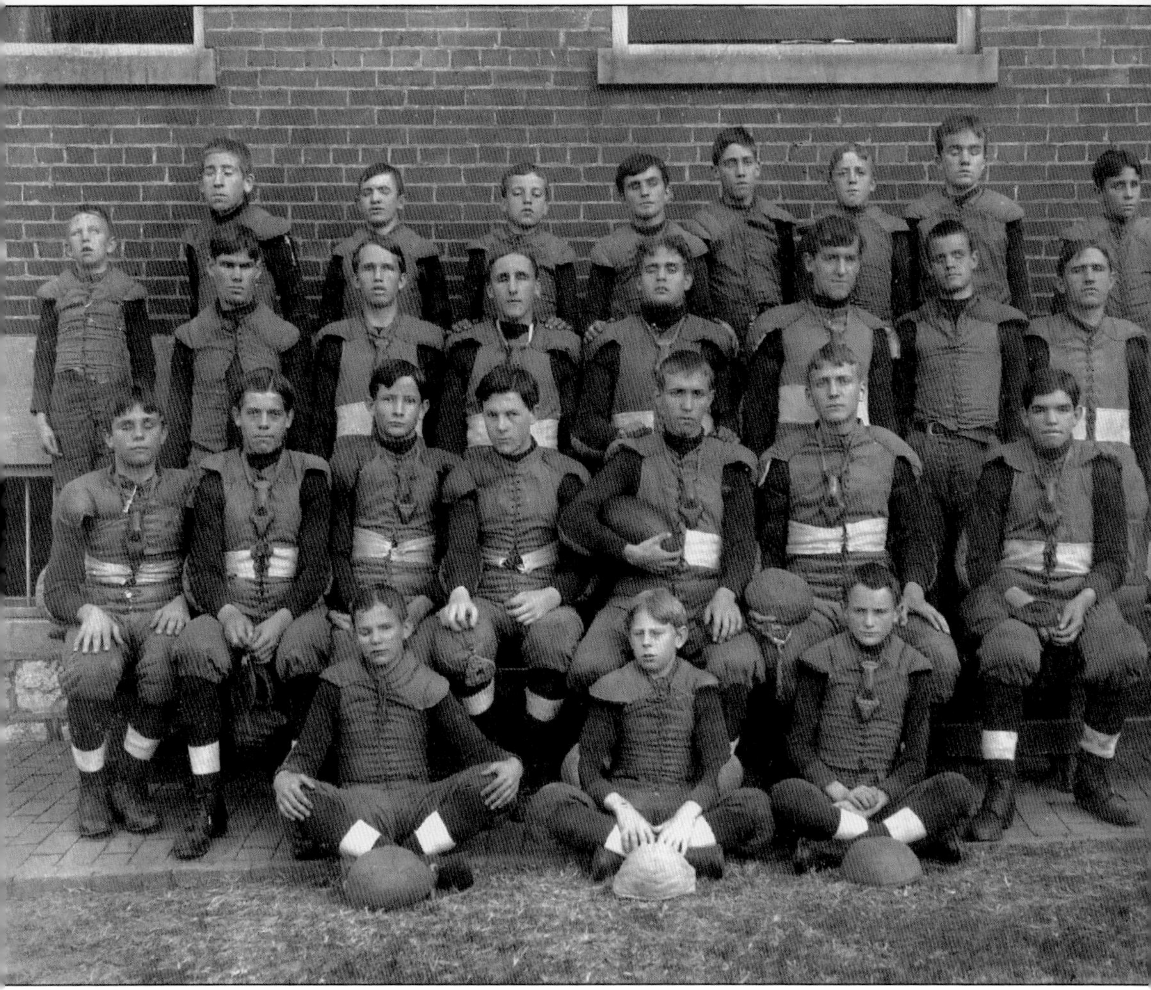

The Maryland School for the Blind had many activities for its students, including this football team in 1895. The devices around the players' necks are nose guards. Although visually impaired and sometimes hearing impaired, the students participated in many of the same activities as sighted children. (Courtesy of the Maryland School for the Blind.)

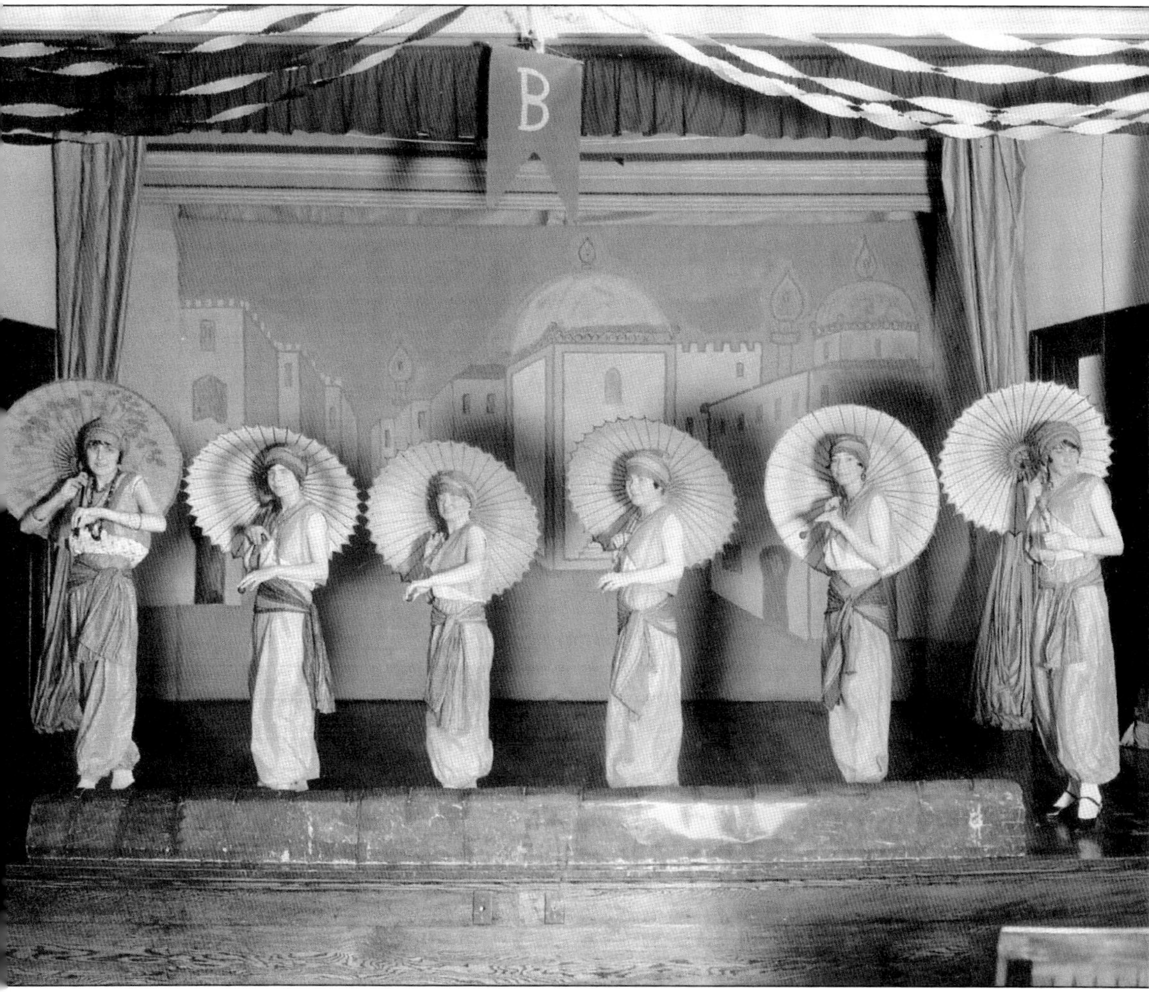

This is a 1920s performance of the girls dramatic group at the Maryland School for the Blind. The structure in front of the stage, although built most likely to hold lights, would have helped the performers to negotiate the edge of the stage and prevent accidents. Along with sports, theater was enjoyed by the vision impaired students of the Maryland School for the Blind. (Courtesy of the Maryland School for the Blind.)

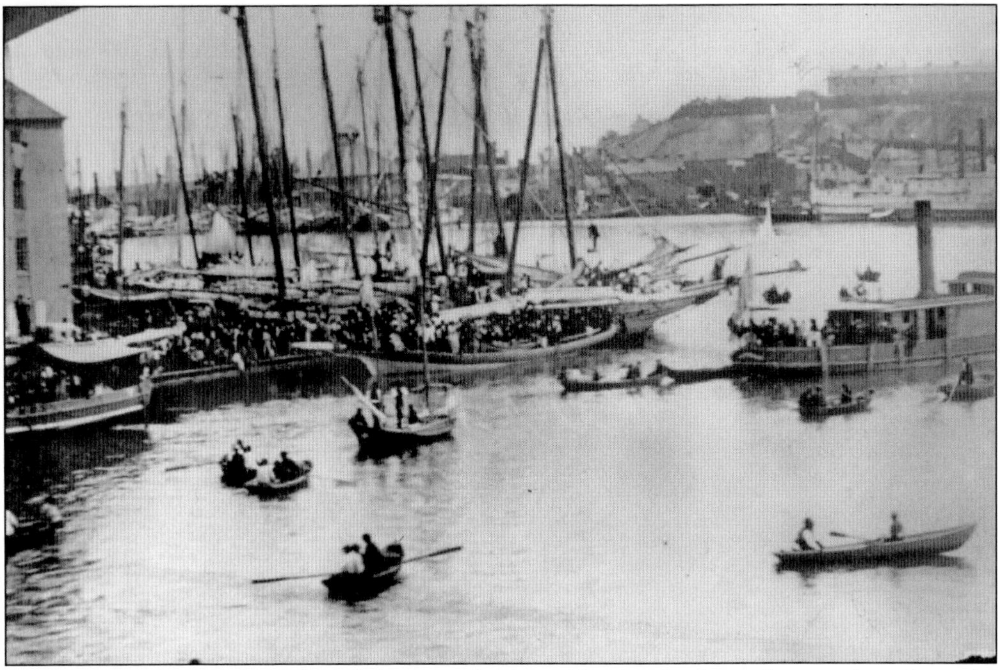

This photo, taken in 1875 by famed photographer David Bachrach, shows the crowd watching the departure of a European-bound ship from the harbor. Federal Hill can be seen across the basin, as can the Civil War barracks that still stand. (Courtesy of the Enoch Pratt Free Library.)

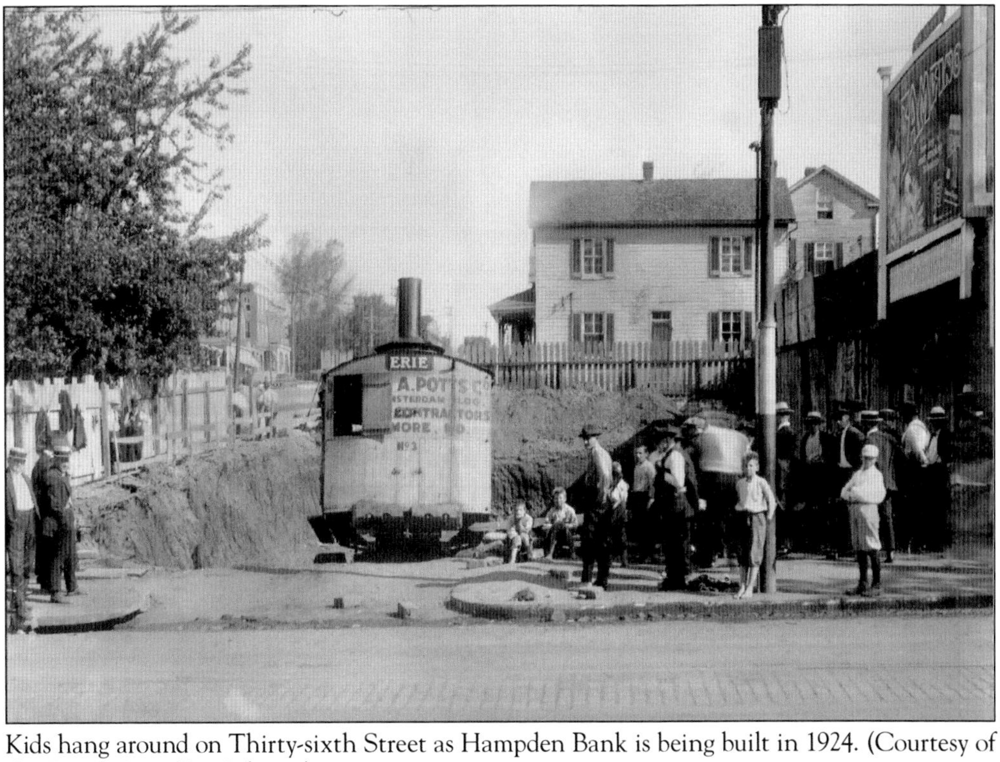

Kids hang around on Thirty-sixth Street as Hampden Bank is being built in 1924. (Courtesy of the Enoch Pratt Free Library.)

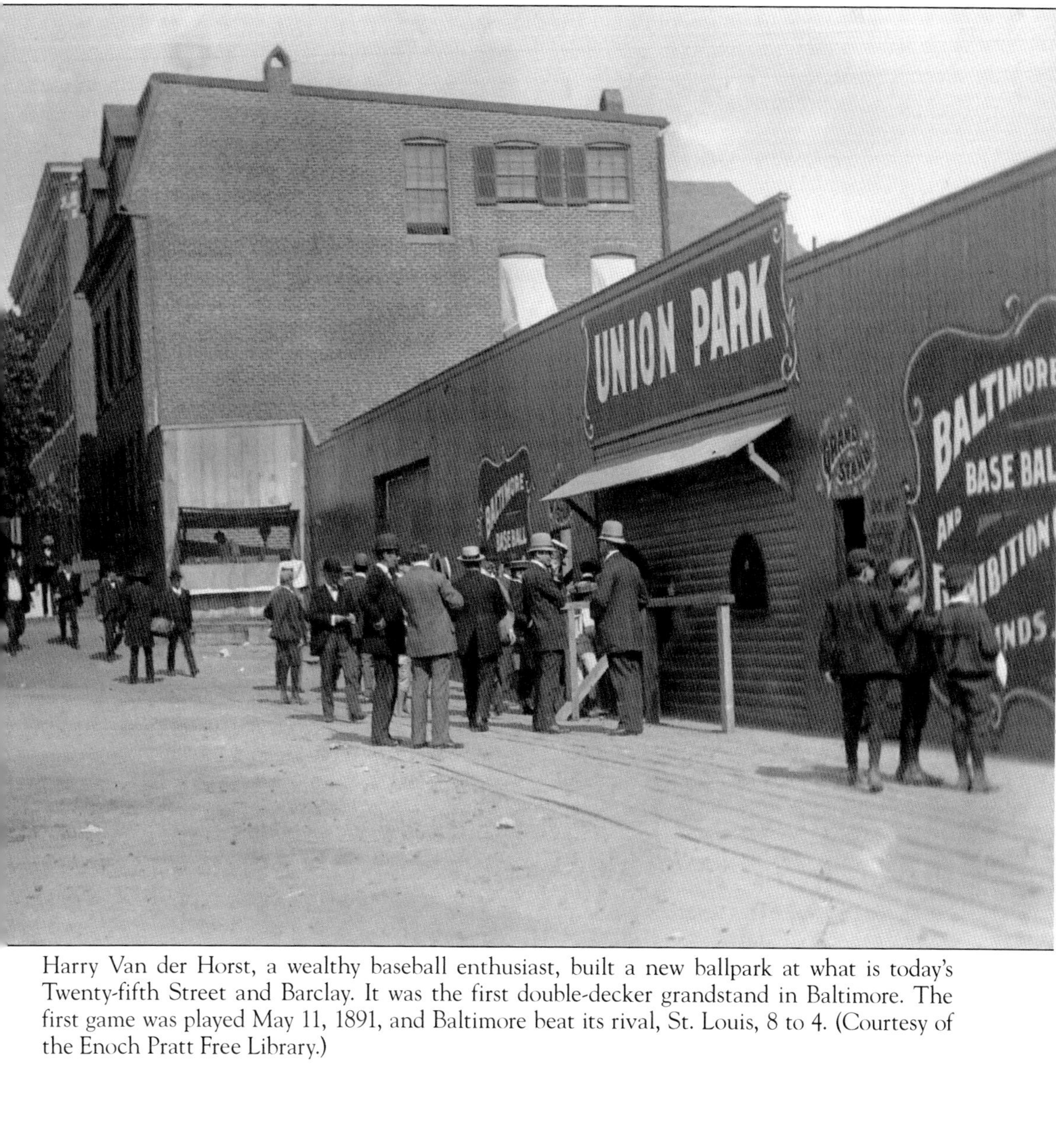

Harry Van der Horst, a wealthy baseball enthusiast, built a new ballpark at what is today's Twenty-fifth Street and Barclay. It was the first double-decker grandstand in Baltimore. The first game was played May 11, 1891, and Baltimore beat its rival, St. Louis, 8 to 4. (Courtesy of the Enoch Pratt Free Library.)

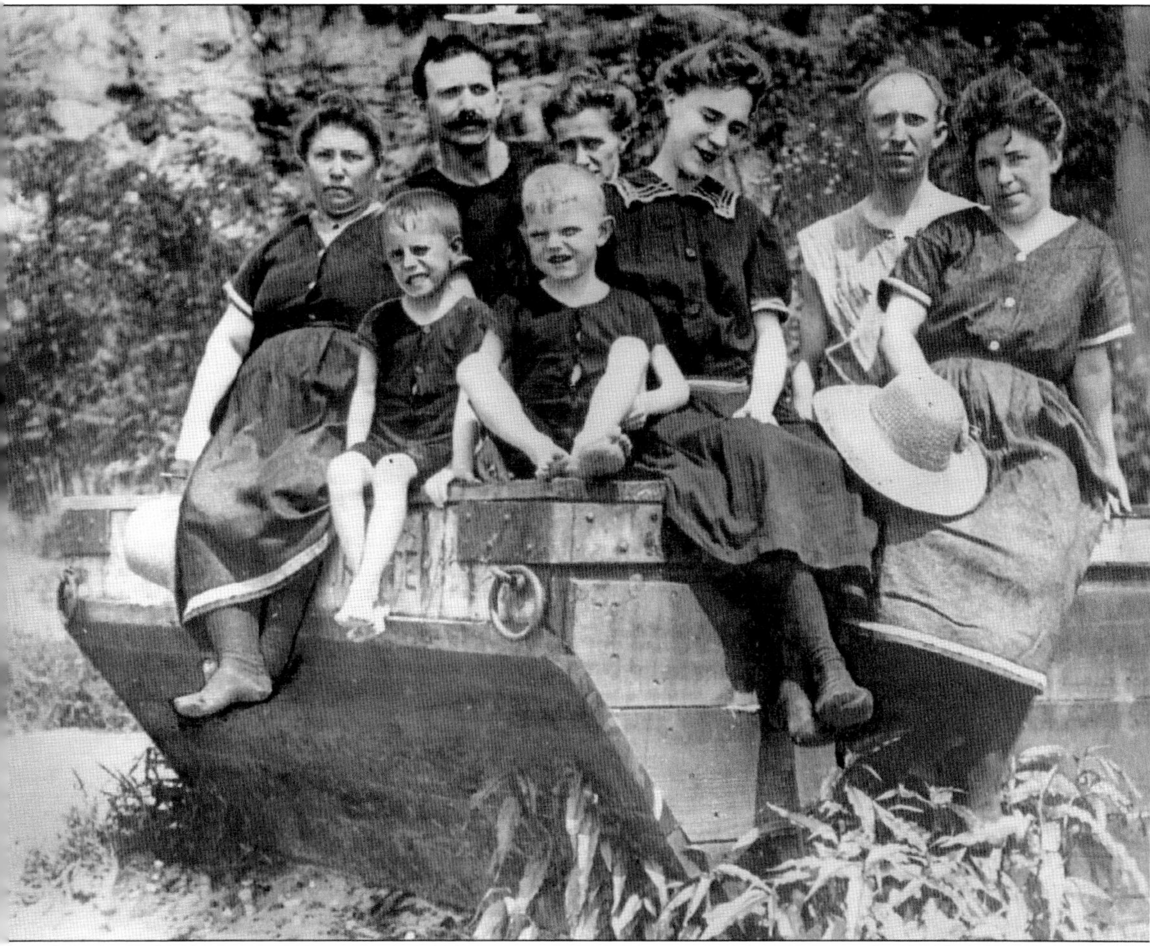

This is the Barnhart family in 1904, sitting in a scow, which is a large open bin used to transport garbage or gravel. (Courtesy of the Enoch Pratt Free Library.)

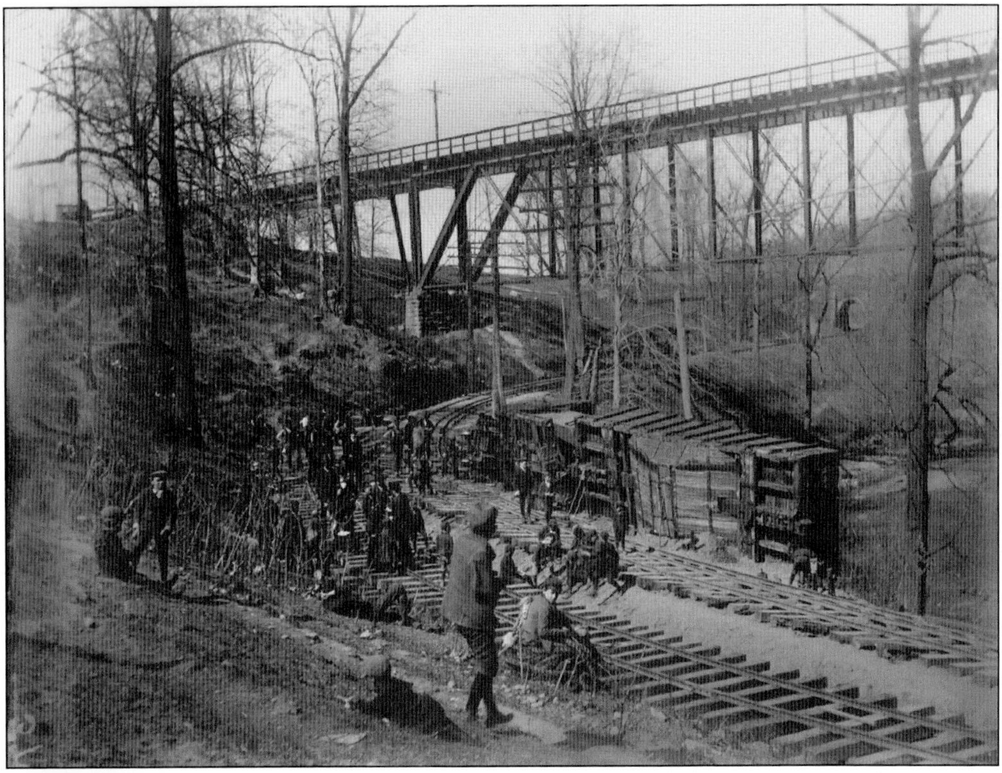

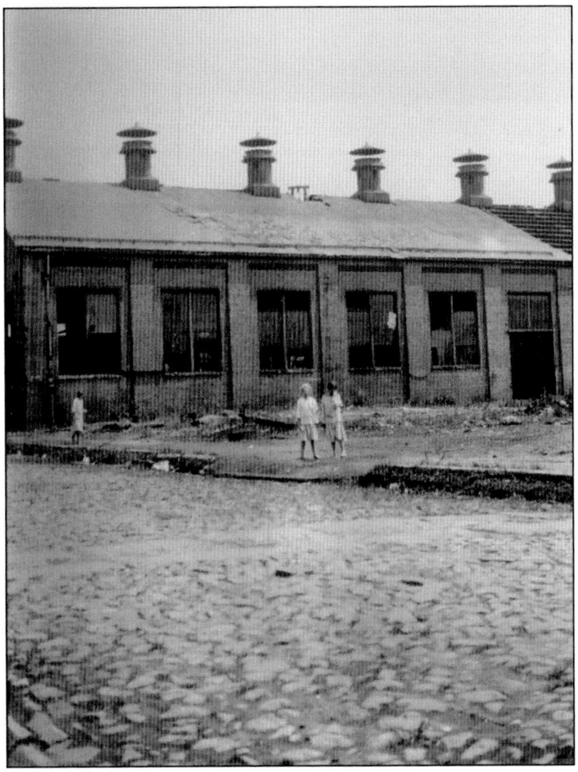

Derailed train cars were always a point of interest for children. At this site of an 1899 accident in Baltimore, kids forage and investigate the wreckage. (Courtesy of the Enoch Pratt Free Library.)

Two little girls search for treasure at the Bartlett Hayward Ammunition Plant site on McHenry Street, c. 1929. Because of Baltimore's industrial past, lead poisoning has always been a big problem for the community. The lead in the soil at this site must have been very high. Although most of the lead poisoning of children was due to the ingestion of paint chips, decades of making shot, ship ballasts, and other industrial production using lead has given the soil of the city a higher-than-natural lead content (Courtesy of the Enoch Pratt Free Library.)

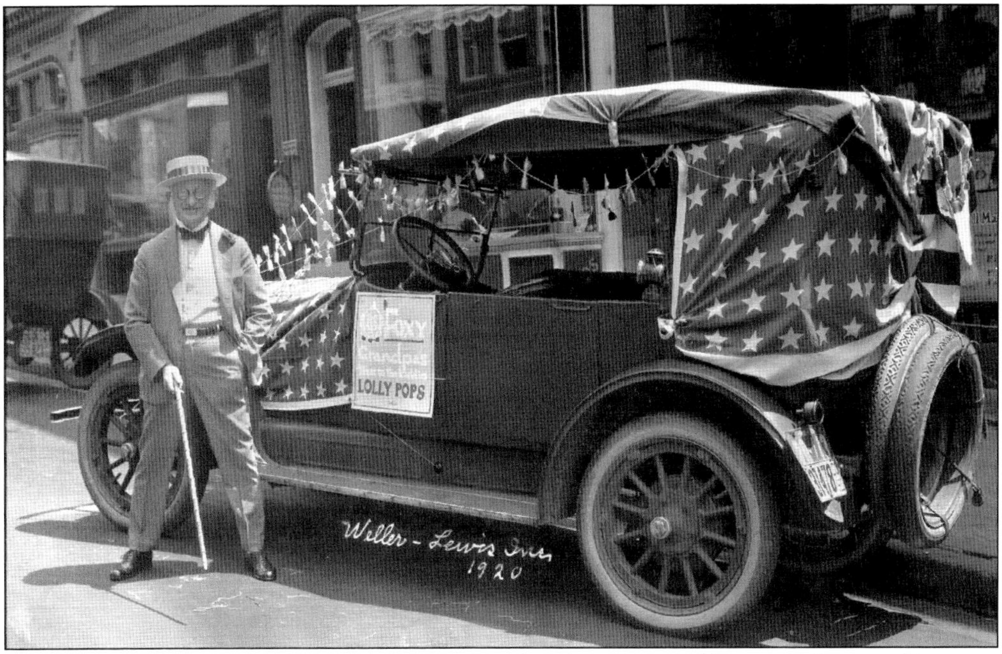

Col. Joseph M. Mann was known as "Foxy Grandpa" by many children in Baltimore. For some time during the early part of the century, the Baltimore Advertising Club held "Poor Kiddies' Outings" throughout the city. This is an event in 1920 at Carlin's Park. Colonel Mann was the owner of Mann Piano Company. (Courtesy of the Enoch Pratt Free Library.)

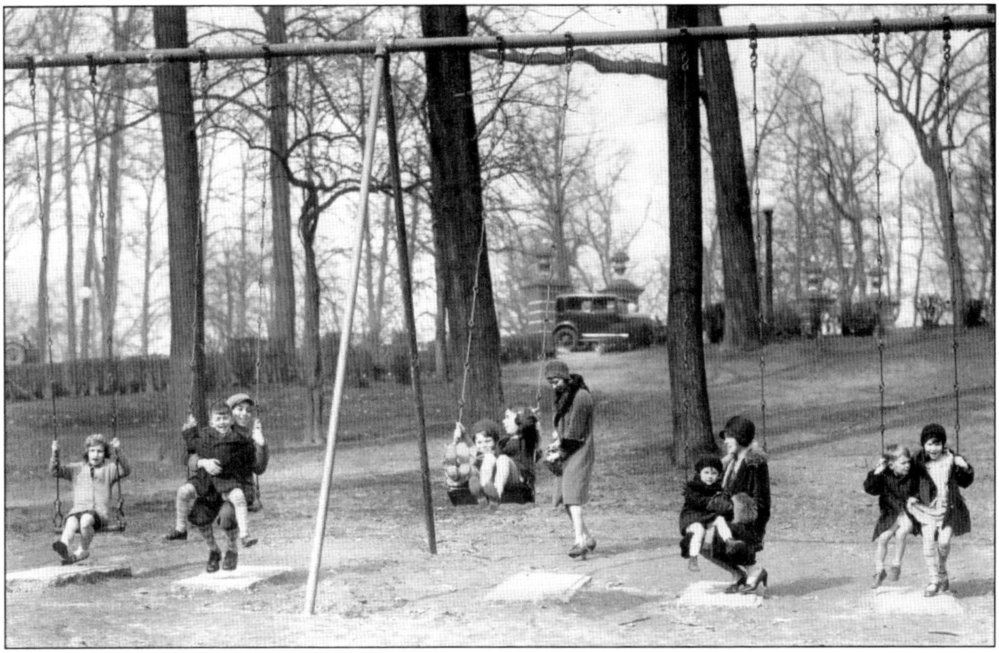

These fashionable 1920s young mothers enjoy an afternoon with their children in Druid Hill Park. In a city so rich in history and with a treasure of parks and spaces for children, there is hope that every child from this incredible place will find some joy growing up in Baltimore as these children did so many years ago. (Courtesy of the Enoch Pratt Free Library.)

BIBLIOGRAPHY

Beirne, Rosamond Randall. *Let's Pick the Daisies: The Bryn Mawr School.* Baltimore: The Bryn Mawr School, 1970.

Board of Commissioners of Public Schools, Diary for 1862. Baltimore: J.W.Bond & Co., 1862.

Bready, James H. *Baseball in Baltimore: The First 100 Years.* Baltimore and London: The Johns Hopkins University Press, 1998.

Clayton, Ralph. *Slavery, Slaveholding, and the Free Black Population of Ante Bellum Baltimore.* Heritage Books, 1993.

Fee, Elizabeth, Linda Shopes, and Linda Zeidman, eds. *The Baltimore Book.* Philadelphia: Temple University Press, 1991.

Friends of Druid Hill Park. *Druid Hill Park Revisited: A Pictorial Essay.* Baltimore: self-published, October 1985.

Hart, Richard H. *Enoch Pratt: The Story of a Plain Man.* A Fiftieth Anniversary Publication. Baltimore: Enoch Pratt Free Library, 1935.

Horowitz, Helen Lefkowitz. *The Power and Passion of M. Carey Thomas.* New York: Alfred A. Knopf, 1994.

Jacobs, Bradford McE. *Gilman Walls Will Echo.* Baltimore: Waverly Press, Inc., 1947.

Kelly, Jacques. *Bygone Baltimore: A Historical Portrait.* Norfolk/Virginia Beach: Donning Company, 1982

Kemp, John R. ed. *Lewis Hine: Photographs if Child Labor in the New South.* Jackson, MS: University Press of Mississippi, 1986.

Krausse, Harry W. *History of Public Education in Baltimore 1860–1890.* Master's thesis. University of Maryland, 1942.

Martin, Mary-Paulding. *The Flag House Story.* Baltimore: Star-Spangled Banner Flag House Association, Inc., 1996.

Maryland: A History of Its People. Baltimore and London: The Johns Hopkins Press, 1986.

Maryland Historical Magazine. Vol. 95, 3 Fall 2000, Maryland Historical Society, Baltimore.

Master Plan Report for Baltimore Zoo and Druid Hill Park. April 1976.

Report of the Commissioners of Public Schools to the City (of Baltimore) 1829–1844. Jacob Small (president), John B. Morris, Fielding Lucas Jr., Joseph Cushing, Wm. Hubbard, John Reese, 31 December, 1829, Office of Commissioners of Public Schools, 1845.

School Plant Directory Volume 1. City of Baltimore Dept. of Ed., Bureau of Research, 1963.

Numerous archival articles from the Baltimore *Sun* and other Baltimore-area publications.